FORCES '89

FORCES '89

N&A

LONDON

IAN ALLAN LTD

Published by Ian Allan Ltd, Shepperton, Surrey
Printed and bound in Italy
First published 1989

ISBN 0 7110 1828 6 (U.K. Edition)
ISBN 0-933852 85 1 (U.S.A. Edition)

Editor   Will Steeds
Assistant Editors   David Girling
                              Caroline Macy
Military Consultant   Geoffrey Cornish

Picture Research   Diane Moore/MARS

Art Editor   Ray Leaning
Designer   Helen James

Production Controllers   Tom Helsby
                              Carol Milligan

Managing Editor   Alan Ross
Consultant Editor   Mark Dartford

**Published in the United States of
America by the Nautical & Aviation
Publishing Co of America, 101 West
Read Street, Suite 314, Baltimore,
MD 21201, USA.**

CONTENTS

The case of the Harrier – a GR.3 is seen here on low-level operations – illustrates the difficulties of equipment planning. Other nations were sceptical about the wisdom of developing the plane, but its worth was demonstrated in a completely unpredicted war – the Falklands.

INTRODUCTION

Even while Iran was signalling her willingness to accept a ceasefire, bitter skirmishing continued in the Gulf War. FORCES '89 examines this most bitter of conflicts, and the prospects for a long-lasting peace. The US Navy's presence in the Gulf, meanwhile, illustrates the USA's worldwide military might – itself exemplified by the USS *Nimitz*. This year's SEA WAR profile provides a fascinating insight into the workings of this most formidable of warships.

Nimitz's capabilities are such that she can detect and identify any threat by referring to a SIGINT-generated database. But as the SPY WAR feature details, today's electronic spies also provide information used by governments to formulate long-term strategies and equipment needs.

On land, the conditions of modern battle continue to change, as the features on the development of the APC and on military medicine show. And even the French Foreign Legion has evolved to become an élite force at the cutting edge of France's military might.

Finally, FORCES celebrates the 70th anniversary of the RAF with a history of Britain's youngest service. FORCES concludes with a behind-the-scenes look at the events and developments of the most crucial military year for decades.

The design criteria for tracked Rapier – to provide rapidly deployable air defence for troops and armour in all terrains – reflect the high-intensity, multi-threat, rapidly moving conditions of today's battlefield.

Chapter 1

SEA WAR:
USS *NIMITZ* – CITY AT SEA

The USS Nimitz carries 86 aircraft, displaces 91,440 tons, has a crew the size of a small city, is powered by two nuclear reactors developing 260,000shp (195,000kW) of power – and cost $1.8 billion (about £782 million) to build. But statistics tell only part of the story: for it is the men who crew this floating city, and their ability to work in perfect harmony with all the ship's sophisticated equipment, who make the *Nimitz* the most formidable warship sailing the seas today.

USS *Nimitz*, the world's largest warship, is a floating city with a maximum 6870 crew. She can travel 700 nautical miles (1297km) in one day and, in theory, only needs refuelling every one million miles (1.6 million km) – yet her basic design dates back to the early post-war years.

The offensive capabilities of the *Hornet* (above) – in 1941 the USN's newest carrier – pale in comparison with *Nimitz*'s (left), whose planes can carry 220 tons of bombs and rockets compared with the *Hornet*'s planes' 20-odd tons.

In *The Final Countdown*, a film made in 1980, the leading role is played not by a human actor, but by a ship – the USS *Nimitz*, the world's largest warship. In the film, *Nimitz* is sailing in the waters off Pearl Harbor when she encounters a 'time warp', and the carrier and her crew are transported back through time to December 1941 – just prior to the surprise Japanese attack that caused the USA to enter World War II. Although *Nimitz* is snatched back through time to the present day again before she has a chance to alter the course of history, it is instructive to compare *Nimitz* with the large US Navy (USN) carriers of that time to illustrate just how much carrier design has changed in the four decades since World War II.

In December 1941 the USN's newest carrier was the USS *Hornet*. Hastily commissioned a mere seven weeks before Pearl Harbor, the *Hornet* had a hectic wartime career before being sunk at the Battle of Santa Cruz in October 1942. Although a large carrier by the standards of the time, *Hornet* was small in comparison with *Nimitz*, as is illustrated by the fact that *Nimitz* can carry the equivalent of the total weight of *Hornet* in fuel, ammunition, aircraft and stores alone.

Although *Nimitz* is much larger than *Hornet* was, she does not operate many more planes – but each of the aircraft she carries is heavier, faster and very much more capable. Fighters, for example, now weigh approximately 27 tons instead of five, and on a maximum-effort 'Alfa' strike a modern plane can carry 220 tons of bombs and rockets 500 miles (805km) to attack a target with a very high degree of accuracy. In 1941 it was considered to be an achievement to find a target at a range of 200 miles (322km), let alone to destroy it with the 20-odd tons of bombs that were all that could be carried that far.

Furthermore, the *Hornet*, equipped with an axial flight deck – with the landing area immediately behind the take-off zone – always had problems if aircraft needed to take off and land simultaneously. In comparison, *Nimitz* can accept and dispatch aircraft simultaneously – and in all but the very worst weather.

Nimitz uses three British inventions that have been perfected by the USN, as well as advanced electronics, to enable it to 'land on' aircraft at the same time as others are taking off: the steam catapult, the Mirror Deck Landing System (MDLS), and the angled deck. The four steam catapults, each 310ft (94m) long, can accelerate the heaviest carrier aircraft to about 150

Nimitz's air wing of 2750 men not only includes pilots (right, in an A-7 Corsair) but also a range of behind-the-scenes specialists such as engineers (above, servicing a Hawkeye) and flight-deck controllers (below right).

knots (278km/h) in two seconds. The MDLS, together with the Carrier Controlled Approach (CCA) system, take much of the guesswork out of trying to catch the 'three wire' (the third of the four arrester wires, counting from the stern, which is the preferred one to use). Finally, the angled deck – where the front end of the landing-run is skewed out at an angle over the port (left) side – enables aircraft to take off and land simultaneously.

Another advantage of the angled deck is that it leaves room around the island (the structure above the flight deck on the starboard side containing the bridge, most of the radars, and the flight deck operations room) for aircraft to be parked without interfering in any way with flight operations.

Only about 40 per cent of a large US carrier's aircraft are carried in hangars. The remainder, when not flying, are stored on deck. In the past, this meant that aircraft had to be pushed forward to get them out of the way for landings, and aft when other planes wished to take off. On *Nimitz*, some rearranging is still necessary, but at least there is room for flying operations to continue while the rearrangements are made.

Perhaps surprisingly, the most dramatic difference between *Hornet* and *Nimitz* – the latter's nuclear power – is the least important in immediate operational terms. Certainly, the ship's nuclear power plant in theory enables *Nimitz* to travel more than one million miles (1.6 million km) before refuelling, but the aircraft and crew still need a regular supply of stores and liquids. So, although *Nimitz* can steam for months on end at high speed, she is as dependent on resupply as *Hornet* was. The most important change, meanwhile, is an almost invisible one. Whereas *Hornet* had two unreli-

able radars and a primitive fighter control system, *Nimitz* has a full range of electronic equipment that not only enables her to detect potential enemies using on-board sensors, but also to combine this with information supplied by her own planes and by other ships in the battle group (CVBG).

The two main systems by which *Nimitz*, her planes, and the ships of the CVBG gather and exchange information are the Naval Tactical Data System (NTDS) and the Air Tactical Data System (ATDS). These feed data to the Combat Information Centres (CTCs) in the various ships of the CVBG and enable the group to use its weapons and aircraft to the best advantage by providing officers with accurate information at all times.

USS *Nimitz* (CVN-68)

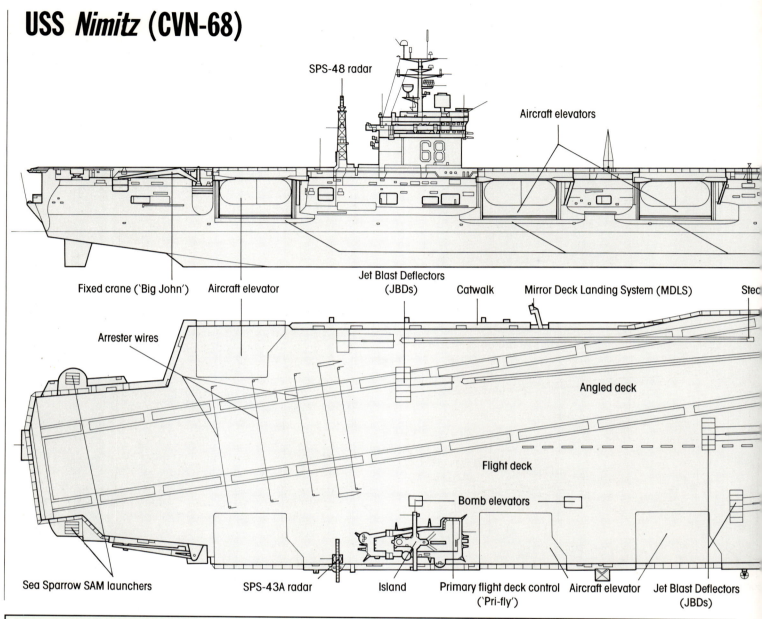

SPS-48 radar

Aircraft elevators

Fixed crane ('Big John')   Aircraft elevator   Jet Blast Deflectors (JBDs)   Catwalk   Mirror Deck Landing System (MDLS)   Ste

Arrester wires

Angled deck

Flight deck

Bomb elevators

Sea Sparrow SAM launchers   SPS-43A radar   Island   Primary flight deck control ('Pri-fly')   Aircraft elevator   Jet Blast Deflectors (JBDs)

USS *Nimitz* (CVN-68): specifications (as built)

Authorized:	Financial Year (FY) 1967 to Ship's Characteristics Board (SCB) 102		**Crew:**	maximum approximately 6870, including air wing and Admiral's staff
Built:	Newport News Shipbuilding and Dry Dock Company, USA		**Armament:**	standard air wing 86 aircraft total capacity 100-plus aircraft three 8-tube Mk 15 Sea Sparrow point defence SAM launchers 2970 tons aviation ordnance 2.5 million gallons (11,250cu. m) JP-5 fuel
Laid Down:	June 22, 1968 **Launched:** May 13, 1972 **Commissioned:** May 3, 1975			

Dimensions:

length:	breadth:	draft:
1040ft lwl	134ft lwl	36ft 8in., full load
(317.1m)	(40.8m)	(11.2m)
1088ft oa	257ft ext	37ft 8in., combat
(331.7m)	(78.5m)	(12.4m)

Displacement: 73,978 tons light   91,440 tons full load

Machinery: two A4W reactors
four General Electric steam turbines approx. 260,000shp (195,000kW) = over 30 knots (55km/h)
four 2000hp (1500kW) diesel auxiliaries

Radar: LN-66 navigation
SPS-10F surface search
SPS-43A 2-D air search
SPS-48 3-D air search
SPN-35/41/42/43/44 Automatic Carrier Landing System (ACLS)

EW: WLR-1H EW warning system
four 6-tube Mk 36 SBROC

oa = overall   lwl = load water line   ext = extreme
All figures are approximate

**The angled flight deck and advanced electronics enable
Nimitz to 'land on' aircraft while others are taking off in all
but the very worst weather. Hornet's axial flight deck and
primitive radars meant that flying from her was a very much
more dangerous hit-and-miss affair.**

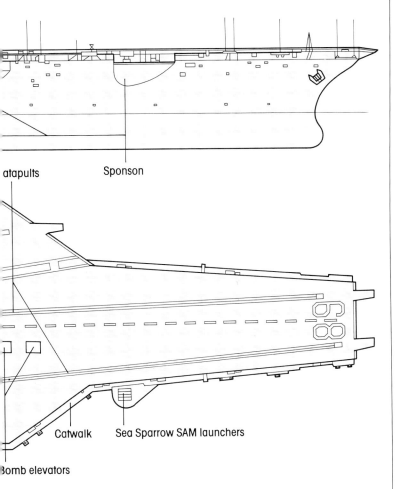

atapults   Sponson

Catwalk   Sea Sparrow SAM launchers

Bomb elevators

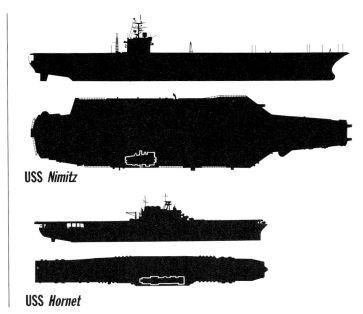

USS Nimitz

USS Hornet

Derivation and design

The USS *Nimitz* is named after Admiral Chester W.
Nimitz, who took command of the USN's Pacific Fleet
just after the Pearl Harbor disaster in 1941. In March
1942, Admiral Nimitz was given responsibility for all
land, sea and air forces in the northern and central
Pacific, and for amphibious operations throughout the
ocean. Nimitz's forces fought across the Pacific and,
given the involvement of the USN's carrier force in the
campaigns he directed, it was entirely appropriate that
the new carrier should be named after him.

US Government authorization to build the USS
Nimitz was given in Financial Year (FY) 1967. The
sixty-eighth fleet carrier to be ordered by the USN,
CVN-68 (as the *Nimitz* was designated) reflects the
experience gained from a programme for building large
carriers which began in the early post-war years.

The first of the truly large US carriers was to have
been the 83,250-ton *United States* (CVA-58), which was
laid down in April 1949 but cancelled five days later. If
completed, she would have been equipped with an axial
flight deck, without an island. Worked stopped on her
because she was designed to take the USN's projected
strategic nuclear bomber, and the US Air Force (USAF)
claimed that this duplicated the task assigned to their
B-36s. Over the next 18 years (the period between the
cancellation of the *United States* and the authorization of
the *Nimitz*), the USN would fight many similar political
battles in its campaign to build a modern carrier fleet.

The cancellation of the *United States* in 1949 represented a low point in the USN's carrier-building
programme – a programme which was only revived
when carriers again proved their usefulness by providing essential air support in the early stages of the
Korean War. The immediate outcome of the revived
programme was the four Forrestal-class carriers. At
78,500 tons full load, these represented a reduced
version of the 83,250-ton *United States*, although they
were still the largest warships in the world when built.
Originally designed with an axial flight deck and no
island, they were completed with an angled deck, steam
catapults (as opposed to explosive), a mirror deck
landing system and a conventional island.

All the large US carriers built since then, including
Nimitz, have been refinements of the Forrestal design.
The first two Kitty Hawk-class carriers, for example,
were basically the same but for a revised flight deck,
with the island being located further aft. This gave more
space for parking aircraft, and easier access from the
elevators to the catapults. CVAN-65, the nuclear-
powered *Enterprise*, was built at the same time to the
same basic design. However, she was larger – 89,000
tons full load, compared to 80,900 tons for the Kitty
Hawk class. Her eight A2W reactors took up no more
space than *Kitty Hawk*'s conventional machinery and
fuel tanks, but *Enterprise* still required the same
number of oil fuel tanks as conventional carriers to act
as underwater protection.

Partly because of her size, partly because of the nuclear reactors, and partly because of her extremely expensive (and unreliable) phased-array SPS-32 and SPS-33 radars, *Enterprise* cost so much that the next two carriers, *America* and *John F. Kennedy*, were conventionally powered half-sisters of the Kitty Hawk carriers. A more compact underwater protection system was introduced on the *John F. Kennedy*, and this has been incorporated in the design for the Nimitz-class carriers. But even the conventionally powered carriers were costing so much by now that powerful arguments were being raised for building either much smaller carriers, or none at all.

However, the carriers once again proved their usefulness – this time in the Vietnam War. If not silenced, the critics were at least chastened, and once Secretary of Defense MacNamara had finally been convinced that another large carrier was necessary, authorization to proceed with *Nimitz* was given.

The *Nimitz* is even larger (though fractionally shorter overall) than *Enterprise*. Improvements in reactor design mean that she only needs two A4Ws to give almost the same power as the 'Big E's eight A2Ws; she also has the more compact underwater protection system introduced in *John F. Kennedy*, so the possibility existed of building a smaller ship.

There are three reasons why, in the end, a smaller ship was not built. First, the big carrier lobby in the USN have always maintained that smaller ships are not only less capable – but also that they are not much less expensive. *Nimitz* cost about $1.8 billion (£782 million) in 1976, but a large part of that cost was for the electronics that a smaller carrier would also need. As the lobbyists also pointed out, the cost of the hull itself is always relatively cheap, and *Nimitz* was deliberately sized as the largest ship that could be built on the existing slipway at the shipyard at Newport News, so that no extra costs would be incurred. The other strand in the argument was that the remaining ships in the CVBG cost about six times as much as the carrier itself, not counting the cost of the Underway Replenishment Group (URG) with its oilers, ammunition and stores ships and *their* escorts, and a multi-product station ship to act as a shuttle between the URG and CVBG.

The second reason for the *Nimitz*'s size is that a smaller carrier would find it difficult to operate the most powerful and sophisticated USN aircraft, such as the F-14 Tomcat. And although a smaller air wing altogether would definitely be cheaper, it would be much less flexible. Up until the early 1970s the USN was able to operate a sufficient number of Essex-class carriers of World War II vintage in the Anti-Submarine

Flight deck operations

Standing on the flight deck, it is so noisy everyone wears a 'cranial' (a leather-and-composite helmet) to protect them, and most have to have headsets too. In addition, everything is colour-coded and organized for safety. Colour-coding extends from the different coloured 'hold-backs' for different types of aircraft, to the jerseys worn by the deck hands: green for marine guards or visitors, green with white trim for plane inspectors (with black letters for catapult or arrester-gear crewmen), yellow for officers in charge of plane handling, catapults and arrester gear. There are red, purple, brown, blue, white and silver jerseys too, some with different-coloured trims, each indicating the task assigned to the person wearing it.

Take-off

After a plane has been put on the catapult, the Jet Blast Deflectors (JBDs) raised behind them, and the weight carefully checked – this makes a vital difference to the catapult speed setting – there is an interchange of hand signals and a three-second wait before the catapult works. The plane, weighing up to 32 tons, is then accelerated to a speed of 130 knots (240km/h) in 310ft (94m), and in less than two seconds.

'Landing on'

'Landing on' is equally violent. Planes are marshalled by the Carrier Air Traffic Control Center (CATCC) behind the carrier, then (unless in EMCON state) guided down a glidescope, often by the Automatic Carrier Landing System (ACLS) on to the 'three-wire' for a 'trap' (a successful arrested landing), the final stage with the aid of the LSO and the Light Landing Device. Each arrester wire, 1½in. (40mm) thick and 110ft (33m) long, lasts for a maximum of 100 landings, and is checked between each one. If a pilot misses the wire he must either do a 'bolter' over the port side to try again – or he flies into the 24-ft (7-m) high nylon crash barrier. The SH-3 Sea King helicopter stands by in case of crashes.

Below: Flight deck crewmen stand by as an F-14A Tomcat is guided on to one of the catapults prior to take off.

CVN-68 AIR WING

F-14A Tomcat

Multi-role fighter
Length: 62ft 8in. (19.10m)
Wing span: 64ft 1½in. (19.54m) unswept; 38ft 2½in. (11.65m) swept
Max speed: 1564mph (2485km/h) at height
Carrier approach speed: 154mph (248km/h)
Principal weaponry: AIM-9 Sidewinder; AIM-7 Sparrow; AIM-54C Phoenix; M61A-1 20mm gun

F/A-18 Hornet

Multi-role fighter/bomber
Length: 56ft (17.07m)
Wing span: 37ft 6in. (11.43m)
Max speed: 1190mph (1912km/h) at height
Carrier approach speed: 154mph (248km/h)
Principal weaponry: AIM-9M Sidewinder; AIM-7 Sparrow; M61 20mm gun

A-7 Corsair

Light attack aircraft
Length: 46ft 1½in. (14m)
Wing span: 38ft 9in. (11.8m)
Max speed: 691mph (1112km/h) at sea level
Carrier approach speed: not available
Principal armament: six underwing ordnance pylons, carrying total 15,000lb (6805kg) load – bombs, missiles and/or rockets; M61A1 20mm gun

E-2C Hawkeye

Early warning and control
Length: 57ft 6¾in. (17.54m)
Wing span: 29ft 4in. (8.9m)
Max speed: 372mph (598km/h) at sea level
Carrier approach speed: 119mph (191km/h)
Principal EW equipment: AN/APA-171 rotodome; AN/APS-138 advanced radar processing system; AN/ALR-73 passive detection system; RT-988/A IFF interrogator; CAINS

A-6E Intruder

All-weather attack
Length: 54ft 9in. (16.69m)
Wing span: 53ft (16.15m)
Max speed: 648mph (1043km/h) at low level
Carrier approach speed: 127mph (204km/h)
Principal weaponry: 5 weapon attachment points. Typical weapon load = 28 × 500lb bombs; Sidewinder, Harpoon, HARM capability

KA-6D Intruder

Tanker
Length: 54ft 9in. (16.69m)
Wing span: 53ft (16.15m)
Max speed: 648mph (1043km/h) at low level
Carrier approach speed: 127mph (204km/h)
Fuel capacity: up to 30,000lb (13,608kg)

EA-6B Prowler

Electronic countermeasures
Length: 59ft 10in. (18.24m)
Wing span: 53ft (16.15m)
Max speed: 610mph (982km/h) at sea level
Carrier approach speed: approx. 130mph (209km/h)
ECM equipment: AN/ALQ-99 jamming system; long-range radar detection equipment in fin-tip pod; central computer for processing signals received

S-3A/B Viking

Anti-submarine warfare
Length: 53ft 4in. (16.26m)
Wing span: 68ft 8in. (20.9m)
Max speed: 506mph (814km/h) at sea level
Carrier approach speed: approx. 120mph (193km/h)
Principal ASW equipment: OR-89 Forward-Looking Infra-Red (FLIR) radar; ASQ-81 MAD; 4 × 46 torpedoes; 60 sonobuoys

SH-3H Sea King

Anti-submarine warfare
Length (rotors turning): 72ft 8in. (22.15m)
Main-rotor diameter: 62ft (18.9m)
Max speed: 143mph (230km/h)
Carrier approach speed: —
Principal equipment/armament: dipping sonar AQS-13; Magnetic Anomaly Detector (MAD) AQS-81; 2 × Mk 46 torpedoes; up to 25 sonobuoys

The new carrier air wing (CVW) deployed from 1987 doubles the number of medium attack aircraft, reduces the number of fighters and light attack aircraft (with F/A-18 Hornets replacing the A-7 Corsairs) and deletes the KA-6D tankers.

STANDARD AIR WING

	Pre 1987			Post 1987	
Fighters:	F-14A Tomcat	24	Fighters:	F-14A Tomcat	20
Fighter light attack:	A-7 Corsair	24	Fighter light attack:	F/A-18 Hornet	20
Attack:	A-6E Intruder	10	Attack:	A-6E Intruder	20
Tankers:	KA-6D Intruder	4	Tankers:		
Electronic Warfare (EW):	EA-6B Prowler	4	Electronic Warfare (EW):	EA-6B Prowler	5
Airborne Early Warning (AEW):	E-2C Hawkeye	4	Airborne Early Warning (AEW):	E-2C Hawkeye	5
Anti-Submarine Warfare (ASW) – fixed wing:	S-3A/B Viking	10	Anti-Submarine Warfare (ASW) – fixed wing:	S-3A/B Viking	10
– helicopter:	SH-3 Sea King	6	– helicopter:	SH-3 Sea King	6
Total		86	Total		86

Warfare (ASW) role to avoid having to carry ASW aircraft and helicopters aboard its CVAs. On June 30, 1975, however, all CVAs, including *Nimitz*, were redesignated CVs (multi-purpose carriers), and this involved embarking ASW aircraft and helicopters in addition to all the other types carried. Although *Nimitz* normally operates a standard 86-aircraft air wing, she has sufficient space to do this and can store and operate more aircraft if required.

The third main reason for the increased size of *Nimitz* is the enlarged magazine and oil fuel capacity. Early experience in Vietnam showed that existing large carriers were using up their stocks of munitions and aircraft fuel at an astounding rate and the Forrestal-class carriers were having to replenish every four days or so. In addition, today's bombs and rockets require more storage space than older types on account of such things as fins, laser designators, and other bulky improvements. Nevertheless *Nimitz*, with almost twice the amount of aviation fuel and one-and-a-half times the magazine space of older carriers, can conduct approximately 16 days' worth of medium-intensity operations before she needs replenishing.

Improved deck layout

The deck layout of *Nimitz* has also been altered. The arrangement of the elevators is retained, with three to starboard (two forward of the island) and one to port. Similarly with the steam catapults: two are located in the bows and two in the waist to port. However, the angle of the landing deck has been reduced to lessen the problems caused by turbulence from the starboard island. In effect, the aft end has been moved to port and the forward end to starboard, thus minimizing the turbulence which planes coming in to land previously encountered. Because of the new deck alignment, the aft end of the bow catapults have had to be slewed to starboard. This prevents aircraft waiting to be launched from fouling planes moving along the landing deck.

In all post-World War II US carriers, the flight deck is actually part of the hull structure, rather than being built on top of it. There are, of course, four large cut-outs in the sides of the hull for the deck-edge elevators, and another at the stern where engines can be tested. The latter area directly connects with the engine repair workshop, which in turn directly connects with the hangar. The flight-deck is covered with a rubber-like non-skid material, and studded with metal tie-downs to secure parked aircraft. There are several Auxiliary Power Unit (APU) connections and 17 refuelling points in the catwalks that run around the edge of the flight deck. The Primary Air Controller – 'Air Boss' – is stationed in the Primary Flight Deck Control – 'Pri-Fly' – room in the bulged port side of the island, with a superb view of the entire flight deck. The bridge is at the front of the island, but the ship is controlled in action from the Combat Information Center (CIC), located below decks.

The *Nimitz* is navigated by means of a number of sophisticated, interlocking systems. Under normal conditions, three main methods are used together to give a total picture not only of the ship's own position, and of all vessels in the CVBG, but also of all air and sea movements over a large area around the CVBG. First, there are the ship's radars, the most important of which (in this respect) is the Marconi LN-66. Then there are the receivers for the information from the NAVSTAR global positioning satellite, and finally there is the Ship's Inertial Navigation System (SINS), a self-contained unit that requires updating from other sources from time to time. SINS also feeds the ship's position into the aircrafts' Carrier Inertial Navigation System (CAINS).

Below: Unmarked RH-53D Sea Stallions – not normally based on *Nimitz* – undergo pre-flight checks on the morning of April 24th, 1980, before flying to join the rest of the Delta Force for the Iranian hostage rescue mission.

The mix of planes in *Nimitz*'s air wing enables strikes to be launched, and threats to be countered, with lethal accuracy. Hawkeyes (above) locate targets and then control the strike by such planes as this F-14 fighter (top).

The offensive role

Until 1987, *Nimitz* carried two squadrons of light attack aircraft, with 24 planes each, and one squadron of medium attack aircraft with 10 planes. At first the light attack aircraft were subsonic A-7 Corsairs, but in the 1980s they have been replaced by the far more versatile supersonic F/A-18 Hornet, which can act as a fighter or light bomber as required. Typical squadrons on *Nimitz* have been VA-82 Marauders and VA-86 Sidewinders – all USN carrier squadrons have names. Until the 1987 refit the medium attack squadron was VA-35 Black Panthers flying A-6 intruders – a long-range, low-level attack aircraft.

The planes' targets are located by a variety of means, including reconnaissance satellites and land-based P-3 Orions. On her 'shakedown' cruise in 1975 *Nimitz* carried a detachment of RVAH-9 Hoot Owl's RA-5C Vigilante reconnaissance aircraft. These were soon phased out, and apart from an occasional A-3 Skywar-rior variant, *Nimitz* had no proper reconnaissance facilities until one of her two F-14 Tomcat fighter squadrons (VF-84 Jolly Rogers) took the Tactical Air Reconnaissance Pods System (TARPS) to sea in 1982.

In addition to masking or jamming enemy radars, the four EA-6B Prowlers – an Electronic Warfare (EW) four-seat variant of the two-seat A-6 Intruder – can perform electronic reconnaissance. EW versions of the A-3 Skywarrior and the ship's four E-2C Hawkeye Airborne Early Warning (AEW) aircraft also have this capability. The Hawkeyes have two further functions: control of the strike, and defence.

If required, the ship's fighters – the F-14 Tomcats and possibly some or even all of the F/A-18 Hornets – can accompany a strike to act as fighter escorts, even carrying bombs or Air-to-Surface Missiles (ASMs) as appropriate. The USN tries to operate with at least two CVs in a CVBG when there is any chance of action.

The escorts are all now being equipped for an offensive as well as a defensive role, with most of the larger ships being back-fitted with Tomahawk SSMs. The majority of the escorts are armed with 5in. guns – which are useful for shore bombardment. They also have Harpoon SSMs with a range of over 60 nautical miles (111km). The CVBG may also be accompanied by battleships armed with 16in. guns.

The weapons systems of the CVBG are linked using the NTDS and ATDS. The intelligence information from the various reconnaissance systems is combined using the Integrated Operational Intelligence System (IOIS) in the Integrated Operational Intelligence Centers (IOICs) afloat or in Hawkeye or E-3 Sentry aircraft. *Nimitz* has been fitted with a Tactical Flag Command Center (TFCC), which has large USQ-81 (V) computer-generated displays to keep track of the battle.

Defence

Most of the aircraft and systems used for attack can also be used for defence. In addition, there are other systems that are solely used for protecting the carrier and its battle group. The greatest possible protection is provided by having a layered defence which in effect places a series of barriers in the path of an attacker.

The outer layer is provided by the carrier's fighters, accompanied by the E-2C Hawkeye AEW aircraft and sometimes by the EA-6B Prowler EW aircraft. Until her 1987 refit (apart from the shakedown cruise), *Nimitz*'s dedicated fighters have always been the F-14A Tomcats of VF-41 Black Aces and VF-84 Jolly Rogers. In the 1980s these have been reinforced by the available F/A-18 Hornets from the ship's two light attack squadrons. Unless a known attack was imminent, there would normally be a maximum of four F-14 Tomcats on two Combat Air Patrols (CAPs). These are guided and controlled by information from the E-2C Hawkeyes and the CVBG's radars and electronic warning devices. There would normally be at least one reinforcement airborne for each CAP, backed by other fighters on 'Alert Five' or 'Alert Fifteen' readiness (that is, ready to take off in five or 15 minutes) parked armed and ready to go, behind the island. At times of high alert, there might also be Deck Launch Interceptors (DLIs) already attached to the catapult, with engines running and fuel pipes connected to the ship so that tanks are kept topped-up, ready for instant launch.

The S-3A Viking ASW aircraft also operate in the outer layer of defence. Their work is sometimes integrated with that of the accompanying SSN (nuclear-powered attack submarine) to find and destroy any cruise missile or attack submarines (such as, in the case of the Soviet navy, Oscar-, Mike- or Charlie-class boats) that might threaten the CVBG. Surface vessels with cruise missiles (in the case of the Soviet navy, Kirov- or Slava-class cruisers) would be the responsibility of the attack aircraft or the SSMs of the SSN or the surface escorts.

The second layer of the defences is provided by the Surface-to-Air Missile (SAM) defence zone – Identification Friend-or-Foe (IFF) and good communications are very important for any friendly planes that wish to pass through this. The missile defence zone is the responsibility of the surface escorts. *Nimitz* normally has one or two guided-missile cruisers (CG or CGN depending on whether conventionally or nuclear powered), one or two guided-missile destroyers (DDG), two ASW destroyers (DD) and one or two guided-missile frigates (FFG). Originally *Nimitz*, like *Enterprise*, was always escorted by at least one CGN, so on her first deployment to the Mediterranean in 1976 *Nimitz* was escorted by CGN-36 *California*. However, CGNs, like

Right: The three-layered defence protects *Nimitz* against airborne, surface and undersea attack – but even if a missile (for example) was to get through, *Nimitz*'s sheer size renders her very difficult to put out of action.

CVNs, are expensive, and the latest escort cruisers, the Ticonderoga-class vessels, with their Aegis system incorporating the fixed-array SPY-1A radar which enables them to track many targets simultaneously, are powered by gas turbines. The guided-missile cruisers, destroyers and frigates (the FFG are normally Oliver Hazard Perry class) are all equipped with Standard SM-2 SAMs. The cruisers, with their superior electronics, are by far the most effective Anti-Air Warfare (AAW) vessels. If the direction of the threat is known, a cruiser or DDG will position itself between the threat and the rest of the CVBG to destroy as many missiles or aircraft as possible, and will then let the CVBG know of any that get through.

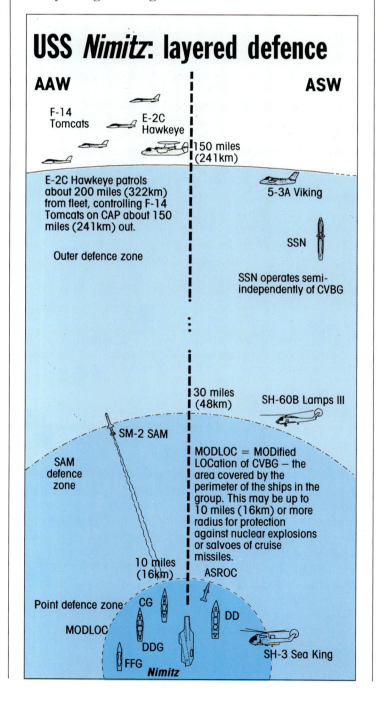

USS *Nimitz*: layered defence

AAW   **ASW**

F-14 Tomcats

E-2C Hawkeye

150 miles (241km)

E-2C Hawkeye patrols about 200 miles (322km) from fleet, controlling F-14 Tomcats on CAP about 150 miles (241km) out.

Outer defence zone

5-3A Viking

SSN

SSN operates semi-independently of CVBG

30 miles (48km)

SH-60B Lamps III

SM-2 SAM

SAM defence zone

MODLOC = MODified LOCation of CVBG – the area covered by the perimeter of the ships in the group. This may be up to 10 miles (16km) or more radius for protection against nuclear explosions or salvoes of cruise missiles.

10 miles (16km)

ASROC

Point defence zone   CG

MODLOC

CG   DD

DDG

FFG

Nimitz

SH-3 Sea King

The second layer of the ASW protection is provided by the SSN, and the LAMPS-1 or LAMPS-III ASW helicopters of the escorts, and the SH-3 Sea King ASW helicopters of the *Nimitz*. These are directed by the SSN and the long-range sonars on the escorts. Until the classes built in the 1980s were introduced, Soviet submarines were relatively noisy and could be detected many miles away under favourable conditions.

The inner layer of the defences is provided by the point defence zone. All the ships in the CVBG have some form of close-in defence weapon. *Nimitz*, for example, was built with three eight-tube Mk 15 Sea Sparrow SAM launchers (she was designed with two twin Tartar medium-range launchers, but these were deleted before completion). These were later replaced by Mk 29 NATO Sea Sparrow launchers. Three Mk 15 Phalanx 20mm Gatling gun Close-In Weapons System (CIWS) firing depleted uranium bullets were also added in the early 1980s. ASROC torpedo launchers and the helicopters provide the inner ASW zone.

The final element is provided by the ship's passive defences. First there is Electronic Counter Measures (ECM) and chaff (clouds of metal foil intended to deceive an incoming missile's guidance system). *Nimitz* has four six-tube Mk 36 SBROC chaff-launchers. Then there are the built-in features of the ship's design: because the ship is so large, her basic structure is massive and extremely resistant to attack without further reinforcement. In addition, *Nimitz* has three armoured decks (including the flight deck); 23 transverse watertight bulkheads dividing the ship into 24 separate watertight areas below the second deck (in carriers, decks are counted up and down from the hangar, or main, deck); over 2000 watertight compartments; and 30 individual damage-control stations. In turn, the hangar is divided into three by bulkheads closed off by fire doors, each area having its own damage-control and fire-fighting equipment.

Protecting the magazines

The major worry with the *Nimitz* design is the very large magazines. The *John F. Kennedy* was designed with the magazines set low down at bow and stern, with the machinery in between. Despite *Nimitz*'s fuller hull-form aft, there is still not enough space to protect a large magazine against underwater attack (the Soviet navy has recently developed some very large wake-homing torpedoes). The *Nimitz*'s two magazines are therefore placed forward of and between the two machinery spaces. Even so, they are still vulnerable, because they are so large that they rise well above the waterline. Large cruise missiles with shaped-charge warheads could potentially penetrate to one of them and set off a catastrophic explosion. The Soviet navy and air force field missiles capable of this, including the AS-6 Kingfisher, the SS-N-12 Sandbox and the SS-N-19. In 1982, *Nimitz* was fitted with Kevlar lightweight armour to improve its chances against such attacks.

Above: Nuclear-powered guided-missile cruiser USS *California* (CGN-36) leads *Nimitz* into Norfolk, Va., after an Indian Ocean deployment in 1980. CGNs are expensive, so the latest escort cruisers are powered by gas turbines.

The ease with which the *Forrestal* withstood the effects of a fire on its flight deck (which resulted in seven holes being blown through into the hangar space by bombs) on July 29, 1967, and with which the *Enterprise* survived a similar accidental fire on January 14, 1969, are often cited to show that large carriers could survive a cruise-missile attack. These incidents do indeed provide impressive evidence of the toughness of the ships (and of their crews) and of the excellence of the USN's damage-control procedures, but they are not the same as horizontal strikes by very large warheads on the most vulnerable parts of the ship. Carriers such as the *Nimitz* are said to be designed to take hits by four of the largest cruise missiles – and to survive. However, all that can be said for certain is that the only ships afloat with a better chance of surviving such damage are the four World War II vintage Iowa-class battleships, which are now once again operational in the Surface Action Groups (SAGs).

In many respects, however, a CVBG's main defence is still not its weapons, aircraft or electronics, but the sheer size of the ocean. Moving at nearly 30 knots (55km/h), a CVBG can travel approximately 700 nautical miles (1297km) in one day in any direction. This means that a strike directed against a carrier is much less certain of success than one directed at, for example, an airfield or a tank concentration. Under EMissions CONtrolled (EMCON) conditions, the CVBG is much harder to find. Nevertheless, signalling by flags and lights, or 'landing on' without using the Carrier Controlled Approach (CCA) radars, makes operations much more hazardous – so there is always a choice to make between active and passive defence.

The crew

CGNs are crewed by some 38 officers and 490 enlisted men, while the reactivated battleships are manned by about 74 officers and 1580 enlisted men. *Nimitz*, however, has a crew of approximately 150 officers and 2500 enlisted men, with another 1000 (or more) officers and men when she is on a war footing. These manning levels are for the ship alone. For when the carrier air wing comes aboard at the start of each deployment, another 2750 officers and men are added to the complement. It is not surprising, then, that the standard complaint about service aboard a carrier is that it is very impersonal – there are too many people and the ship is too big.

Depending on how you count them, there are 11 different deck levels in the hull, not counting the island. Despite the four-digit alphanumeric code (introduced by the USN in 1949) which indicates which end, side and level in the ship any particular compartment is on, it is still very difficult for those who have never been to sea before to find their way around. Unfortunately, a very large percentage of the enlisted men are 19-year-olds who fall into this category. The USN receives approximately 100,000 volunteer recruits a year, who receive nearly eight weeks of basic training at either San Diego, California, Great Lakes, Michigan, or Orlando, Florida. Many of them have come from the central states of the USA and have never even seen the sea before, let alone sailed on it.

Even when they are on the carrier, few of the crew see much of the sea. The flight deck, for example, is a dangerous place for the unwary, and all new carrier deck hands attend the 'P-School', which is a short course on flight-deck operations. Much time, then, is spent below-decks, and perhaps as a result there have been many problems with drugs. Alcohol abuse is not usually a problem, as the USN is teetotal – except for an award of two cans of beer per man per day when a ship has not touched port for 100 days. There have also been racial tensions. *Nimitz* has a Human Resources Control composed of men from different departments to iron out problems, and the Command Master Chief (the senior enlisted man aboard) acts as a link between the enlisted men and the ship's senior officers.

The *Nimitz*'s officers are divided into two categories: the Unrestricted Line Officers (the non-specialists who can, if they are lucky, cap their careers by commanding a fleet); and the Restricted Line officers (specialists such as Engineering Duty Officers) and Staff Corps Officers (technical or logistics specialists) who do not command ships or fleets. There are several ways that officers can join the USN, but high-flyers normally enter via the US Naval Academy at Annapolis. Each branch of the service has its own training establishments, such as the Engineering Duty School at Mare Island, California, for Junior Engineering Officers.

Nimitz's captain, like all USN carrier captains, has to have been a flyer, as do the 'Air Boss' and the Landing

Daily life

The ship's crew is divided into a number of departments, such as the deck department (consisting of seamen), the operations department, the engineering department, and so on. Each department is subdivided in turn into divisions. The XO organizes them by issuing a Plan Of the Day (POD) – which details who is working where, and when.

The main crew mess and the officers' wardroom are beneath the hangar on the second deck aft; the Chief Petty Officers' (CPOs') mess is one deck below the wardroom. There is another mess and wardroom forward for those who do not have the time to change from their dirty overalls before eating. The ship is so large that the Food Service Division has more than 250

Below and right: Nimitz-class carriers are crowded (as the picture of the sleeping quarters shows), noisy and dangerous, so every effort is made to provide the best food, medical care and entertainment for off-duty personnel. Shown here are the dental surgery, mess E-6, one of the galleys and the main store. The ship also produces its own newspaper and TV shows, using onboard facilities.

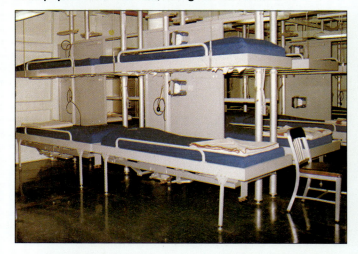

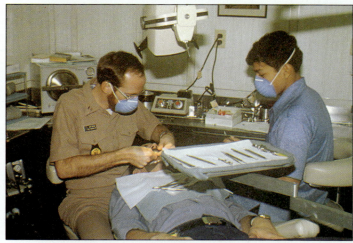

men working in the galleys. About a hundred of these are mess management specialists and the remainder are drawn on a rota from the non-specialist crewmen (so far, the USN has not sent women to sea in carriers).

There are considerable onboard facilities for entertainment, including multi-channel TV and radio stations. There are also three extensively stocked shops, and for the more serious-minded there are civilian teachers on hand to help any young crew-member who wishes to continue with his high school or college studies so that he has more qualifications when he leaves the Navy. There is a chapel that serves all denominations and a hospital and pharmacy and a dental department.

There are few places where a ship the size of *Nimitz* is able to tie up, but that does not stop the 'liberty boat' from taking crew and air wing personnel ashore. The Sixth Fleet's main base is at Naples in Italy, where there is a large USN community, but other places that are visited include Portsmouth in England, Rota in Spain, Piraeus in Greece, Tel Aviv in Israel, and a number of other ports that it is felt advisable to make visits to. At regular naval bases, it is understood that sailors will always behave like sailors, but on goodwill visits everyone has to be on their very best behaviour.

Signals Officer (LSO) in charge of the 'meatball' – the Optical Landing System. To become the captain of a carrier, it is necessary to have served for about 24 years in the Navy. On the way, the officer in question will have commanded a squadron and a CVW, been the Executive Officer (or XO; the man in charge of running the ship and its discipline under the captain), and will probably have commanded one of the multi-purpose stores ships. For example, Captain Maudlin, who commanded *Dwight D. Eisenhower* (CVN-69) on its first overseas deployment, had previously (as a Commander) been XO of *Nimitz* for its first year in service, and had then commanded the AOE *Seattle* before moving on to CVN-69.

Air wing personnel

Traditionally, there is always bad feeling between a carrier's crew and the air wing personnel, a situation which is not helped by the crowded conditions under which they all live. The air wing is composed of many specialists, and there are twice as many aircrew as there are aircraft for intensive operations, with ready rooms for the various types of squadron. Then there are the groundcrew, the photo-interpretation specialists, and the armaments, operational planning and electronics experts. Perhaps most surprising of all, there are manufacturers' representatives onboard to advise on various pieces of equipment.

Aircrew go through primary, basic and advanced training with Naval Training Command, flying initial 'carquals' (carrier qualifications) on the ageing Essex-class training carrier *Lexington* in the Gulf of Mexico before going on to the replacement training squadrons, which train them to fly their particular type of operational aircraft.

Operating from a conventional carrier is the most dangerous form of peacetime flying, and there have been a number of serious accidents on *Nimitz*. Such accidents can happen in many different ways. For example, an F-14 Tomcat of VF-84 Jolly Rogers crashed into the sea during the deployment off Iran on May 3, 1980, because of a catapult problem, as did an A-7E Corsair on February 24, 1987, in the Mediterranean. Meanwhile another F-14, this time from VF-41 Black Aces, was lost when it came in too low and hit the ramp on landing on October 3, 1977. However, one of the worst accidents was the crash of the EA-3B Skywarrior on January 25, 1987, when an inexperienced pilot attempting to go round again clipped the top of the crash barrier and went into the sea; all seven crew were lost. The worst accident of all occurred when an EA-6B Prowler of VMAQ-2 crashed into the deck park on May 26, 1981. Thirteen people were killed, 11 aircraft were destroyed or badly damaged, and there was also a serious outbreak of fire.

Marine squadrons, such as VMAQ-2, are regularly deployed on USN carriers and sometimes replace equivalent USN squadrons for the whole deployment.

City at sea

Whatever you want, *Nimitz* and her sister ships (these pictures are of the *Dwight D. Eisenhower*) have got – except female company, alcohol and relief from the noise. Although many sailors still eat 'sliders and rollers' – hamburgers and hot dogs – there is a wide variety of food readily available. There are the stocks of the ship's own massive store-rooms and freezers, and fresh food is supplied by the regular visits of the station ship.

Another contact with the outside world is the Carrier On-board Delivery (COD) plane, which not only brings visitors and urgently needed spares, but carries other high-priority items such as mail and new videos. The ship's own radio and TV channels, meanwhile, do their best to keep the crew informed of everything going on in the outside world.

Below and right: The working day is split into five five-hour watches and two two-hour 'dog watches' between 4pm and 8pm; the XO decides who will work where. Shown here are Nimitz-class carrier *Dwight D. Eisenhower*'s information receiving room (where all the information received from the various sources is collated), the air traffic control centre, the bridge and the ship's post office.

Most officers and petty officers have to do some administration work as part of their jobs, but the carrier is so big and has so large a crew that approximately 20 per cent of the entire crew is devoted to enabling the other 80 per cent to man the ship and its various systems and weaponry. Men are always joining and leaving the ship, and keeping the paperwork up to date is a major headache.

Although most time off watch is spent sleeping – unless the ship is in port and there is shore leave – everything possible is done to keep up morale. One advantage of serving on a carrier is that entertainers can be flown on by the COD plane or by the ship's helicopters. There is also plenty of room (either on the flight deck or in part of the hangar) for concerts and parties. Any carrier, and particularly a nuclear carrier, has power to spare for lighting, as well as superbly equipped workshops to produce any props that may be required for parties or concerts.

Most of the crew wear dungarees, with the specially coloured jerseys for those working on the flight deck, and radiation badges for those working near the reactors. Bunks are more comfortable than they used to be, but carriers are more crowded than most modern warships, so there is less privacy than either the crew or the staff who designed *Nimitz* would like. However, until planes need less maintenance and flight deck operations can be automated, carriers will always need large crews: crowding goes with the job, unless you are fortunate enough to be an admiral.

Nimitz in action

Compared with many USN carriers, *Nimitz* has had a very straightforward career. From 1975 to 1987 she was in the Atlantic Fleet, and since her 1987 refit she has been assigned to the Pacific Fleet. Whereas most carriers have had a number of different air wings (CVW) assigned to them, *Nimitz* has only had CVW-8 – though this Atlantic Fleet air wing has now been assigned to CVN-71, the new improved Nimitz-class *Theodore Roosevelt* carrier, and *Nimitz* will host a Pacific Fleet air wing. Not only did CVW-8 (tail identification letters AJ) remain attached to the *Nimitz* for more than a decade, so did many of the squadrons in it – particularly VF-41 Black Aces, VF-84 Jolly Rogers, and VA-35 Black Panthers. Electronics squadrons such as VAQ-134 Garudas (flying EA-6B Prowlers on the hostage mission deployment in 1979-80), and VAW-124 with E-2C Hawkeye, VS-24 Scouts with S-3A Vikings and HS-9 Sea Griffins with SH-3 Sea King helicopters – all aboard for the 1985 6th Fleet deployment – were less regular visitors. The air wing came aboard before each

deployment, and at the end of it returned ashore again along with all its personnel, normally to Naval Air Station (NAS) Oceana in Virginia, close to *Nimitz*'s base port (from 1975 to 1987) of Norfolk, Virginia.

As is normal with most USN carriers, the *Nimitz* spent the 18 months following her refit in a shakedown cruise before her first operational deployment to the Mediterranean. Then followed a regular cycle of approximately six months with the Sixth Fleet in the Mediterranean, followed by a spell in Norfolk, Va., and then nine months in the Second Fleet on the Atlantic coast. The first alteration to this routine came on her third deployment, when *Nimitz* was sent to relieve the USS *Kitty Hawk* (CV-63) which was in the Indian Ocean keeping watch over the situation in Iran. In April 1980 RH-53D Sea Stallions flew from *Nimitz* to join the doomed Iranian hostage rescue mission.

The next deployment in 1981 was equally exciting – and far more satisfying. *Nimitz* had already chalked up a number of 'firsts'; for example, in November 1977 the first ICAP EA-6B Prowler deployment with VAQ-135 Ravens, and on this 1981 deployment the first use of TARPS by VF-84 Jolly Rogers, but far more gratifying – at least to the air wing – was the first F-14 Tomcat combat success during a coat-trailing exercise in the Gulf of Sidra, when two Libyan SU-22s were shot down.

Following a relatively uneventful deployment between November 1982 and May 1983, spent mainly on 'Bagel Station' off Lebanon and in further exercises off

Below: RH-53s practise formation take-offs prior to the abortive Iranian hostage rescue mission in 1980. In another dramatic action, F-14s from *Nimitz* shot down two Libyan SU-22s (inset) over the Gulf of Sidra in 1981.

Libya, *Nimitz* underwent a major refit lasting from June 1983 to September 1984. This refit was followed by three more deployments to the Mediterranean.

In August 1985, it was announced that *Nimitz* and her CVBG were being transferred to the Pacific Fleet, with effect from March 1986. Under a new policy, they were to go to the new carrier base at Bremerton, on Puget Sound in Washington State, rather than to California – a move which would have involved some 9000 USN personnel, 8500 dependants, 15 ships, and cost more than $300 million (£162 million). The move was postponed, but *Nimitz* has now been assigned to the Pacific Fleet, and has been replaced at Norfolk, Va, by the brand-new *Theodore Roosevelt* (CVN-71), which has taken over *Nimitz*'s old air wing, CVW-8.

The future

Nimitz (CVN-68), was followed by the almost identical *Carl Vinson* (CVN-70) and *Dwight D. Eisenhower* (CVN-69). The *Eisenhower* was delayed, like the *Nimitz*, by problems in the development of her A4W reactors and only finally commissioned in 1977, while the *Carl Vinson* (CVN-70) was commissioned in 1982. The next three USN carriers reveal slight changes in equipment and detailed layout, but are otherwise to the same design. *Theodore Roosevelt* (CVN-71) was commissioned on October 25, 1986, and has recently replaced *Nimitz* in the Atlantic Fleet. *Abraham Lincoln* (CVN-72) was launched in February 1988 and will be

Below and inset: Celebrating the launch of Nimitz-class carrier *Abraham Lincoln* (CVN-72) in 1988. With the approval of funding for further CVNs, the role of the super-carrier within the USN is assured well into the 21st century.

commissioned in 1990, and *George Washington* (CVN-73), laid down in September 1986, will be commissioned towards the end of 1991.

This massive influx of new supercarriers is the result of pressure by the USN for an enlarged and modernized fleet – the '600-ship Navy'. On December 22, 1987, Congress approved long-term funding for two further improved Nimitz-class vessels – CVN-74, to be authorized in FY 1991 and CVN-75, to be authorized in FY 1993. However, whereas the USN wanted these ships to be part of a phased 'cascading' of the oldest carriers into training roles, then retirement – so maintaining an increased force level of 15 deployable carriers – budgetary restraints are forcing a rethink.

However, although fewer CVBGs may mean that *Nimitz* and her sister ships are used more intensively, given a 40-year life (*Midway* and *Coral Sea* have already been in service for longer), *Nimitz* will last until 2015, and CVN-75 until about 2040.

The mix of aircraft within the air-wing is certainly changing. The new carrier air wing (CVW) for the late 1980s doubles the numbers of medium attack aircraft (which can also be used as tankers) while deleting the specialist KA-6D tankers and reducing the numbers of fighters and light attack aircraft. The aircraft that will see the USN into the 21st century, meanwhile, will include the relatively conventional General Dynamics/McDonnell Douglas A-12 advanced tactical aircraft (the replacement for the A-6 Intruder) and the improved F-14D Tomcat, as well as (possibly) such radically different types as the tilt-rotor V-22 Osprey. As all of these will require carriers to operate from, supercarriers will still be sailing well into the 21st century.

Chapter 2
FORCES LIFE:
THE FRENCH FOREIGN LEGION

Cynically founded in 1831 as a means of disposing of Paris's human flotsam, the Foreign Legion soon became legendary both for its bravery in action in inhospitable parts of the globe and for its esprit de corps. Today's Legion is still expected to fight anywhere, at any time, and many Legionnaires are still of foreign origin but, far from being an expendable force, today's superbly trained and equipped Legion is at the cutting edge of France's armed might in its role as that country's rapid action force.

Convoy duty in the fierce heat of Chad, Central Africa. In this campaign, the French Foreign Legion faced many adversaries, including the rebels, a lack of fuel and spares – and hepatitis caused by contaminated water.

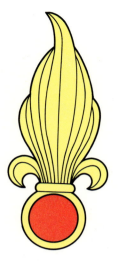

Above extreme left: Badges worn with pride by the Legion, a cap badge (left) and a pocket badge.
Above: The first full dress uniform of 1831, and the uniform worn in Mexico during the 1860s.

Few military organizations have been founded with such cynicism, or betrayed so often by their political masters, as the French Foreign Legion. When Marshal Joseph Soult signed the Legion into existence in 1831, one of his aims was to get rid of a rabble of foreigners who were terrorizing Paris.

The rabble consisted of refugees from failed revolutions in half a dozen countries, the remnants of Napoleon's armies, and French soldiers who remained loyal to Charles X, who had been forced to abdicate. Hungry mobs had also joined the disaffected soldiers in rioting and looting food stores. Soult, who was War Minister and needed soldiers to conquer France's new empire in North Africa, perceived this mob's potential: 'So they wish to fight. Then let them bleed or shovel sand in the conquest of North Africa.'

Soult also decreed that the Legion 'should not be employed in the continental territory of the kingdom'. In other words, the Legion could die in the service of France abroad – but would not be allowed to set foot in France. Here then, right at its inception, the men of the Foreign Legion realized that they could not rely on France, but only on the Legion. It was from this realization that the spirit of the Legion grew.

When a man joined the Legion no questions were asked about his past. He gave loyalty to the death and, in return, the Legion gave him a home, a family and returned his loyalty. The curious who asked a Legionnaire where he came from would be told: 'The Legion is my country.'

The early days

The original Foreign Legion was predominantly German – as it has remained until recently – and it was packed off to become part of the newly formed Armée d'Afrique. For the next four years the Legionnaires did as Soult had dictated: they died in mercilessly fought skirmishes in North Africa. When they were not fighting, they built roads across the virgin territory.

In 1835, the Legion was sent to fight in the Carlist civil war in Spain, on behalf of the infant Queen Isabella,

and ceased to be part of the French army. The cost of feeding, paying and kitting-out the Legion was also transferred to its new owners, who felt that while it was proper for the Legionnaires to die for them, it was not necessary for them to be fed.

Despite the attitude of its new masters, the Legion – by now comprising 123 officers and 4021 men – fought until it was virtually wiped out; this, they deemed, released it from the obligation the French Government had made on its behalf. In January 1839 the remnants, 63 officers and 159 other ranks, marched into the French garrison town of Pau to report for duty.

Nobody had expected them to survive. Moreover, while they had been in Spain a new Legion had been raised to meet the demands for more and more men to fight France's increasing number of colonial wars. The survivors of the Spanish civil war were eventually allowed to join the new Legion.

It was at this time that the foundations of the romance which surrounds the name of the Foreign

Legion began to be laid, and in those days the romance was not far removed from reality. P.C. Wren's *Beau Geste*, with its fight to the last in the isolated Fort Zinderneuf, reflected the fate of many Legionnaires sent into the desert to hold strategic points with inadequate force. The *cafard* – desert madness – also took its toll.

The Legionnaires learnt to survive and fight in the desert, marching many miles a day at the slow sand-pace of 85 steps per minute. Their watchword became 'March or Die', for they knew that any man who dropped out would die slowly under the knives of the tribesmen's women.

It was here, in Algeria, that the Legion built its home, the depot of Sidi-bel-Abbès. Behind the depot's white walls recruits were inculcated with the remarkable *esprit de corps* which seemed to galvanize the Legion in battle, but which was eventually to lead to its political disgrace more than one hundred years later.

In 1854 the Legion was sent out of Africa again, but this time as part of the French army fighting in the Crimean War. The men of the 1st and 2nd Regiments fought alongside the British Army at the Battle of the Alma and took part in the Siege of Sebastopol. The pretty wife of the Legion's commander, Brigadier Bazaine was an accomplished pianist and accompanied her husband to the war with her grand piano where she entertained the Legionnaires with her piano-playing.

At the end of the Crimean War the Legion returned once again to the desert, and to the old life of back-breaking labour interspersed with brutal skirmishes. In 1862, however, the opportunity arose for the Legion to take part in another foreign adventure.

The public's perception of life in the Foreign Legion ranged from the romanticism of the Hollywood adventure film, *Beau Geste* (above) to the strip cartoon humour of *Beau Beep* (below extreme left).

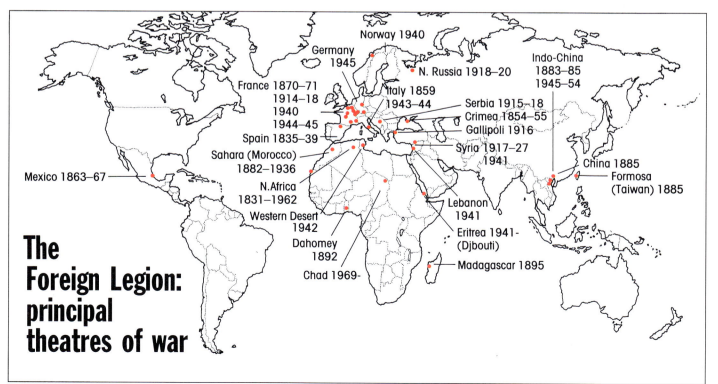

The Foreign Legion: principal theatres of war

Norway 1940
Germany 1945
France 1870–71 1914–18 1940 1944–45
Italy 1859 1943–44
N. Russia 1918–20
Indo-China 1883–85 1945–54
Serbia 1915–18
Crimea 1854–55
Gallipoli 1916
Spain 1835–39
Sahara (Morocco) 1882–1936
Syria 1917–27 1941
China 1885
Formosa (Taiwan) 1885
Mexico 1863–67
N.Africa 1831–1962
Western Desert 1942
Dahomey 1892
Lebanon 1941
Eritrea 1941- (Djbouti)
Madagascar 1895
Chad 1969-

Left: Bayonet fixed and ready for action – a fusilier from the French Foreign Legion, Mexico 1863.

Mexico and Danjou's hand

After a quarrel with Mexico, caused by the failure of its revolutionary leader, Benito Juarez, to pay the interest on a series of loans, Napoleon III dispatched an expeditionary force which defeated the regular Mexican army and established the Habsburg princeling, Maximilian, as king of Mexico. The Legion had not been included in the original expedition but its officers, bored with road-building, petitioned Napoleon to be allowed to go. Three battalions under Colonel Pierre Jeanningros were landed at Veracruz on March 31, 1863 – and were relegated to garrison duty along the fever-ridden route from Veracruz to Mexico City.

Malaria and yellow fever raged through the Legion and morale slumped. They were refused permission to take part in the siege of Puebla, whose capture would open the way to Mexico City. The Legionnaires took their revenge by dealing harshly with the guerrilla forces that ventured out to attack them. It was in this unpromising situation that the Legion fought the battle which was to become the focus of its ethos. In size it was nothing: in bravery it was an epic.

The great day began with a typically boring task. Colonel Jeanningros was ordered to supply an escort for a special convoy which was making its way up from Veracruz to Puebla. Consisting of 60 carts and 150 mules, it carried not only heavy siege guns to batter the walls of Puebla, but also three million francs in gold.

Jeanningros, based at Chiquihuite half-way between Veracruz and Puebla, sent two companies, both weakened by fever, to meet the convoy as it plodded up from the coast. Alarmed by reports that the Mexicans had assembled a large force of regular infantry and cavalry to ambush the convoy, he ordered the 3rd Company of the 1st Battalion to reinforce the guard. The 3rd company had also been seriously weakened by fever, and none of its officers was fit to march. The battalion adjutant, Captain Jean Danjou, the paymaster, Sous-Lieutenant Jean Villain and an officer of the 1st Company, Sous-Lieutenant Clement Maudet, nevertheless volunteered to lead the half-strength company. Aged 28, Danjou was a veteran of the Crimean War, and had lost his left hand at Sebastopol. He had replaced it with a cleverly jointed wooden hand, on which he wore a spotless white glove.

Danjou and his men left Chiquihuite in the early hours of April 30. It was soon to become unbearably hot. At first all was quiet. After six hours' marching, the Legionnaires halted just outside the broken-down village of Camerone to make breakfast. Suddenly, Mexican cavalrymen appeared and it soon became obvious that they were part of a large force. Danjou abandoned breakfast and led his men into Camerone, where they formed a square to fight off the cavalry, as they had learned to do in Algeria. They then took refuge

in the village's ruined hacienda. By this time the supply mules had bolted and 16 men had been captured, leaving only 49 men and the ammunition they carried in their pouches. This ill-equipped band had to defend the farm buildings against a Mexican force of 1500 men.

The Mexicans called on Danjou to surrender. He replied in true Legion style: 'We'll die first'. And so he did, shortly afterwards. However, before he was shot he made his men swear that they would not surrender.

Sous-Lieutenant Villain took over command and the battle raged furiously, with the Legionnaires suffering badly from thirst. Villain himself was killed in the early afternoon. Maudet, a dissident journalist who had joined the Legion to escape imprisonment, took command. More Mexican regulars arrived. Still the Legionnaires held out, although by now they were split into small groups, each fighting its own battle. By five o'clock there were only 12 Legionnaires left standing.

Colonel Milan, commander of the Mexican forces, harangued his troops, and ordered a general assault. But still the Legionnaires held out, although by now there were only five able to continue the fight. Just after six o'clock they ran out of ammunition and, after nine hours of fighting, they fixed bayonets and with Maudet at their head, charged the Mexican lines.

Legionnaire Constantin, an Austrian, threw himself in front of Maudet and died with 19 bullets in his body. Maudet was mortally wounded. A German, Wenzel, a Pole, Katau, and a French corporal, Maine, survived when a Mexican officer who had trained in France held off his men and asked the remaining Legionnaires to surrender. Corporal Maine agreed, on condition they would not have to surrender their arms.

When the men were taken before Colonel Milan and

he was told that they were the only survivors, he exclaimed: 'Truly, these are not men, but devils'. The survivors – there were 32 in all, including the wounded and those taken prisoner earlier – were treated kindly, despite the fact that they had so badly mauled Colonel Milan's force that he had to abandon his plans to ambush the convoy.

The following day, Colonel Jeanningros led a relief column to Camerone where he found Danjou's drummer, Lai. Bleeding from bullet and lance wounds, Lai had hidden under a pile of corpses and had crept out only after the Mexicans had marched away.

The importance of this minor skirmish in an insignificant war lay in the willingness of the defenders to die fighting. Every man became a hero, and the fight became a legend. Danjou's wooden hand was found and it became a totem to the Foreign Legion, a bizarre but tangible reminder of a day of great glory.

Fittingly, every year on April 30, Danjou's wooden hand is paraded by the 1st Regiment at the Legion's modern depot at Aubagne in Provence, where it 'takes the salute' as the Regiment marches past. Indeed, wherever in the world a unit of the Legion is based on that day, it too celebrates Camerone Day. The ceremony is always the same: first there is a parade in full uniform; then a reading of the story of Camerone; and finally, a feast. Camerone *is* the Legion.

Above left: Captain Jean Danjou, the battalion adjutant, who served with distinction in Algeria, the Crimea and Italy, before meeting his death at Camerone in 1863.
Below: April 30, Camerone Day Parade at Aubagne, France.

Europe and Africa

In 1867, the French pulled out of Mexico, leaving the hapless 'Emperor' Maximilian to be captured and shot by firing squad. Three years later Marshal Soult's orders that the Legion should never be used in France had to be abandoned when France went to war with Prussia. But even in that emergency the Legion was at first kept in Africa as more than half of its men were German. To begin with, a new regiment of the Legion was formed in France from non-German volunteers, but eventually the 'real' Legion was sent for, and the Germans in its ranks fought bravely for their adopted country against the Prussians. The Legion was also employed in the brutal repression of the Communards, who had seized Paris after the French defeat by the Prussians in 1870.

It was with some relief that the Legion returned to its more usual empire-building role after this period in France, and in the next 40 years it served all over the world, as France turned her attention to acquiring new overseas possessions. The Legion saw service in them all and Indo-China became its second home. Its new leader, General de Negrier, in a brutally frank comment made at this time, told his men: 'You Legionnaires are soldiers in order to die and I am sending you where you can die.'

One of the strangest wars in which the Legionnaires were sent to fight was in Dahomey, where King Glé-Glé, encouraged by the Germans, tried to drive out the French. The King's ambitions were soon thwarted, but when he died one of his sons, Behanzin, mounted a

Below: the colour party of the 1er Régiment Etrangers at Sidi-bel-Abbès, Algeria in 1910. The Legion left its HQ for the last time in October 1962.

guerrilla campaign against the French. They retaliated by sending a column to sack his capital, Abomey, located deep in the jungle some 155 miles (250km) from the coast. The 2nd Battalion of the 2nd Foreign Legion Infantry Regiment was ordered from Sidi-bel-Abbès to join this force, which set out confident of its superiority.

The campaign was not to prove as easy as the Legionnaires imagined, however, for nobody had told them about Behanzin's corps of shock troops – who were just as brave and just as willing to die as the Legionnaires themselves. The difference was that they were women. For the rule in Dahomey was that when girls reached the age of 15 they went before a selection board. The best-looking were sent to the King's harem, the misshapen and sick were killed, and the rest underwent two years' of rigorous training as warriors. They were formidable foes. 'They were like mad creatures', one French officer wrote in his memoirs. 'Even bayonets did not seem to stop them. Some tried to claw their way up the blades skewering them to get to grips with their enemy . . .'

World Wars I and II

It was in relatively minor colonial wars such as that in Dahomey that the *Régiments Etranger* learnt and plied their trade in the years leading up to the great blood-letting of World War I. Some 30,000 Legionnaires died or were seriously wounded on the Western Front, but despite the horrendous casualties no Legionnaire took part in the mutinies of 1917, which came close to destroying the French army. For once the Legion was officially honoured in Paris.

After the war, the turmoil in Europe brought a new influx of recruits. So many former Russian officers joined that a Russian battalion was created, and it was not uncommon to find former generals serving in the ranks. The depression of the 1930s brought another wave of recruits, and this time many of them were British and Americans seeking food and shelter and a restoration of their pride.

These Legionnaires fought in North Africa just as their predecessors had done, but this time against the charismatic desert warrior Abd el-Krim, in French Morocco. They also saw action in France's new mandated territory of Syria. In short, it was business as usual for the Legion right up to the outbreak of World War II.

The Legion's fate in World War II reflected that of France itself. Bitterly divided, torn between its loyalty to the official French Government of Vichy and the Free French Forces of General de Gaulle, the Legion lost its sense of direction. The victorious Nazis took 2000 German Legionnaires and incorporated them into the Afrika Korps. Free French Legionnaires fought against Vichy Legionnaires in Syria. Others sat out the war in remote outposts.

One action, however, restored honour not only to the Legion but to the whole of the Free French Forces.

Above: Victory in the Western Desert at Bir Hakeim, Spring 1942: a Free French Legionnaire poses, with his banner attached to his rifle, at the end of the battle.

Five hundred men of the 13th Demi Brigade of the Légion Etranger, as part of the 1st Free French Brigade, behaved with great valour at Bir Hakeim in the Western Desert in May and April of 1942.

The French, under the command of the former Legionnaire, General Pierre Koenig, held out for 15 days against Rommel's tanks, guns and planes in a battle conducted with panache by the French at a time when British forces were fleeing before the Afrika Korps. When their position became untenable, they broke out. At the break-out, General Koenig was driven by his English woman driver, Susan Travers, who later became the only woman ever to become a full member of the Foreign Legion. Another of those to escape was Legionnaire Captain Pierre Messmer, who was later to become Prime Minister of France. Even when he had attained this exalted post, however, his wife said of him: 'He is still my Legionnaire. He smells of the desert.'

Post-1945: Indo-China

When World War II finished, the French attempted to reoccupy their lost empire. This involved a return to Indo-China where, with several notable exceptions,

French honour had been sullied by collaboration with the Japanese. The returning French army, composed mostly of foreign troops from the Armée d'Afrique, immediately clashed with the Viet Minh. This nationalist, communist force had emerged during the war as the only effective resistance to the Japanese. They were now prepared to fight the French for independence.

The ensuing colonial war soon became a disaster for the French. The nadir was reached at Dien Bien Phu where, in the spring of 1954, men of the Foreign Legion once again found themselves fighting against insuperable odds. The French commanders in Hanoi, seeking to bring the Viet Minh to a decisive battle, completely misread their enemy's capabilities and boasted that they would destroy the Viet Minh attackers with gunfire and

Below: Legionnaires attack an enemy stronghold. More often than not, the Legionnaires would reject a steel helmet and go into battle wearing their kepis.
Bottom: Amphibious vehicles were used by the Legion during the hostilities in Indo-China.

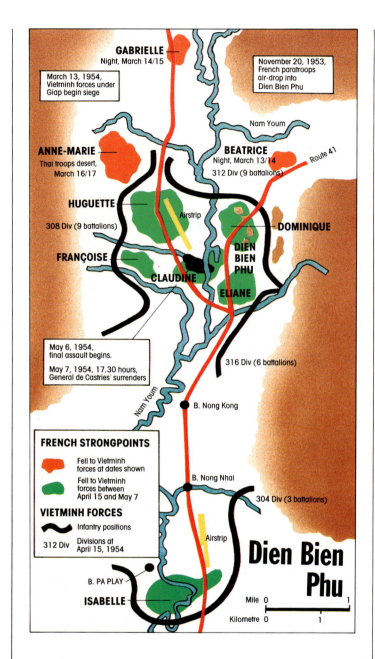

GABRIELLE
Night, March 14/15

March 13, 1954,
Vietminh forces under
Giap begin siege

November 20, 1953,
French paratroops
air-drop into
Dien Bien Phu

Nam Youm

ANNE-MARIE
Thai troops desert,
March 16/17

BEATRICE
Night, March 13/14
312 Div (9 battalions)

Route 41

HUGUETTE

Airstrip

DOMINIQUE

308 Div (9 battalions)

DIEN
BIEN
PHU

FRANÇOISE

CLAUDINE

ELIANE

May 6, 1954,
final assault begins.

May 7, 1954, 17.30 hours,
General de Castries' surrenders

316 Div (6 battalions)

Nam Youm

B. Nong Kong

FRENCH STRONGPOINTS

Fell to Vietminh
forces at dates shown

Fell to Vietminh
forces between
April 15 and May 7

B. Nong Nhai

304 Div (3 battalions)

VIETMINH FORCES

Infantry positions

312 Div   Divisions at
April 15, 1954

Airstrip

Dien Bien
Phu

B. PA PLAY

ISABELLE

Mile 0   1

Kilometre 0   1

Above: Plan of the Dien Bien Phu campaign in Spring 1954. The barrage of artillery rounds crushed the Legionnaires who were unable to retaliate successfully.

Below: The French were surrounded and trapped in the valley of Dien Bien Phu by the Viet Minh.

Above: Since the casualties could not be evacuated during the siege of Dien Bien Phu, they were patched up by the medical staff and then the soldiers returned to the fight.

air attack. But it was the Viet Minh commander, General Giap, who was to do the destroying.

On the first morning of the assault the Beatrice fortress, held by men of the 13th Demi Brigade of the Foreign Legion, was pounded by Giap's well-camouflaged guns. The position's artillery, two 105mm field guns, were knocked out and Beatrice's commander, Colonel Gaucher, was killed. Viet Minh sappers then blew holes in the barbed wire and masses of infantry poured through the breaches, regardless of casualties, overrunning bunkers and dug-outs in hand-to-hand fighting with bayonets and grenades. Of the 800 Legionnaires manning the fortress, only 200 were able to reach the main French lines after the rout.

The fall of Beatrice foreshadowed the fate of Dien Bien Phu. The siege lasted 56 days, and by the time the guns had fallen silent it had cost the French 2000 dead, and 7000 wounded and missing. A further 7000 had been taken prisoner, many of whom died as they were marched through the jungle under cruel conditions. Dien Bien Phu represented more than just a lost battle. It brought about the fall of the government in Paris; the end of the French empire in Indo-China; and set in motion the process which led to the USA's involvement, and defeat, in Vietnam.

For the Legion it meant a return to North Africa to lick its wounds, and to absorb the military lessons of Indo-China. However, they were not the only ones to learn the lessons of Indo-China, for Algeria's own nationalist movement – the Armée de Libération Nationale (ALN) – now emerged, and the agony of Algeria's battle for independence from France began.

The Legion in Algeria

The Foreign Legion was involved in the vicious Algerian war from start to finish, and at the end came close to being destroyed by its dedication to the ideal for which it had first been formed: *Algérie Française*, French rule over Algeria.

In 1960, for the first time in its history, the First Regiment of Foreign Legion Parachutists (1er REP) mutinied against General de Gaulle – they felt that they were being betrayed by his government. The Legion had virtually defeated the ALN on the field of battle, only to see the politicians offer to relinquish the *Algérie Française* for which they had shed so much blood. Paris was plunged into a state of panic on hearing of the mutiny. Airfields were blocked in case the Legion's paras flew from Algeria to take over France itself.

The Legionnaires, however, saw themselves as once more fighting a noble battle against great odds. They were prepared to die for what they, as foreigners, saw as their duty to the true France, which had been betrayed by politicians. They had considerable initial success in Algiers, but the air force and the navy were totally opposed to them, as was the French conscript army serving in Germany. De Gaulle then did what he could do so well: he broadcast to the nation. 'Frenchmen and women,' he intoned, 'France is in peril. Frenchmen, Frenchwomen, help me!' It was a very powerful, emotional speech – and it was effective. The mutiny collapsed, and the 1er REP drove off to prison singing the Edith Piaf song which had become the regiment's own: 'Rien! Je ne regrette rien.'

A few Legionnaires went underground, sheltered by the *Pieds noirs* settlers, and committed acts of terrorism as the 'Delta Force'. Most of them were tracked down eventually. Some went before the firing squad and others served long terms of imprisonment.

Below: During the 1950s, the Legion fought to keep Algeria under French rule, to the extent that, in 1960, they mutinied against the French government and caused panic when it was thought they would invade France.

which has a crew of two and carries ten fully equipped men. The VAB is extremely adaptable. Some are fitted to carry a 120mm mortar, others have a 20mm turret gun and another variant has a roof-mounted radar.

The 3e Régiment Etrangers d'Infanterie, an infantry battalion about 500 strong, has the task of looking after French military interests in South America. Its headquarters is at Fort de France on the island of Martinique. The 4e Régiment Etrangers is the training regiment which takes recruits through their basic training at Castelnaudry, near Carcassonne. The 5e Régiment Etrangers d'Infanterie, a battalion about 600 strong based on Tahiti, in the Pacific, has responsibility for the protection of the islands where France carries out nuclear tests. The 6e Régiment Etrangers Genie (REG) is the Legion's own regiment of engineers, based at L'Ardoise. The 13e Demi Brigade Légion Etrangers (DBLE), is an all-arms group (equipped with its own tanks and artillery) permanently based at Djibouti, headquarters of France's East Africa Military Region. The 2e Régiment Etrangers de Parachutistes (REP) is the Legion's only surviving paratroop unit. This regiment did not take part in the mutiny in Algiers and so survived de Gaulle's anger.

The parachute regiment

The 2e Régiment Etrangers de Parachutistes is regarded as the élite of the Legion today – and it is at the tip of France's rapid action force, the Force d'Action Rapide (FAR). The FAR is designed to play a role in both the European theatre and in 'out-of-area' operations. The latter involves defending the French Overseas Territories and the former French colonies, notably those in Africa, with whom France has treaties.

The 2e REP is based at Calvi in Corsica, where the mountainous terrain provides a training ground just as arduous as the desert. It is certainly more relevant to the Legion's modern tasks, for 2e REP now has teams of frogmen and specialized mountain warfare units in its ranks. Indeed, there are similarities between the Special Air Service (SAS) and the 2e REP, and it is noticeable that there is a high proportion of Britons serving in the regiment.

The 2e REP only accepts volunteers from the best of the recruits who survive their basic infantry training at the 4e Régiment Etrangers base at Castelnaudray. They are then put through a gruelling series of tests – which only about three out of ten pass.

These go to the regiment's Corsican headquarters, Camp Rafalli, where they are trained in all the techniques of a modern para-commando.

Camp Rafalli is ideally placed for para-training. It has an airfield with rifle and mortar ranges close at hand. Specialists also practise free-fall parachuting for behind-the-lines 'insertion' operations.

The Foreign Legion today

After the Algerian mutiny, the 1er REP was disbanded. Indeed, de Gaulle was minded to do away with the Foreign Legion altogether, but Pierre Messmer reminded him what a political debt he owed the Legionnaires for their stand at Bir Hakeim, and the Legion was allowed to live. It has, however, become a very different force. Officers classed as 'unsound' were hounded out of the army, and the Legion was dispersed throughout the remnants of the Empire. When, in 1966, it was finally brought back to occupy its first depot on French soil at Aubagne, not far from Marseilles, it was much more closely integrated with the French army.

The Legion now consists of 8500 fighting men, organized into infantry, cavalry, parachute, engineer and headquarters units. These are: The 1er Régiment Etrangers de Cavalerie (REC), which is equipped with AMX-10RC amphibious armoured cars mounting 105mm guns. This regiment is based at Nimes, while the 1er Régiment Etrangers d'Infanterie (REI) is based at the Aubagne depot.

The 2e Régiment Etrangers d'Infanterie is a mechanized infantry unit equipped with the Vehicle de l'Avant Blindés (VAB) amphibious armoured personnel carrier,

Above: Rigorous training of Legion recruits ensures a skilled and highly motivated force to be reckoned with.
Right: On patrol in the rain forests of French Guiana, where the 3e REI built the French rocket launching base.

Once fully trained, the Legionnaires are assigned to one of six companies in the 1300-strong regiment. While these companies fulfil their normal para-commando function in time of war, they also have different areas of expertise.

No. 1 Company specializes in street fighting and night operations, with emphasis on heliborne assault and behind-the-lines operations. No. 2 Company specializes in mountain warfare, and its men are trained in climbing and skiing techniques. No. 3 Company is the amphibious company, and its men are trained as para-swimmers and in the use of small boats. No. 4 Company's special duties include sabotage and demolition, and its men are trained in 'stay-behind' missions. Each of these companies is based on the normal platoon and section structure and has its own Milan section with two launcher teams. Primarily an anti-tank weapon, it can also be used in a bunker-busting role. Each of the sections is armed with a 7.62mm F1 light machine gun, and an 89mm anti-tank projector. The personal weapon is the ultra-modern 5.56mm FA MAS assault rifle.

Service and support companies

In addition to the four rifle companies, the 2e REP has two specialist companies: the CCS service and support company and the CEA reconnaissance and tactical support company.

CCS runs the base at Calvi and carries out all those logistic and administrative functions that enable any regiment to take to the field. However, and here there is another similarity with the SAS, the CCS also runs its own communications network giving its deployed teams instant access to regimental command at Calvi.

The CEA, meanwhile, provides the fire-power punch for the regiment. Apart from its reconnaissance platoon mounted on French-built jeeps, the company has an air-defence section armed with Roland Surface-to-Air Missiles (SAMs) and four 20mm twin anti-aircraft guns which can also be used against ground targets; two vehicle-mounted Milan platoons with a total of 16 launchers; and a towed mortar troop with eight 81mm and four 120mm mortars.

There is another aspect to this company which is very SAS in style and role. Called Commandos de Renseignement et d'Action dans la Profondeur, it rejoices in the acronym of CRAP – much to the amusement of its British members. CRAP's teams are trained to operate deep behind enemy lines, preparing the way for the advancing rifle companies, or in 'sticks' on special operations. Every CRAP member is also trained in High Altitude, High Opening (HAHO) parachute techniques, so that they can be released miles from their targets and fly on to them undetected. Each 'stick' consists of men with individual skills and will include a medic, a signaller, a demolitions expert, and any other expert whose speciality is required.

All members of 2e REP are also trained in helicopter work. The navy's Super Frelons are used to airlift the heavy mortar teams, with the army's Pumas being used to carry 12 fully equipped Legionnaires.

Above: The Legionnaires have always constructed their own camps and built roads, when not on active service. Below left: The 2e REP were quickly flown to Kolwezi, in May 1978, when help was needed to control rebels.

Today's Legion in action

The Foreign Legion has not been deprived of action in modern times. It has been part of the peace-keeping force in the Lebanon, where one of its tasks was to supervise the withdrawal of the Palestinian Liberation Organization (PLO) after its defeat by the Israelis.

In 1976, meanwhile, men of the 13 DBLE, stationed at Djibouti, carried out a classic rescue operation when 29 children of French families living in Djibouti were held hostage by Somalian terrorists.

The operation was complicated by the fact that the children's bus was parked alongside Djibouti's border with Somalia; there was a chance of interference from Somalia. To prevent this, a screen of 1er REC's armoured cars drew up along the border while men of the 2e REP carried out the rescue of the children. They stormed the bus while marksmen of the French police anti-terrorist unit, the Groupement d'Intervention de la Gendarmerie Nationale (GIGN), who had flown in from Paris, picked off the terrorists.

The Legion has also been involved in the confused fighting in Chad where the French government, in its usual pragmatic fashion, has supported first one government and then its rival successor. The Legionnaires' constant enemy in Chad, however, has been Colonel Gadhaffi's Libyan Army, which has been pursuing that country's claims on its southern neighbour's territory. The fighting here has smacked of desert warfare – with the terrain representing as much of an enemy as the Libyan army and their rebel supporters.

The most famous of the Legion's interventions, however, was in Zaire in May 1978, when France mounted Operation Leopard to rescue 2500 Europeans from a 1000-strong column of Zairean rebels. The rebels, from Zaire's copper-rich state of Katanga, had been exiled to neighbouring Angola, where they had been armed and trained. They came rampaging over the border to seize the mining town of Kolwezi, where they

indulged in an orgy of looting and rape and murder.

The 2e REP was assigned the task of saving the Europeans. They arrived to find that their parachute harnesses were not compatible with Zaire's Hercules aircraft, from which they were to jump into action. They rigged up jury gear and, after two nights without sleep, made their jump just outside Kolwezi. At Kolwezi they almost came into conflict with a Belgian force which had arrived on the same mission.

It was left to the Belgians to round up the white population and fly them to safety; in the meantime the Legionnaires went hunting the rebels. While doing so they came across groups of hostages, both white and black, who were being held under threat of immediate execution. Sometimes the Legionnaires were too late. In one building they found the butchered bodies of 38 men, women and children. Such sights brought an even greater sense of urgency to the Legion's mission, but after a couple of days of brisk fire-fights, the rebels began to disperse.

The 2e REP spent some time winkling out those responsible for the worst of the atrocities. They then handed over responsibility for the area to a multi-national African force.

The regiment was awarded an official battle honour for this operation although – like all battles – it showed up flaws in planning and weaknesses in equipment. Nevertheless, it demonstrated that France's Force d'Action Rapide is truly effective. Most important for the Legion was that Operation Leopard and its battle honour represented a clear sign of official forgiveness for the mutiny in Algeria all those years ago. The Foreign Legion is again an élite force, trusted to fight – and die – for France.

Above: The 2e REP carried out Operation Leopard, in Kolwezi, Zaire, with the loss of only five men, but with the capture of considerable rebel equipment.
Below: From the dry heat of the desert to the humidity of rain forests, the Legionnaires disembark to begin a tour of duty in French Guiana.

Other operations

The Legion also continues with its tradition of digging when it is not fighting. The 5e REI, the guard force for the Muratoa Atoll in the Pacific where France carries out its nuclear bomb tests, has been involved in a massive programme of building. The construction of fall-out shelters, roads and the shoring-up of atolls crumbling under the impact of repeated nuclear explosions are all tasks which have been assigned to the Legionnaires.

In South America, meanwhile, the men of 3e REI have laboured in the dark rain forests of French Guiana to build the launching base for France's Ariane rocket.

Another area of operations for the Legion is Corsica. Here, the Corsican National Liberation Front (CNLF) has been engaged for years in a campaign of bombings – and occasionally murder – against French settlers on the island. The Legion has never been used in an anti-terrorist role against the CNLF, however. Perhaps the memory of Algeria still remains too fresh in the minds of the government. Instead, the Legion plays a more low-key policing role. But despite this, on at least one occasion the Legion has been the object of the CNLF's attentions. In 1982, one Legionnaire was shot dead and another wounded by masked CNLF terrorists at a Legion rest camp at the village of Sorbo-Ocagnano.

Life in the service today

There is no lack of recruits to the Legion today. Germany and the Eastern European countries provide some 16 per cent of new recruits, with the British contingent steadily increasing in recent years, under the impact of unemployment to around 5 per cent. But what is interesting about the national composition of the modern Legion is that more than 50 per cent of its

Top right: On patrol in Djibouti. The motorized vehicle has replaced the Legionnaire's mule as transport.
Below: Dismantling, cleaning and reassembling his rifle must become second nature for a Legionnaire, since it is possible that his life could depend on it.

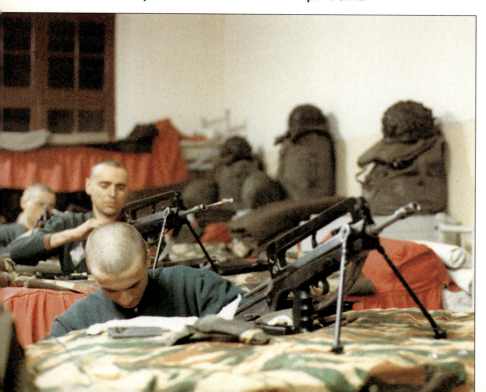

strength is made up of Frenchmen. Today's Foreign Legion, then, is no longer truly foreign.

One of the reasons for this is economic. The Legion is better paid than the rest of France's armed forces, and indeed troops of the 2e REP receive special allowances which mean that their salary is one third higher than for the rest of the Legion.

Legionnaires sign on for a five-year engagement, and it is still true that no questions are asked about a recruit's background. At the end of the five-year term, a Legionnaire can either retire with a pension or sign on again. Overall, those who join the Legion are no longer regarded as the brutalized sweepings from every corner of the globe, and many choose to marry French wives and settle down in France on retirement.

The officers remain mainly French, but the old tradition by which the Legion took the six officers who passed highest out of the military academy is no longer followed. Indeed, even young men doing their national service are now accepted as officers – so long as they measure up to the Legion's standards.

It remains difficult for a foreigner to be commissioned into the Legion, and those who are offered commissions must adopt French nationality. Even then, it is doubtful if they would ever rise above the rank of captain.

To be an officer in the Foreign Legion is to know that you have dedicated men behind you. This is important, given that a Legion officer is always expected to lead from the front: any officer who is unable to do this is finished. In this respect the Legion is similar to another famous band of mercenaries, the Gurkhas. They will give their lives for their officers so long as the officer is willing to lead them into battle.

A military organization such as the Foreign Legion obviously depends a great deal on tradition and ritual to mould its *esprit*, and the modern Legion is proud of the old Legion's traditions. The songs sung at the slow desert-marching cadence figure largely in today's Legionnaires' training, even though they now go to war by parachute. The story of Camerone is still drilled into every recruit.

Above: Ceremony and tradition are all part of the esprit which continues to bind men from many countries into a single élite force like the modern French Foreign Legion. Below: The old and the new. A Legionnaire with his 5.56mm FAMAS semi-automatic rifle, stands outside a desert fort in Chad, Central Africa.

The future

Today's Foreign Legion is a highly professional, well-equipped force, motivated by its history and its ability to provide young recruits with a home and a family – in return for the recruit's willingness to fight and die. But is there a place for such a force in the French army of today, and will there continue to be if the Western European defence forces are amalgamated?

The answer lies, as it always has for the Foreign Legion, with the politicians. It was created, at a stroke of the pen, for political purposes; it could be disposed of just as easily. However, given France's commitments to her former colonies – colonies which remain bound to metropolitan France by economic, social and military ties – and to those places which remain French dependencies, there is clearly a continuing need for a rapid intervention force such as that which is provided by the Legion.

In Europe, too, a rapid deployment force affords French commanders greater flexibility in emergencies, enabling them to deploy highly mobile units at great speed – not only in pursuit of France's own military objectives, but also as part of a multi-national force.

Given the laws restricting the use of the conscript army (it is forbidden by law to operate abroad except in time of war) it is essential for France to possess a force such as the Foreign Legion. If it were disbanded, some similar force would have to be cobbled together, without tradition, without *esprit*. The Legion, purged of its mutineers, more domesticated, and composed of 'hi-tech' soldiers would, therefore, seem to be safe.

It is not that France loves the Legionnaires – many socialists and communists still regard them as dangerous brutes and regret that they were ever allowed to establish a home base in France. Nevertheless, the Legion performs a necessary function for France, and it will survive as long as it remains useful – and loyal. As for the Legionnaires, they still believe in the lines of their poet Pascal Bonetti, written as so many of them went off to die in 1914: 'Has not this foreigner become a son of France,/Not by blood inherited, but spilled.'

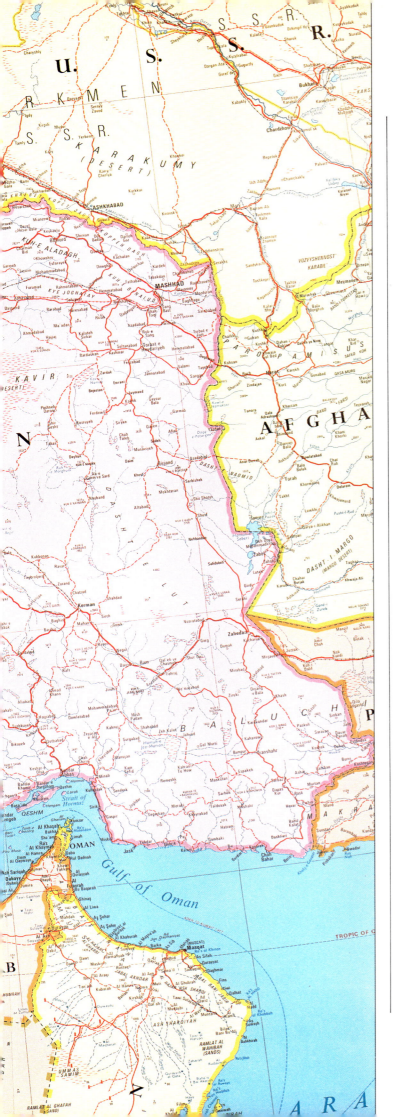

Chapter 3
CONFLICT:
WAR IN THE GULF

The capture and re-capture of the Faw peninsula, the powerful pictures of tankers burning in the Gulf, the horrific scenes of the effects of chemical warfare – these images sum up the Iran-Iraq conflict for many people in the West. Yet what are the causes of this, the 20th century's longest-running war? What forces does each side possess – and who is arming them? Such questions must be answered if a lasting peace is ever to return to the Gulf, for the future stability of the Middle East, and perhaps of the whole world, is at stake.

Iran and Iraq occupy strategically crucial positions in the Gulf and the outcome of the war between them will affect the political balance of the entire Middle East – and thus the availability of oil supplies to the West.

Above: A woman soldier of the National Liberation Army – an Iranian rebel force, backed by the Iraqis, dedicated to the overthrow of Khomeini's regime. The rebels scored some notable successes in the summer of 1988.

To most outsiders, the war between Iran and Iraq is almost a complete mystery. A few dramatic highlights may stick in the mind, but despite what is shown on television, the public discussions in the West about sending warships to the Gulf, the arms scandals, 'Irangate', there is little understanding of the causes of the war or its possible consequences.

Yet this is a major conflict between two large and important countries. It has already lasted eight years. There have been more than one million men killed or wounded on the battlefield and major damage to both side's cities and economies. For Iran and Iraq the war is already a disaster, and one with no obvious end.

It is also a disaster for many of their neighbours – particularly those caught up in the tanker war. It is also a worry for the world. The USSR has a common border with Iran, and the USA and the West cannot ignore events in a region that possesses more than half of the world's proven oil reserves.

Setting the scene

The war came about because of miscalculations by both sides. Iran and Iraq differ from the other Gulf oil states in having large areas of fertile land as well as vast tracts of desert. The former supports large populations – Iran's is about 50 million, Iraq's 16.5 million. The two countries have a history of rivalry, which was reinforced before and after World War II by the decline of British power in the area, culminating in that country's complete withdrawal in 1971.

Iran, under Shah Mohammed Reza Pahlevi, aimed for what he termed 'strategic Autarky' (*sic*). By this, he meant the domination of Iran not only over the Gulf but also over the Arabian Sea. By the time the Shah was overthrown by a popular revolution spearheaded by fundamentalist Islamic mullahs (he left for Morocco on January 16, 1979), Iran had bought arms worth $17.6 billion (£880 million) from the USA alone, and almost as much again was on order or projected. Iraq, buying arms mainly from the USSR, could not hope to match the power of the Shah's well-trained armed forces and in signing the Algiers Agreement (or Treaty of Baghdad, as it is also known) on March 6, 1975, she effectively accepted second place.

The setting up of the Islamic republic on April 2, 1979, changed the balance between the two sides. There was a power struggle between the civilians led by President Abolhasan Bani-Sadr and the fundamentalists led by Ayatollah Ruhollah Khomeini – a struggle not finally resolved until Bani-Sadr was replaced in June 1981. There was also a purge of those not supporting the revolution in the armed forces – a purge that continues to this day. Over 5000 officers were removed, including 30 generals and over half the middle-ranking officers in the army. The navy was not too badly affected, but the air force, all of whose pilots were officers, suffered particularly badly. The wholesale cancellation of arms on order, the removal of the USA's 50,000 technicians and instructors and the immediate shortages of (American-built) spares added to the confusion. Some military units such as the Imperial Guard and the Immortals Brigade (Javidan) were disbanded completely, and the Pasdaran (the Revolutionary Guards) were set up.

Iran's leaders then miscalculated in two ways. First, they thought that the fervour of the Pasdaran made up for the chaos in the regular army, so that there was no more reason to fear the power of Iraq than there had been before. Second, they thought that the Iraqi Ba'athist dictatorship was as unstable as the Shah's regime in Iran had been. There are two main branches of the Islamic faith – Sunni and Shia. Over half the population of Iraq is Shia, as is the overwhelming majority of Iran's. Less than a third of Iraq's population, but almost all its leaders, are Sunni. Moreover, most of these leaders come from a small area round Takriti in central Iraq and have come to power in a series of coups – the latest (led by the current President, Saddam Hussein) taking place in July 1979. Iran therefore tried to overthrow the Ba'athist regime by encouraging the Shiites in the south of Iraq to rebel and by organizing assassination attempts. One such attempt, in April 1980 – a month when Ayatollah Khomeini called on the Iraqi armed forces to overthrow Saddam Hussein – nearly killed Tariq Aziz, the second most powerful man in Iraq.

Between April and August 1980 there were a series of frontier incidents involving tank and air battles, and the Iraqis began to consider taking advantage of Iran's obvious problems to solve the long-running dispute over rights to navigate the Shatt al-Arab (the waterway leading to Iraq's main port, Basra) while further weakening Iran. Although most of the frontier between the two countries has remained the same since 1637, the Shatt al-Arab has proved a constant source of trouble. It provides Iraq's only major access to the sea (her total coastline is a mere 36 miles (58km) long, but it also provides the route to the sea from Iran's refineries in the Abadan area. The Algiers Agreement forced Iraq to accept less than they felt they needed in rights over the Shatt al-Arab.

Saddam Hussain therefore proposed to take advantage of the situation in Iran to seize a large part of the Iranian province of Khuzestan, giving Iraq a much larger coastline and putting the Shatt al-Arab entirely under Iraqi control. Within a week of the outbreak of full-scale hostilities on September 22, 1980, his army had done that, but he had made two major miscalculations.

First, the Iraqis thought that the inhabitants of the mainly Arab province of Khuzestan, who had been agitating for autonomy from the rest of Iran (which is mainly non-Arab), would welcome the Iraqis (who are mainly Arab). The inhabitants, however, did not see it that way.

The second miscalculation by the Iraqis was to assume that the revolution had so weakened the Iranian armed forces that they would not have the capacity to make effective counterstrokes. The regime in Tehran would thus be forced to recognize the *fait accompli* presented to them by Iraq and negotiate a settlement. It would not matter that a considerable part of the Iraqi army was tied down in the north of the country to prevent a Kurdish uprising.

Below: An Iranian Scud-B – an SSM used by both sides in the War of the Cities – being paraded through Tehran. Bottom: Iraqi casualties have been lower than Iran's, but as many as 50,000 Iraqis have been taken prisoner.

The Gulf War: sequence of events

	Land war	Oil war	City war
1980			
Sep	Iraq invades Iran	Iraq bombs oil facilities including Kharg Island	Iraq bombs Iranian cities
Oct	Khorramshahr captured and Abadan besieged by Iraqis	Iranian navy and air force destroy Iraqi Gulf oil terminals, and Iran threatens to mine Straits of Hormuz	Iran bombs Baghdad. First use of missiles against cities (by Iraq)
1981			
Jan	First Iranian counter-offensive near Susangerd		
May	Heavy fighting along southern front		
Aug		Iranian air force hits Iraqi oil installations	
Sep	Operation Thamin ul-A'imma by Iran lifts siege of Abadan		
Oct		First Iranian air force attack on Kuwait	
Nov	Operation Tariq ul-Quds by Iran near Susangerd		
Dec	Offensive by Iranians near Qasr-e-Shirin		
1982			
Jan		Iraq's pipeline through Turkey sabotaged	
Mar	Operation Fath ul-Mobin by Iran near Dezful (large gains)		
May	Iran reaches Iraqi border on southern front		
Jun	Iraq withdraws unilaterally from remaining land held in Iran		
Jul	Operation Ramadan by Iran towards Basra	Iraqi air force raids Kharg Island for second time in war	Major attacks on cities by both sides
Aug	Operation Ramadan continues		
Sep–Oct	Operation Muslin Ibn Aqil by Iran near Qasr-e-Shirin		
Nov	Operation Muharram by Iran near Dezful		
1983			
Feb–Apr	Operation Val Fajr by Iran near Basra		
Jul	Operation Val Fajr 2 by Iran in Kurdistan		
Aug	Operation Val Fajr 3 by Iran near Mehran		
Oct	Operation Val Fajr 4 by Iran in Kurdistan	France loans Iraq five Super Etendards	
1984			
Feb	Operation Val Fajr 5 by Iran on wide front around Mehran Operation Val Fajr 6 by Iran	Major Iraqi air attacks begin on Kharg Island and tankers	First War of the Cities. Iraq fires missiles at Dezful, Iran shells Basra then temporary ceasefire on civilian targets
Mar	Iraqi counter-offensive in south	Iraq steps up tanker war Aerial siege of Kharg Island proclaimed. First Iraqi use of Super Etendards	
Apr		Iraq steps up tanker war even further	
May		Temporary ceasefire in tanker war then Iran starts retaliatory attacks in southern Gulf	
Jun	Pause until Oct while Iran reorganizes land forces	Another temporary ceasefire sponsored by UN, then continued Iraqi attacks make Iran set up tanker shuttle to southern Gulf	Another temporary ceasefire sponsored by UN
Oct	Operation Val Fajr 7 by Iran near Mehran		
1985			
Jan	Iraqi offensive near Qasr-e-Shirin	Tanker war continues	Iraqi air strikes on Iranian cities; Iranian first use of missiles
Feb			Iran shells Basra
Mar	Operation Fatima Zahra by Iran in south, briefly reaches Highway 6 north of Basra		Second War of the Cities, lasts until June. Iraqi strategic bombing campaign
Jul		Iraqi navy attacks Cyrus offshore oilfield south of Kharg Island	
Aug	Small Iranian offensives in north and central fronts		
Sep	Small Iranian offensives in north and south	Iraqi pipeline to Saudi Arabia opened	
Oct–Dec		Iraqi air force maintains offensive against Kharg Island	More attacks by both sides on cities

1986

Jan
Iran uses helicopters against tankers in southern Gulf

Feb
Operation Val Fajr 8 by Iran in north fails, in south captures Faw
Operation Val Fajr 9 in Kurdistan

Apr
Iraqi counter-offensive at Faw fails

May
Iraqi offensive takes Mehran
Major Iraqi raid on oil refineries in Tehran

Jun
Operation Kabarla 1 by Iran recaptures Mehran
More tanker attacks

Jul
Third War of the Cities. Many Iraqi air raids against cities

Aug
First long-range Iraqi strike hits southern end of tanker shuttle at Sirri. Iran moves southern terminus to Larak, Iraq strikes that too. Iraqi attacks on Kharg also increase

Sep
Operation Kabarla 2 by Iran in Kurdistan
Operation Kabarla 3 by Iran near Faw
More Iraqi raids on Lavan and Kharg. Iran detains Soviet freighter *Pytor Yemstov*

Oct
More heavy Iraqi air strikes.
Iranian frigates use Sea Killer SSMs against tankers

Nov
Iraq continues air strikes
Iraqi air strikes against cities
Occasional Iranian missile attacks

Dec
Operation Kabarla 4 by Iran near Basra
More Iraqi air attacks. Iran shells Basra

1987

Jan
Operation Kabarla 5 by Iran in south
Operation Kabarla 6 by Iran near Qasr-e-Shirin
Iran buys more tankers for shuttle.
Iraq continues long-range strikes
Iran hits Kuwaiti oil installations
Large-scale Iraqi air attacks against Iranian cities

Feb
First (premature) US announcement about reflagging Kuwaiti tankers
Ceasefire in attacks on cities only holds for five days

Mar
Operation Kabarla 7 by Iran in the north

Apr
Operation Kabarla 8 by Iran near Basra and Fish Lake
Operation Kabarla 9 by Iran near Qasr-e-Shirin
Operation Kabarla 10 by Iran in Kurdistan
Iranian Silkworm SSMs operational

May
Soviet tanker *Marshall Chukhov* hits mine.
USS *Stark* hit by Iraqi Exocet ASM. Tanker *Texaco Caribbean* hits mine just outside Straits of Hormuz

Jun
Minor Iranian operations in north

Jul
Kuwaiti tankers reflagged.
Bridgeton hits mine off Kuwait
West starts sending MCMVs to Gulf

Aug

Sep
Iran Ajr seized by Americans

Oct
US helicopters sink three Iranian gunboats
Iranian Silkworm SSM hits tanker *Sea Isle City*. US warships destroy two Iranian oil platforms

1988

Feb
Iranians resume attacks on tankers by fixed-wing aircraft
Restart of War of the Cities. Air attacks and first missile attacks on Tehran by Iraq. These continue with Iranian missile reply until April

Apr
Iranian offensive in Kurdistan
Operation Ramadan Mubarak by Iraq retakes Faw
USS *Samuel B. Roberts* hits mine
US Navy destroys two oil rigs and one missile boat belonging to Iran and badly damages two Iranian frigates.
America announces it will protect all neutral shipping in the Gulf

May
Iraqi offensive east of Basra drives Iranians back
Missile and air attacks against cities resume

Jun
Iranian attack in the south defeated by the Iraqis who push the Iranians back to the frontier. Iraq also makes gains on the central and northern fronts
Iraqi planes destroy many Iranian oil and gas facilities to the south of Bushehr. Iranian gunboats attack neutral tankers in Gulf

Jul
Iraq regains more territory in Kurdistan
Iran accepts UN-sponsored ceasefire
Iraq attacks the Kharg Island shuttle, hitting several tankers. USS *Vincennes,* while engaging Iranian gunboats, shoots down Iranian civilian Airbus by mistake

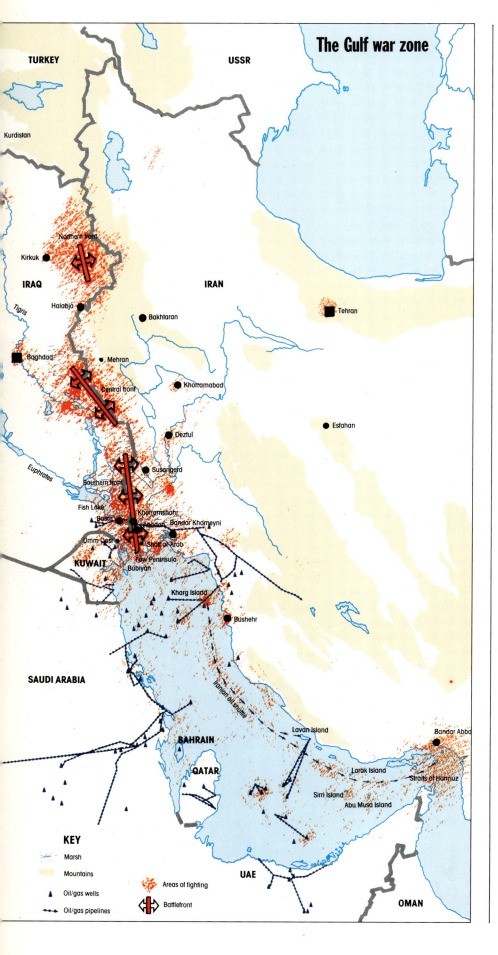

The Gulf war zone

TURKEY

USSR

Kurdistan

Kirkuk
Northern front
IRAQ
Halabja
Tigris
Baghdad
Mehran
Central front
Euphrates
Southern front
Fish Lake
Basra
Khorramshahr
Umm Qasr
Abadan
Shatt-al-Arab
KUWAIT
Faw Peninsula
Bubiyan

IRAN
Bakhtaran
Tehran
Khorramabad
Esfahan
Dezful
Susangerd
Bandar Khomeyni
Kharg Island
Bushehr

SAUDI ARABIA

Iranian oil shuttle

Lavan Island
Bandar Abbas
BAHRAIN
QATAR
Larak Island
Straits of Hormuz
Sirri Island
Abu Musa Island

UAE

OMAN

KEY
Marsh
Mountains
Oil/gas wells
Oil/gas pipelines
Areas of fighting
Battlefront

The campaigns

On September 28, 1980, only six days after the start of the war, Saddam Hussain announced to Iraq that all their goals had been reached. He went on to say that Iraq was willing to cease hostilities and negotiate. The Iranian response was very different. They quickly deprived Iraq of most of its capacity to export oil (and therefore of most of its income), and the Pasdaran in particular showed an ability to inflict a level of casualties (admittedly at the cost of many more casualties to themselves) that the Iraqis were not willing to tolerate. The Iraqis have spent the past eight years trying to force the Iranians to accept a negotiated settlement that will ensure the survival of the Iraqi regime, while the Iranians are trying to overthrow it.

The course of the war has largely been determined by these incompatible aims, and by geography and the advantages that each side started with. This has meant that the war has been fought on three separate fronts along the land border, has extended down the Gulf to the Straits of Hormuz, and has involved air and rocket strikes on each other's cities. Both sides have also encouraged bombing campaigns by opposition groups in each other's countries.

There are very few places where it is convenient to fight battles, but most of the 730-mile (1175km) border between Iran and Iraq is even more unsuitable than most. The south is a mixture of palm grove, waterway and marsh, extending 70 miles (113km) up from the Persian Gulf to Basra and beyond. It is extremely hot in summer (May to October), exceeding 95°F (35°C) almost every day in the shade. The flat alluvial plain extends north-west up the Tigris and Euphrates valleys, flanked along the border by mountains. These start about 60 miles (100km) north of Basra and continue to the Turkish frontier in the north. For most of their length there are few practicable passes for an army, and in the far north the peaks reach up to 10,000ft (3000m). Khuzestan is the only convenient place for armoured warfare, but even there the dust in summer and heavy rainfall in winter cause problems.

Iraq's major geographical disadvantage is that the vast majority of its fertile, populated area is in the east. This has seemed an advantage in border disputes with her north-western neighbour, Syria, but means that her capital, Baghdad, is little more than 40 miles (65km) from the Iranian border. Basra and the Kirkuk oil fields are equally vulnerable.

Although much of Iran's population is in the western, Iraqi side of the country, Iran is much bigger, so the distances are greater. Her capital, Tehran, is nearly ten times as far from the border as Baghdad. Her coastline stretches over 1240 miles (1995km) along the Persian Gulf and out into the Indian Ocean. The Straits of

Left: The war began when Iraqi troops invaded Iran in September 1980. It has been fought on three fronts along the land border, has extended down the Gulf to the Straits of Hormuz, and has involved the War of the Cities.

Hormuz – the entrance to the Gulf – is more than 700 miles (1130km) from the nearest airfields in Iraq.

Iran has used its size and manpower first to protect it from the worst effects of the Iraqi attacks and then to push the Iraqi forces back while maintaining a flow of oil exports (and therefore money to buy weapons). Iraq has used the skills of its (relatively) unpurged armed forces and scientific community to withstand the superior manpower and fervour of the Iranians and to devise ways of overcoming the geographical problems: for example, by trebling the range of its Scud-B rockets so that they can reach Tehran, or by creating a chemical warfare industry from scratch.

The land war: the southern front

The land war has proceeded in several phases. The first, lasting until December 1980, was the Iraqi invasion, followed by six months of bloody fighting that did not really change the status quo. From mid-1981 to mid-1982 the Iraqis were gradually driven back, until in July 1982 the Iranians were in a position to invade Iraq. The next 20 months saw the Iranians nibbling at the Iraqi positions, but in mid-1984 there was a pause while Iran reorganized its forces. Then came a return to the cycle of attacks on Iraq with, in February 1986, the successful crossing in strength of the Shatt al-Arab and the seizing of almost the entire Iraqi coastline. There had been limited counter-attacks and minor gains by Iraq, but nothing comparable to the sudden recapture of the Faw peninsula in April 1988, followed by several lesser victories for Iraq.

Geography dictates that the south has been the site of the largest battles and greatest number of casualties. Besides, there is a major oilfield, part of which is in Iran, part in Iraq, and a potentially unreliable population (the Shiites in Iraq and the Arabs in Iran). Both armies have had to adapt – painfully – to the difficult conditions of this semi-submerged region, much of which was virtually uninhabited pre-war.

Iraq's initial assault was certainly not an all-out attempt to conquer Iran. It only involved about a third of the Iraqi army and, despite some early successes, it quickly became bogged down in the major towns of Abadan and Khorramshahr. Most of what was left of Iran's regular army was not on the Iraqi frontier, but the Pasdaran, despite heavy casualties, managed to inflict significant losses on the Iraqi armoured division that invaded Khuzestan. The Pasdaran were particularly effective in the towns: for example, destroying 16 armoured vehicles in one action in Khorramshahr alone before it finally fell on October 18, 1980. The Iraqis had to commit their crack Special Forces Brigade and Presidential Guard units to win Khorramshahr, and they never captured Abadan, whose siege was raised by the Iranian operation Thamin ul-A'imma in late September 1981. The Iranian defence was greatly assisted by their helicopter gunships and the few fixed-wing aircraft they could get operational. An attempted pre-emptive strike

Jubilant Iraqi troops celebrate an early victory in the Shatt al-Arab (top). The Iraqis have generally failed to capitalize on their superiority in armoured forces against Iran's poorly equipped but zealous Pasdaran (above).

on Iranian airfields had failed dismally, although the Iraqi air force did manage to destroy the Iranian gunboat force based on the Shatt al-Arab.

After this, lack of spares and shortages of pilots greatly reduced the effectiveness of the Iranian air force. (Many of the pilots had been imprisoned, exiled or had defected – including Colonel Mohammed Mo'zzi, who came out of prison to become a war hero and finally defected in his F-14 Tomcat in late June 1981, with the deposed President Bani-Sadr in the rear cockpit.) This had a knock-on effect on the Iranian ground forces, making it dangerous to mass formations of tanks or troops. During the Al Dawa (dawn) 8 offensive that led to the capture of Faw by the Iranians, they lost large numbers of M-60 tanks and armoured vehicles.

Although the Iranian army has not done quite as badly as might have been expected, considering the effects of the purges, it has taken a long time to recover a degree of competence. In early January 1981, during the first major Iranian counter-offensive, about 100 M-60 and Chieftain tanks were lost and a further 150 captured by the Iraqis when the Iranians drove into an Iraqi trap near Susangerd. Nine months later, a further 150 Iranian M-48A5 tanks were captured during the otherwise successful Thamin ul-A'imma offensive when they were abandoned by their crews. In a bizarre twist, these tanks were later sold by the Iraqis to a middleman (they needed the money to buy equipment) and then resold to the Iranians in 1987.

For several years, Iran relied on revolutionary and religious zeal to win the day for the Pasdaran and Basij, who tried to overwhelm the Iraqis by sheer weight of numbers. With casualty rates similar to those of World War I battles, they did manage to push the Iraqis back, first to the frontier, and then to the outskirts of Basra. Here they were stalled by the enormous earth and water barriers built by the Iraqis, and by the immense Iraqi superiority in the air and in firepower on the ground. There are now about 120 square miles (310sq. km) of water barriers around Basra, including the vast artificial Fish Lake. Although the Iranians briefly cut Highway 6 – the vital Iraqi lifeline between Basra and Baghdad – in the Fatima Zahra offensive of March 1985, they were unable to hold these advanced positions.

By this time, all parts of the Iranian army were showing rather more skill at using their strengths – for example, when they took Faw, an area of marsh better suited to men than machines – but the terrible casualties have taken their toll. With more than 300,000 dead and 600,000 wounded, many of the most skilled and daring have been put out of action. The use, from 1983, of chemical warfare by Iraq (later copied by Iran), cannot have improved morale, though it has caused relatively few casualties.

The central and northern fronts

To the Iraqis, the central and northern fronts are places which they need to hold against Iran, rather than springboards for attack. The goals have been the nearest towns, Mehran and Qasr-e-Shirin, or defensible mountain passes. The earliest assaults, in September 1980, were to distract the Iranians from the southern front, but later attacks have been ripostes to Iranian probes in these vulnerable areas.

For the Iranians, unlike the Iraqis, there is a potential strategic advantage in attacking on the central and northern fronts. In the centre, there is always the possibility of pushing the Iraqis out of the foothills and advancing on their capital, Baghdad. The north is even

Below: One of the M-60s captured by Iraq from Iran in 1981; some were later re-sold to Iran via a middleman.
Inset: Kurds with a captured Iraqi soldier. With Iranian help, the Iraqi Kurds resisted the 1984 Iraqi offensive.

more tempting. In Iraqi Kurdistan live most of Iraq's approximately four million Kurds. Mullah Mustapha Barzani formed the Kurdish Democratic Party (KDP) in 1958, and since 1961 the KDP's militia, the Pesh Merga, has been in almost constant conflict with the Iraqi security forces. Helped by Iran, they successfully resisted the Iraqi offensive that began in August 1974. Although Iranian (and CIA) help was largely withdrawn after the Algiers accord of 1975, the Iraqi defeats in 1981 and 1982 saw a resurgence of Kurdish militancy.

Led first by Mustapha Barzani's eldest son Idris, then after Idris's death in 1987 by another of his sons Masud, the KDP has a fighting strength of about 15,000 irregulars. There are also the forces of the KDP's rival, the Patriotic Union of Kurdistan (PUK). Between them, the KDP and PUK hold down approximately 300,000 Iraqi regular soldiers and paramilitary forces – a dilution of their strength that the Iraqis can ill afford.

If the Iranians did break through in Kurdistan, they could cripple the Kirkuk oilfield, and the competence shown by the Pasdaran in the north in the past two years has given them significant gains. This has led to the use of chemical warfare by the Iraqis against not only military but also civilian (Kurdish) targets, such as the town of Helabja.

Below and inset: Kurdish victims of an Iraqi chemical attack on Helabja. The Kurds are the only civilians to have suffered such attacks so far, but the Iraqis have used chemical weapons extensively against Iranian troops.

As in the south, the Iraqi army has sometimes shown a surprising lack of competence – and with far less excuse than the Iranians. For example, their first assault on the central front since the first weeks of the war – against Qasr-e-Shirin – failed badly, and when they did succeed in capturing Mehran in May 1986, the local commander failed to take simple tactical precautions or capture the high ground around it. The Iranians rejected the Iraqi offer to exchange Mehran for Faw and in Operation Kabarla 1 overran the two brigades defending Mehran in early July 1986, going on to make gains in Iraqi territory to the west.

The oil war

Without oil exports, neither side could afford to buy the weapons, such as tanks, missiles, aircraft and ships, that they need to fight the war. The Iranians immediately adopted a strategy of trying to stop all Iraqi oil exports and have kept it up for the past eight years. The Iraqis, faced with more problems, first tried to do as much damage as they could to the Iranian oil industry and only later started the long distance Gulf air-raids as a way of pressurizing Iran to negotiate. Tit-for-tat in the Gulf has become a way for both sides to involve the international community in the war – with both Iraq and Iran hoping that the rest of the world will support their own side in order to secure oil supplies.

Iraqi aircraft struck at Iranian oil targets in the opening hours of the war, and the combined effect of air

Top: An Iranian oil platform burns following an Iraqi attack. Both sides must maintain oil exports to pay for the war, but the Iraqis have failed to destroy Kharg Island (above), from where Iran exports most of her oil.

and land attacks destroyed the Iranian refineries at Abadan and Bakhtaran early on. Later air raids have destroyed the refinery at Masjid-I-Sukin as well. Although the Iranians have managed to put some part of Bakhtaran and Masjid-I-Sukin back on line they are still having to import refined oil, while exporting crude.

The initial Iraqi blockade of the Gulf only affected the northern sector – mainly Bandar Khomeini (formerly Bandar Shahpur), Bushehr and Kharg Island. Their air force and navy were effective against ships trying to reach Bandar Khomeini, much less so in the early years against Bushehr and Kharg Island. Kharg Island has been responsible for approximately 90 per cent of Iranian oil exports during the war and on the face of it would seem quite an easy target to hit. However, not only is it a round trip for Iraqi aircraft of about 400 miles (640km) (more or less the limit for the high-performance attack aircraft available to Iraq in the early

part of the war when carrying an effective bomb-load), it is also an obvious target and thus heavily defended.

Not until early 1984 was the Iraqi air force able to mount a campaign against Kharg Island, and it was not until 1985–86 that Iran seriously started trying to create new routes for exporting the oil. Meanwhile, Kharg was even better protected, with less vulnerable loading buoys and moored radar-reflecting decoys to attract the AM-39 Exocet and AS-30 missiles which Iraq was using against the tankers. At the same time Iran had organized a shuttle of tankers from Kharg Island to Sirri Island, nine-tenths of the way down the Gulf, where, they thought, Iraq would not be able to hinder foreign tankers loading from the shuttle.

August 12, 1986, was a triumph for the Iraqis and a disaster for their opponents. On that day, the Iraqi air force showed its mastery of its new Mirage F-1EQs by flying them the length of the Gulf, attacking Sirri (and, accidentally, a neutral oil rig) and returning home. The Iranians immediately moved the end of the shuttle to the very entrance of the Gulf, to Larak Island, but the Iraqis hit this too. Because of the lack of storage facilities at Larak, the Iranians have hired large supertankers to store oil: usually nine for crude at Larak, and seven for refined products at Hormuz itself.

Lack of sufficient aircraft and pilots, the problems of attacking the heavily defended Kharg Island and the sheer difficulty of the 1500-mile (2400-km) round trip to Larak Island in the single-pilot, single-engined Mirage F.1s mean that Iraq cannot completely cut off Iran's oil exports. She can close Kharg Terminal for a time, as she did in September and October 1986, but cannot maintain the pressure to make it permanent.

Iran initially had much more success. Despite losses comparable to those of the Iraqis, her navy established, and has mostly maintained, effective dominance over the northern Gulf. To the shocked surprise of the Iraqis, they effectively destroyed the Iraqi oil-exporting terminals around Faw in October 1980. With the Shatt al-Arab closed (there are still more than 70 merchant ships laid up in it now), the Iraqis could not export oil by sea. The Iranians then persuaded Syria – never one of Iraq's friends – to close Iraq's main pipeline to the Mediterranean. In January 1982, they managed briefly to sabotage the remaining pipeline through Turkey. This was backed up by air and rocket attacks on Iraqi oil installations.

Apart from the rather over-optimistic purchase of four oil mooring buoys to enable exports to be quickly resumed should the Gulf be reopened to Iraqi tankers, Iraq has taken other measures to maintain the flow of oil. First they expanded the capacity of the Turkish pipeline. Then they built a new pipeline from the Basra oilfield to the Saudi Arabian port of Yanbu, and some oil is also trucked out through Jordan. Attempts have also been made to persuade Syria to reopen her pipeline, but Iran – partly by not demanding repayment for oil supplied to Syria – has managed to keep it closed.

War of the Cities

The first four years of the war saw sporadic attacks on the cities of each side, but since February 1984 there have been four distinct 'Wars of the Cities', in which Iraq has tried to force Iran to the negotiating table by destroying civilian morale. Iran has retaliated, more or less effectively, to each attack and each of the 'Wars' has been followed by a period when both sides have agreed not to make such attacks.

In the first days of the war the Iraqi air force used its bombers to attack all the main Iranian towns to slow down the mobilization of the Iranian reserves and volunteer forces. This soon escalated into attacks by both sides on military, economic and purely civilian targets in each other's countries. On October 15, 1980, Surface-to-Surface Missiles (SSMs) were used for the first time (by Iraq, against Dezful), and towns within artillery range have been shelled without much regard to civilian casualties.

The first War of the Cities took place in early 1984, when Iraq launched Scud-B SSMs against Dezful, and Iran shelled Basra in reply. A United-Nations-sponsored moratorium in June 1984 lasted, more or less, until January 1985, when Iraq launched air raids against Iranian cities, to which Iran responded with Scud-B SSM attacks. The second quarter of 1985 saw the second War of the Cities, when Iraqi planes were hitting targets all over Iran: Ahwaz, Bakhteran, Bushehr, Dezful, Hamadan, Isfahan, Shiraz, Tabriz and other towns, but especially Tehran, which was receiving an average of two air raids daily.

Top: A school in Mianeh, northern Iran, following an Iraqi Scud-B attack. Between February and May 1988 the Iranians fired only about 40 Scuds against Iraq, compared with the latter's total of 170. Fired mainly at Tehran, the Iraqi attacks have undermined Iranian morale.

The last two months of 1985 saw sporadic exchanges of raids but, apart from the important Iraqi strike on Tehran refineries in May 1986 (that forced Iran into becoming a major importer of refined petroleum products), there was a relative lull in the Wars of the Cities until July 1986, when Iraq restarted major air raids on Iran. This third War of the Cities was one-sided, the Iranian air force now being so weak that the only major response was to fire a few Scud-B SSMs at Baghdad.

This phase lasted until early 1987, and it was followed by a lull of almost a year before the next War of the Cities began in February 1988. The Iraqi strikes have undoubtedly had an effect on Iranian morale (the lesser Iranian efforts have not affected Iraq quite so much), and this has been intensified by fear of chemical attack – so far only used against civilians in Kurdistan. However, these strikes still have not driven Iran to negotiate.

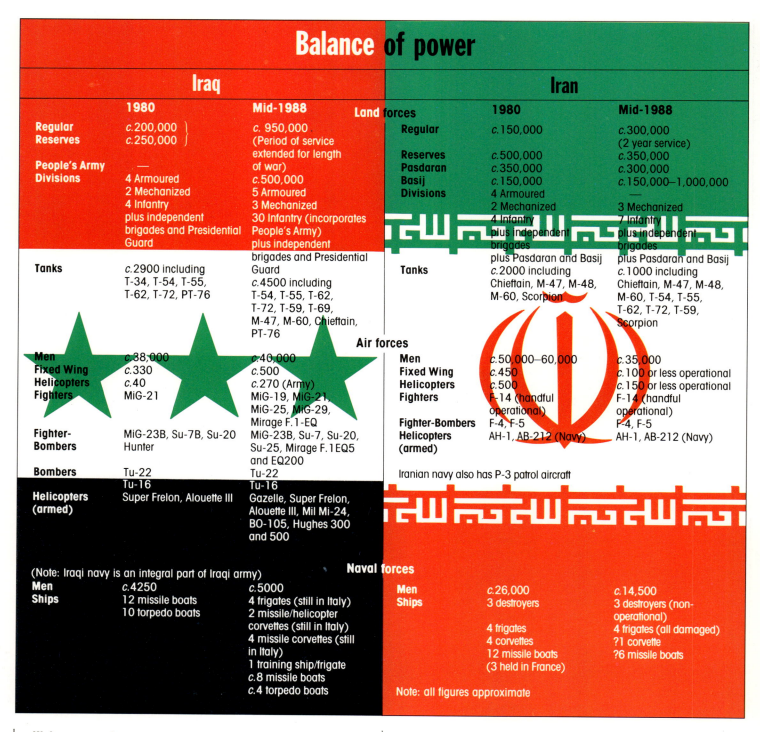

Balance of power

Iraq

	1980	Mid-1988
Regular	c.200,000	c. 950,000
Reserves	c.250,000	(Period of service extended for length of war)
People's Army	—	c.500,000
Divisions	4 Armoured	5 Armoured
	2 Mechanized	3 Mechanized
	4 Infantry	30 Infantry (incorporates People's Army)
	plus independent brigades and Presidential Guard	plus independent brigades and Presidential Guard
Tanks	c.2900 including T-34, T-54, T-55, T-62, T-72, PT-76	c.4500 including T-54, T-55, T-62, T-72, T-59, T-69, M-47, M-60, Chieftain, PT-76
Men	c.38,000	c.40,000
Fixed Wing	c.330	c.500
Helicopters	c.40	c.270 (Army)
Fighters	MiG-21	MiG-19, MiG-21, MiG-25, MiG-29, Mirage F.1-EQ
Fighter-Bombers	MiG-23B, Su-7B, Su-20 Hunter	MiG-23B, Su-7, Su-20, Su-25, Mirage F.1EQ5 and EQ200
Bombers	Tu-22 Tu-16	Tu-22 Tu-16
Helicopters (armed)	Super Frelon, Alouette III	Gazelle, Super Frelon, Alouette III, Mil Mi-24, BO-105, Hughes 300 and 500

(Note: Iraqi navy is an integral part of Iraqi army)

	1980	Mid-1988
Men	c.4250	c.5000
Ships	12 missile boats	4 frigates (still in Italy)
	10 torpedo boats	2 missile/helicopter corvettes (still in Italy)
		4 missile corvettes (still in Italy)
		1 training ship/frigate
		c.8 missile boats
		c.4 torpedo boats

Iran

Land forces

	1980	Mid-1988
Regular	c.150,000	c.300,000 (2 year service)
Reserves	c.500,000	c.350,000
Pasdaran	c.350,000	c.300,000
Basij	c.150,000	c.150,000–1,000,000
Divisions	4 Armoured	—
	2 Mechanized	3 Mechanized
	4 Infantry	7 Infantry
	plus independent brigades	plus independent brigades
	plus Pasdaran and Basij	plus Pasdaran and Basij
Tanks	c.2000 including Chieftain, M-47, M-48, M-60, Scorpion	c.1000 including Chieftain, M-47, M-48, M-60, T-54, T-55, T-62, T-72, T-59, Scorpion

Air forces

	1980	Mid-1988
Men	c.50,000–60,000	c.35,000
Fixed Wing	c.450	c.100 or less operational
Helicopters	c.500	c.150 or less operational
Fighters	F-14 (handful operational)	F-14 (handful operational)
Fighter-Bombers	F-4, F-5	F-4, F-5
Helicopters (armed)	AH-1, AB-212 (Navy)	AH-1, AB-212 (Navy)

Iranian navy also has P-3 patrol aircraft

Naval forces

	1980	Mid-1988
Men	c.26,000	c.14,500
Ships	3 destroyers	3 destroyers (non-operational)
	4 frigates	4 frigates (all damaged)
	4 corvettes	?1 corvette
	12 missile boats (3 held in France)	?6 missile boats

Note: all figures approximate

High command

The Iraqis have had a relatively simple political and military structure throughout the war. The Ba'athist regime, led by Saddam Hussain, has a firm control over the way the country and the war are run. At times, President Hussain has assumed personal leadership in the military campaigns, such as in the first two years of the war. At other times, such as during the immediate aftermath of the loss of Faw, he has delegated this to others. As head of state, prime minister, commander-in-chief of the armed forces and head of the Revolutionary Command Council, Hussain has effective control over everything Iraq does. Although he cannot evade responsibility for the major military failures Iraq has, in general, done well enough for him not to be in any serious danger, so far, from an internal coup.

The situation in Iran is very different. The power struggle between the political and religious leaders of the revolution was won by mid-1981, when Bani-Sadr was deprived of his position as commander-in-chief and President, but it has left a very complicated command structure. The situation has been further complicated by the desire of the religious leaders to limit the power of the conventional armed forces. The unique position of Ayatollah Ruhollah Khomeini is recognized in his roles as supreme religious and political leader and head of the Supreme Defence Council. There have been many shake-ups inside the ruling élite, such as the execution of Foreign Minister Ghotbzadeh in September 1982 and the purge of those around Khomeini's chosen successor, Ayatollah Hussein Ali Montazeri, in late 1986. None of these has seriously affected the control of the current leadership of Iran, even though lack of consistent direction from the top has made Iraq's task that much easier.

The armies

Iraq started the war with an army of about 200,000 men, with a further 250,000 in the reserves. As soon as it was realized that it was likely to be a long war, there was a frantic scramble to increase the number of men under arms. Each successive crisis saw a more stringent combing-out of the civilian sector, culminating (after the loss of Faw in 1986) in the liability of all men under 50 and some women for conscription. Although the Iraqi casualties have only been a fraction of those suffered by Iran (about 400,000 compared with one million or more), they have been enough to worry the regime. There have also been large numbers of Iraqis taken prisoner – 50,000 is not unlikely. Iraq has taken great care to try to make life at the front as comfortable as possible, with television, good food, and regular relief – something made easier by the short distance between the Iraqi cities and the front.

Iraq retains large numbers of paramilitary forces and the separate, élite Presidential Guard brigades, as well as a People's Army – an emergency, lower-grade, theoretically volunteer force, about half the size of the regular army. However, this does not compare in size or importance with either the Iranian Pasdaran force, or their Basij. The cutting edge of the Iranian war machine is undoubtedly the Pasdaran. This force was set up as the revolutionary counterbalance to the regulars and substituted fervour for training. After the horrendous casualties early on (rates of up to 30,000 dead were not unusual for a short offensive), the Pasdaran were given more training and reorganized in 1984. Even now, however, the lack of heavy weapons and training make the Pasdaran less effective than they might be and goes far to explain the lack of success near Basra.

The Basij are basic cannon-fodder. Mostly very young (youths of 14 and under are quite common), they are used to fill out the numbers of regulars and Pasdaran. In the past year or so they have become much harder to recruit, as war-weariness begins to appear. Conditions for Iranian soldiers are, in general, not as good as those enjoyed by their enemies. Not only are there more of them further away from their bases, but Iraqi control of the air and the Iranians' greater enthusiasm for the fight make it more difficult and, at the same time, less necessary to provide comforts.

Immense Iraqi superiorities in armoured forces and firepower have, if anything, increased during the war. Both sides have lost more tanks and other Armoured Fighting Vehicles (AFVs) than they possessed at the outset but, whereas Iraq has been able to replace her losses and indeed expand her armoured forces relatively easily, Iran's armoured force has rapidly declined, both in quantity and quality. In both cases, the lack of a major arms industry and problems with existing suppliers have made for a diverse arsenal.

Iraq entered the war with an armoured force almost entirely equipped by the Soviets, with a few World War II T-34s, the majority being T-55s or T-62s and the rest being the modern T-72s with its 125mm smooth-bore gun. When she invaded Iran, the USSR refused to supply arms (except on a small scale through Poland and East Germany) until February 1984. As a result, Iraq turned to France, who provided among other things AMX-30 tanks and SS-11 Anti-Tank (AT) missiles. She also bought tanks: the T-59 (T-54-copy) and T-69 (T-62-copy) from China. Also in service are considerable numbers of the British Chieftain and some US tanks captured from Iran.

Below: Iranian troops with an 81mm mortar near Abadan, where the Iraqis' initial assault of the war faltered.
Bottom: An Iraqi T-55, supplied by the USSR. Iraq has also purchased tanks from France (AMX-30s) and China.

Above: While only a few of the 80 F-14As delivered to the Iranians between 1976 and 1978 remain operational, the Iraqis have found it easy to obtain spares and sophisticated weapons systems (such as Exocets) for their planes.

In the case of Iran, the USA had already pulled out of supplying arms, leaving Iran with large numbers of M-47, M-48 and M-60 tanks but little back-up. She also had about 700 British Mk 3/3P and Mk 5/5P Chieftains. By 1983, Iran had captured nearly 1500 Soviet tanks from Iraq and had in addition acquired more from countries such as Libya, but she had lost so many AFVs that she was reduced to three armoured divisions. In 1985, T-59 and T-69 tanks arrived from North Korea and China. Whereas Iraq has been able to buy on credit and has had generous financial support from other Gulf states such as Saudi Arabia (which has proved useful in dealing with the USSR whom Iraq has had to pay for all the arms it has supplied), Iran has had to pay cash on the nail for most of its supplies.

Also, Iran cannot get some types of sophisticated weapons from the West, except under rather strange circumstances. Israel has been of great help to Iran in supplying quantities, though never enough, of spare parts for American weapons. The USA herself supplied (among other things) some 2000 Tube-launched, Optically-tracked, Wire-Guided (TOW) AT missiles as part of the 'Irangate' arms-for-hostages deal. These vitally needed, sophisticated missiles made a difference in the next few battles, but no more have been supplied.

In general, whereas Iraq has been able to buy whole weapons systems with a relatively assured supply of spare parts, ammunition and training, Iran has had to shop around, mainly on the black market, and accept what little she can get. Although rather more has been supplied to Iran than is generally admitted (engine parts for Chieftain tanks are but one example), the Iranians' difficulties with arms supplies have had a definite effect on their battlefield performances.

It would be easier to list those countries that have *not* sold arms to one side or another during the war. For example, Portugal and Spain have provided light arms and ammunition to Iran, who has also acquired jeeps and tents from India, ex-US equipment from Vietnam, and so on. Some countries, notably China (which is seeking hard currency to buy sophisticated equipment for its own armed forces) and France, have sold considerable quantities of arms to both sides. In general, Iraq has received about half of its weapons from the USSR, a quarter from France, and the rest from other sources. Iran originally had no major supplier, but in the past four years China and North Korea have supplied well over half of what Iran has been able to obtain.

Air forces

The differing abilities of the two countries to obtain sophisticated weapons has been even more important as regards air-power. The purges, the departure of the US technicians and the loss of US spares had crippled the Iranian air force, whereas the Iraqi air force entered the war fully trained and equipped. While Iran has experienced even more difficulty obtaining aircraft and helicopters than land weapons, Iraq has integrated sophisticated Western weapons systems, such as the AM-39 Exocet carried by the Mirage F.1EQ5, into its combat forces with devastating effect.

However, as well as flying deep-penetration missions into Iran, the Iraqi air force has also been required to make up for the army's weaknesses and errors. For example, in two days during the loss of Faw in early 1986, the Iraqi air force flew over 500 close-support missions. These were not particularly effective because of the lack of Iranian targets. For the marshy ground made it easy for troops who had experienced air attack before to dig in effectively, and the use of men rather than vehicles made targets difficult to find and not particularly worth attacking when they had been found. However, the Iraqi losses were heavy, as they were when Israel and the USA supplied Iran with replacement Hawk missiles in early 1986.

Even so, the Iraqi problems have been tiny compared with those experienced by the Iranians. Many pilots defected, and there are now elaborate precautions to try to prevent this. Morale has been further reduced by such problems as the shooting down of an Iranian Falcon 20 jet transport by mistake when it was landing at the Iranian Omidiyah air base – not, unfortunately, an isolated incident. In fairness, it should be said that keeping even a proportion of their aircraft operational – particularly the F-14 Tomcats, only flown otherwise by the US Navy – has been a real achievement. The problem for the Iranians is that apparently minor problems such as the lack of spare parts for radars makes even the aircraft they can fly less effective than they ought to be. The contrast between the Iraqi air force, commanded by an air marshal, and the Iranian, whose fear of their own officers is reflected in their having an aircraftsman as deputy commander for a time in 1987, is complete.

Below: With ships such as this Saam-class frigate, built in Britain by Vickers, the Iranian navy controlled most of the Gulf – until the US Navy stepped in to damage two frigates, sink one missile boat and scuttle the *Iran Ajr*.

The navies

Partly because it was less affected by the purges than the air force, the Iranian navy has, in general, performed well. Initial exchanges in the first few months of the war cost them two Bayandor-class corvettes and two (possibly three) Kaman-class missile boats, as well as numbers of smaller craft. However, one of the corvettes (sunk by an AM-39 Exocet from an Iraqi Super Frelon helicopter) and many of the smaller craft were lost to air attack rather than to the Iraqi navy, and they sank at least four Iraqi OSA missile boats as well as six torpedo boats and other vessels. The result was that the Iraqis, apart from a few sorties such as the one in 1985, retreated to their base at Umm Qasr by the Kuwaiti border, and the Iranian navy has more or less controlled the Gulf ever since.

The Iranians' superiority has enabled them to destroy the Iraqi oil facilities on the Gulf, support the Iranian land forces in their crossings of the marshes south of Basra and, with their missile boats based at Bushehr, to defend their own facilities at Kharg Island against all but the occasional tip-and-run raid. The only major actions involving ships have been the 'tanker war' and the actions taken by the US Navy.

For the Iraqis, the tanker war has been almost entirely conducted by air attack. When the action was all in the northern part of the Gulf, the Super Frelon helicopters were used. They used their AM-39 Exocets to good effect, but as the action in the Gulf moved south, fixed-wing attack aircraft were needed. The French loan of five Super Etendards (the aircraft used by Argentina in the 1982 Falklands War) from October 1983 – they were first used operationally at the end of March 1984 – and the subsequent purchase of the French Mirage F.1s enabled the Iraqis to make effective strikes against tankers first around Kharg Island and then all the way to the Straits of Hormuz.

Iranian tactics have been very different. When they started their retaliatory strikes against Saudi and Kuwaiti tankers in 1984 (and it should be noted that neither side has attacked tankers thoughtlessly or at random), they used F-4 Phantoms with AGM-65 Maverick TV-guided missiles. Shortages of aircraft and missiles meant that the next wave of attacks, starting in January 1986, were by AS-12 missiles fired from Augusta-Bell 212 helicopters based on the Rashadet oil platform in the Rostam oil field. Tankers avoided this by passing at night, so the helicopters were moved to Abu Musa Island nearer the entrance to the Gulf.

When tankers were routed to avoid this too, the Iranian navy took over, using Sea Killer SSMs from their Saam-class frigates. Since they are beam-riding missiles, the Sea Killers could be, and were, used at night. Meanwhile, the Pasdaran, based on offshore oil rigs and islands, had started 'nuisance' raids using speedboats and other light craft.

In the past two years, US retaliation against Iranian missile and mine attacks on Kuwait and the reflagged tankers and on her own forces, has led to major losses for the Iranian navy. The Gulf is easy to mine (as is the Red Sea, in which pro-Iranian forces planted mines in July 1984). Both sides mined the northern Gulf, but it was while mining the south that the Iranians lost the *Iran Ajr* – captured by the US Navy on September 21, 1987, and scuttled by them after a close examination. In October 1987, in the northern Gulf, helicopter gunships sank three Iranian gunboats which had fired on a US observation helicopter, but it was the actions on April 18, 1988, that caused the greatest loss, with a Kaman-class missile boat sunk and two Saam-class frigates seriously damaged. This damage was more important than the 40-plus casualties, because these last remaining large warships of the Iranian navy (the three destroyers have been immobilized through lack of spares since before the start of the war) have only been kept operational by using electronics and weapons systems from those sister-ships which still worked.

The wider war

The first and worst effects of the war outside the two combatant countries have undoubtedly been felt by the other states bordering the Gulf. Then gradually, as the war has progressed, almost all the major countries in the world have become involved in one way or another.

The state most threatened has undoubtedly been Kuwait. With as many proven oil reserves as Iraq and Iran combined, it has a tiny population, outnumbered almost four to one by foreign workers. For years it was threatened by Iraq, but in July 1977 the two countries signed an agreement over the disputed Kuwaiti islands of Waribah and Bubiyan that lie near Iraq's naval base of Umm Qasr. As a Sunni-ruled sheikdom, it has also been threatened by Iran, and was first bombed by Iran in October 1981. Since then there have been many attacks, plus airline hijackings in 1984 and 1988.

Support for Iraq led to attacks both on Kuwaiti-owned tankers and on tankers trading with Kuwait. These began in May 1984, the *Umm Casbah* and *Bahrah* being the first casualties. Sheik Jabah, meanwhile, survived an Iranian-inspired assassination attempt in 1985, and from October 1986 to mid-1987 the only ships attacked by Iran were Kuwaiti-owned. The USA offered the protection of its flag to the Kuwaiti fleet in February 1987, which was rejected, but in a balancing act Kuwait simultaneously hired three Soviet tankers and reflagged 11 of its fleet of 22 tankers under the US flag.

The size and sophistication of its armed forces have enabled Saudi Arabia to cope better with the problems posed by Iran, but the location of the holy city of Mecca on Saudi territory has been the cause of many difficulties, including riots by Iranian pilgrims in 1987, when well over 400 died. The Saudi rulers, although fundamentalist, belong to the Sunni branch of Islam, which has caused many tensions with Shiite Iran.

Major arms purchases from the USA, including F-15 Eagle fighters, E-3A Sentry Airborne Warning And Control System (AWACS) aircraft and missile corvettes, plus French tanks and frigates and the purchase of Tornadoes from Britain announced in July 1988, have made Saudi Arabia a major regional power, as was demonstrated on June 5, 1984, when Saudi F-15s guided by an E-3A on temporary loan from the USA shot down an Iranian F-4 Phantom, after which Iran virtually ceased attacking Saudi ships.

Both Kuwait and Saudi Arabia are major financial supporters of the Iraqi war effort, not so much to support Iraq as to prevent Iranian domination. Saudi Arabia is also the terminal of one of Iraq's oil pipelines. Although Saudi Arabia relies heavily on US support, she has also demonstrated her independence by purchasing from China 90 Deng Feng 3 ballistic missiles with a range of 1900 miles (3000km).

The other important Gulf state, Oman, controls the south side of the Straits of Hormuz. It signed an agreement over the control and policing of shipping in the Straits with Iran in 1977, and the international shipping lanes both in and out of the Gulf pass through Omani territorial waters. Close ties with Britain have led to much British support for the small but efficient navy; the USA has greatly improved facilities at Masirah Island and other bases (although mostly for her own Central Command (USCENTCOM).

The Gulf Co-operation Council, formed in January 1981 and comprising Saudi Arabia, Kuwait, Oman, Bahrain, Qatar and the United Arab Emirates (who lost the Tanb and Abu Musa Islands to Iran in 1971) are a loose affiliation of the Gulf states not actively involved in the fighting. They have held military exercises (the first 'Peninsula Shield' exercise was held in October 1983) and considered the purchase of minehunters, but a proposal to form a regional defence force has come to nothing, partly because the smaller states do not want to replace Iranian by Saudi dominance.

The West

Britain formally withdrew from the Gulf in 1971, but the war caused a permanent naval presence, the Armilla Patrol, to be set up on October 22, 1980. For several years this consisted of two warships – normally a destroyer and a frigate, plus a Royal Fleet Auxiliary in support. Four minesweepers sailed briefly in early 1984 to counter Iranian threats to mine the Gulf, and a higher profile was adopted in 1986. Early in 1987 a second frigate was added, and in June of that year the rules were altered so that the ships (which 'accompanied' rather than convoyed the merchant vessels) were allowed more latitude to respond to hostile acts. In 1987

alone they accompanied more than 400 British-flagged and mainly British-owned ships through the southern Gulf. In August 1987 (after the mining incidents) four Hunt-class minehunters and their support ship *Abdiel* sailed to reinforce the British presence.

At first the Iranians maintained a purchasing mission in Britain, but this was later forced to leave. However, despite a policy of trying to restrict sales to either side, tank engine spares have been supplied to both sides, as well as other equipment. Iranian hovercraft were overhauled in Britain in 1984, and in the same year three Iranian naval vessels – *Kharg*, *Lavan* and *Tanb* – were finally released to Iran.

France has sold large quantities of arms to both sides, although the greater part, including the most sophisticated equipment, has gone to Iraq. The loan of the Super Etendards and sale of Mirage F.1s with their Exocets, as well as the AMX-30 tanks and guns, missiles and radars, have all been of inestimable value to Iraq.

France has maintained an occasional naval presence in the Gulf throughout the war, stepping it up in conjunction with the British in 1987. France sent an aircraft carrier, *Clemenceau*, and her escorts, as well as mine-warfare vessels (MCMV). More MCMVs were sent in late 1987 by Belgium and Holland, and Italy also sent a naval force after one of her merchant ships was attacked in the Gulf.

Below: HMS *Beaver*, one of the vessels making up Britain's Armilla Patrol, tasked to accompany British-flagged ships through the Gulf. Other European nations with naval forces in the Gulf are France, Italy, Belgium and Holland.

Above: A US corporal participating in Bright Star 83, held to test the ability of US forces to respond to any crisis in the Middle East. Sufficient supplies are held at Diego Garcia to support a force of 15,000 for 30 days.

The USA's role

The USA has been involved in the Gulf as far back as World War II. Ever since then there has always been at least a flagship (currently the converted landing dock platform *La Salle*), normally accompanied by two destroyers, stationed in these waters. Massive support for the Shah of Iran culminated in the pull-out of 1979. In November that year the Iranians stormed the US Embassy in Tehran and seized the American staff as hostages. A carrier battle group (CVBG) was stationed permanently in the Indian Ocean, and there was the abortive hostage rescue mission (Operation Eagle Claw) on April 24–25, 1980.

Although the hostages were released in January 1981, relations with Iran remained soured, not being improved by constant Iranian threats to close the entrance of the Gulf. The US-led attempt to prevent arms reaching Iran, Operation Staunch, began in 1983 and had considerable success in 1985–86. However, it was undermined not only by arms shipments from the Israelis (to them, any enemy of Iraq was worth supporting) but also by the USA's clandestine arms-for-hostages deal, which led to the exposure of 'Irangate' and the disgracing of Robert McFarlane, Admiral Poindexter and Lt. Col. Oliver North, among others.

Above: A Soviet spy ship and minesweeper in the Gulf. Above left: USS *Vincennes*, which shot down an Iranian civilian Airbus by mistake in July 1988. US Navy personnel board an Iranian mine-layer (left).

US naval forces in the region were gradually increased in response to the escalating tanker war in the Gulf. Embarrassments in the early part of 1987 – the accidental attack by an Iraqi Exocet-armed Mirage F.1 which nearly sank the frigate USS *Stark* (FFG-31), with the consequent disgracing of her senior officers, and the mining of the *Bridgeton*, underlining the US Navy's shortcomings in mine-hunting equipment – have given way to much greater success. In October 1987, four US destroyers shelled two oil platforms. In April 1988, the cruiser *Wainright* (CG-28) shelled more oil rigs and sank a missile boat, and A-6 Intruders from the US carrier *Enterprise* (CVN-65) damaged the Saam frigates in retaliation for the mining of the US frigate *Samuel B. Roberts* (FFG-58). These retaliations have served to underline the USA's determination to keep the oil flowing through the Gulf.

Apart from the massive US naval presence, including

battleships and their surface action groups, there are also the forces already in position for any US land involvement in the area. The Gulf is halfway round the world from the USA and very difficult to reinforce in a hurry. The USA therefore developed the maritime pre-positioning concept. Since the early 1980s the US Navy has based sufficient supplies aboard converted merchant vessels at Diego Garcia in the Indian Ocean to support a Marine Amphibious Brigade of 16,000 men for 30 days. These ships, originally named Near Term Pre-positioning Ships, are now known as the Marine Pre-positioning Squadron. There are also base-rights and equipment in Kenya, Somalia, Egypt, Oman, Bahrain and Saudi Arabia. Reinforcements would come from what was originally known as the Rapid Deployment Joint Task Force, and the concept has been tested in exercises from Bright Star 82 to Solid Shield 87. Command of US forces in the Gulf area comes under USCENTCOM, set up on January 1, 1983.

The USSR

Not only her long common frontier with Iran but also her intimate involvement in Afghanistan from December 1979 has made the USSR particularly sensitive to events in the Gulf. Much of the southern USSR is Moslem, giving rise to serious concern over the spread of militant Islamic fundamentalism. Active involvement, apart from the resumption of direct arms sales to Iraq in February 1984, was limited to the occasional visit by a warship from the Soviet fleet in the Indian Ocean.

However, since the brief detention of the Soviet freighter *Pytor Yemstov* by Iran when carrying arms to Iraq in September 1986, the USSR has had a permanent naval presence in the Gulf which consists of a few frigates, minesweepers and auxiliaries.

Other neighbours

Turkey, with the Iraqi pipeline running through it, a large Kurdish minority, and a common frontier with both the opposing sides, has been active – especially in recent years – in trying to make peace between them. Syria, only bordering Iraq and traditionally hostile to her, has acted very much on the side of Iran. She has closed the oil pipeline and indulged in the occasional border incident. However, Syria does have problems with Iran, particularly in Lebanon. Once part of Syria, Lebanon is seen by Syria as being very much her preserve. Iranian backing for Hezbollah in Beirut and southern Lebanon in rivalry with the Syrian-backed Amal (these are the two major Shia groupings in the Lebanon) has caused many tensions.

The uncertain future

There have been many attempts to stop the fighting already. Iraq has tried to get out of the war almost ever since she started it and has made over 20 serious peace offers. Iran feels she has to insist on the overthrow of a regime which she sees as totally responsible for the war before she will make peace. The result – in the absence of any military victory and despite UN-sponsored partial truces and ceasefires – has been stalemate.

The USA was only prepared to accept Iranian domination of the Gulf when Iran was a client state. An Iran capable of closing the Gulf has led to US intervention on a large scale, including the supply of much intelligence material to Iraq. Both the USA and the USSR, as well as the other Gulf states, have in general supported Iraq (especially after it began to lose the land war in 1983–84) not for her own sake but to control Iran. The result again was stalemate.

A worry that still existed was the possibility that either side might develop nuclear weapons in an attempt to break the stalemate. For Iran the effects of the revolution and the cancelling of reactor construction at Bushehr in 1979 put a temporary stop to her plans. Iraq was much further advanced until the Israelis launched Operation Babylon on June 7, 1981. In a perfect pin-point strike, eight F-16 Fighting Falcons escorted by eight F-15 Eagles virtually destroyed the nearly complete reactors (capable of producing weapons-grade plutonium) at Al Tuwaitha.

A worry that had already been realized was the use of chemical weapons. Banned by the Geneva Protocol of 1925, mustard gas H and the nerve gases Tabun and Sarin have been produced and used by Iraq to improve her tactical position on the battlefield. They have also been used in retaliation by Iran, but not yet by either side on a large scale against civilians.

Neither side wanted the war to go on. Iraqi war-planning is clearly demonstrated by the order of a considerable fleet (four frigates, six missile corvettes and supply vessels) from Italy in December 1980. Obviously intended for post-war domination of a Gulf in which Iraq would have a larger coastline and a larger role, they remained in Italy (much to that country's embarrassment) because Iran continued to control the entrance to the Gulf. It was to have been a short, victorious war. Because it was not, Iraq found herself with an unusable fleet, massive overseas debts and a regime that might be vulnerable if the war continued much longer.

Iran, plagued by internal differences and considerable war weariness, also wanted the war to finish. Although her debts were nothing like as large as Iraq's, her economy was in bad shape. What Iran was looking for was a clear-cut military victory to force a quick end to the war. The help from the superpowers, and from Iraq's supporters in the Gulf, as well as Iraq's own military performance, were enough to prevent this. Indeed, the Iraqi success in the middle months of 1988 in forcing Iran back to its borders along the entire front, created a situation where an end to the war at last seemed possible.

Iranian war-weariness and strategic sterility, combined with the constant Iraqi pressure against the cities and oil targets as well as on the land front, prompted Iran to ask for an unconditional ceasefire agreement in July 1988. Constant US pressure in the Gulf and on the diplomatic and economic fronts also played their part in this development. However, while a ceasefire changes the immediate situation, the underlying tensions between Iran and Iraq will go on causing problems for many years to come.

Below: While Hashemi Rafsanjani, Speaker of the Iranian parliament, discussed Iran's acceptance of the UN ceasefire resolution with senior Iranians on July 18, 1988, skirmishing between the two countries' forces continued.

Chapter 4

MILITARY MEDICINE:
BATTLEFIELD REPAIRS

In the 1st century AD the Romans included an 'extractor of arrows' in each cohort. Yet, even in the 19th century, provision for those wounded in battle remained primitive, and it was common for an army to lose as many men from disease and infection as on the field of battle itself. The role of the modern military medic remains simple – to prevent infection and to contain damage – but with airportable hospitals, the latest equipment and drugs and superb training, all but the most badly wounded will survive to be taken behind the lines for full treatment by today's miracle-working surgeons.

Troops unload medical supplies from Hercules transports before setting up a field hospital during a Reforger exercise in 1983. These exercises provide the US forces with valuable experience of reinforcing their units in West Germany quickly.

63

The whole purpose of an army is to defeat an enemy by force. This is achieved by killing and injuring as many members of the opposing side as possible. Very rarely, however, are these terms used – they are disguised by talk of neutralization, destroying equipment or knocking out vehicles or positions.

The medical service of any army is very different in its approach from the other parts of that force. Its aim is to undo the damage inflicted by the enemy and thus to restore morale and increase the will to win. Throughout history this has been the case. As societies have become more sophisticated, so they have become less prepared to accept death and injury fatalistically. At times this can be overridden by, for example, religious fanaticism, under the influence of which death is felt to be glorious. Nations are also more ready to accept casualties if their survival is at stake. Conversely, in more limited wars, the expectation of casualties may be very low: in the Falklands War, for example, every casualty had to be seen to be being provided with the very best treatment. In a more extensive war, it is regarded as an acceptable consequence that a proportion of casualties will inevitably receive less than ideal treatment.

Treatment of the injured is only part of the story. It is just as important to prevent ill health by maintaining hygiene both in the field and in barracks. But medical support has not always had a high priority. A Colonel Walton, in his *History of the British Standing Army* of 1909, commented that 'There are two branches of administration which unlike the other administrative branches are not absolute essentials to an army. These branches are the medical and religious branches. An army could exist without either.'

Early history

A rudimentary medical organization was introduced by the Romans who, when they invaded Britain in AD 43, included an 'extractor of arrows' in each of their cohorts. In each legion there was a higher grade of physician. The Romans also introduced a hospital system, to the extent that in each fortress there was a *valetudinarium* to accommodate the sick and wounded. As with many Roman developments this organization fell into disuse after the legions had left Britain during the final disintegration of the Roman Empire.

It was not until the Norman Conquest in the 11th century that a simple form of medical attention is again recorded. Each Norman lord had a force of retainers, which included a 'leech' – usually a monk, who included bleeding by the application of leeches among his arts. However, a papal edict of the 12th century directed that monks were no longer to shed blood and the blood-letting passed to the barbers. Only the teaching and administration of medicine remained with the monks.

In the wars of the Middle Ages, physicians and surgeons were engaged for the duration of a particular conflict and were generally part of the king's entourage.

The sick and wounded were sent to monasteries for care and recuperation. In 1253, a Thomas Weseman 'who knew how to cure wounds, a science particularly useful in the siege of castles' was among the forces assembled by King Henry III. It was about 1300 that panniers first received a mention as a means of carrying medical stores, and records of the injured being evacuated from battles begin to occur. Following the siege of Calais (1346-47), large numbers of sick and wounded were shipped home. Indeed, the practice of evacuating the injured from the battlefield almost led to defeat in the battle of Poitiers (1356), when the English were attacked as they were carrying out the operation.

The development of gunpowder and gunshot brought about a wider range of injuries and some primitive treatments for gunshot wounds were soon developed. These usually involved cauterization with boiling oil of elders mixed with treacle; boiling pitch was used to stop bleeding after amputation. Despite the recognition that bleeding from wounds had to be stopped, the practice of blood-letting was continued for several hundred years.

Left above: A skeleton found at Maiden Castle, Dorset, has a Roman arrowhead embedded in its spine. Some 14 centuries later, an engraving (above) shows a surgeon extracting an arrow while the battle still rages.
Left: A knight carries a comrade to a monastery, the source of medical knowledge in the Middle Ages.

By the time of Elizabeth I, each company in the army had its own surgeon and at least some medical equipment. However, the Civil War saw the introduction of the first medical system organized by regiment, whereby each regiment was assigned a surgeon assisted by surgeon's mates. A few military hospitals were set up in which the sick were looked after by attendants appointed from among the womenfolk of the soldiers. An expedition to the West Indies at about this time included the first hospital ship.

The standing army

The restoration of the monarchy in 1660 also resulted in the formation of a permanent standing army: for the first time, the army was organized on a proper regimental basis. Permanent commissions were offered to regimental surgeons, although they, like other officers, had to purchase them. The career in prospect for a surgeon once he had obtained such a commission, however, was still far from attractive, and only those in the Guards regiments had any possibility of promotion.

The pay could only be enhanced by drawing the salary of a combatant officer as well as that of a surgeon. The status of a medical officer of that time was low.

The regimental surgeon was his own supplier, although the state made a small grant for equipment. The regimental hospital was run by the medical officer, with the assistance of a warrant officer and three helpers. These hospitals were really no more than store-rooms set aside for the surgeon, where he could deal with the worst cases. In fact, the main function of the medical services in peacetime was to attend all floggings – to ensure that they were carried out properly, and then to deal with the results.

The next major development in the provision of military medical services came in the early 18th century, when the Duke of Marlborough introduced a system of camp hygiene and medical relief. Hospitals were established and carts and barges used to evacuate casualties from the battlefield to the hospitals. Casualty-collecting posts and regimental aid stations were reported at the Battle of Blenheim (1704).

Developing facilities

One important figure in 18th-century military medicine was John Hunter. Famous for his work in the fields of anatomy and surgery, he played a key role in the scientific foundation of surgery. Less well known, however, is the part he played in the development of military medicine. Suffering from tuberculosis, he joined the army to improve his health, and soon saw the need for mobile hospitals and for a system of medical transport. Hunter's main aim was not so much to carry the wounded back from the battle, but to move medical facilities forward, and in order to make his point more forcefully he wrote directly to the commander-in-chief rather than through the normal military channels.

Although his initial military career was quite short, Hunter returned later in life as Surgeon-General to the Land Forces and as Inspector-General of Hospitals. He was particularly opposed to the then current practice of primary amputation of limbs wounded by bullets, believing that a more conservative approach which tried to preserve the limbs would be sufficient.

Wellington's armies

The Peninsular War, fought under the generalship of the Duke of Wellington in the early 19th century, produced two notable medical men, James Guthrie and Sir James McGrigor.

Guthrie began his remarkable career with the 29th Foot and ended it as Deputy Inspector-General. He started as an apprentice at the age of 13, had become a hospital mate by 15, and passed the examinations of the Royal College of Surgeons at 16. He was wounded at the Battle of Vimeiro – an experience which affected his view of military medicine, for even after leaving the service he continued to pay special attention to the training of military doctors. His lectures at the Royal

College, for example, were open to them without fee.

When he joined for service in the Peninsular War only two carts were needed to transport the medical equipment for the whole army, and there was no transport available to move the wounded. The hospitals were filthy – he described one particular hospital as a slaughterhouse. Following John Hunter's principles, he was a supporter of conservative treatment for wounds, avoiding amputation where possible and strongly opposing the practice of bleeding.

Unlike Guthrie, McGrigor was primarily an administrator, and his great contribution to military medicine was to improve the primitive transport arrangements for the injured on the battlefield. He not only insisted that military vehicles should be set aside for the movement of casualties, but also set up hospitals along the evacuation route. Perhaps the best testimony to the efficacy of his changes was that some five thousand men were actually returned to the battle from the sick list. At the end of the Peninsular War, in recognition of his achievements, McGrigor was made Director-General of the Medical Services.

The Battle of Waterloo took place in 1815, and for most of the medical men involved this was their first experience of war. Moreover, McGrigor was back in London and his influence was sadly lacking from the

Below: A sketch of a man wounded at the Battle of Waterloo who has received a sword wound in the neck. The wounded were evacuated mainly by regimental bandsmen and they faced a long and painful journey to the medical officers who were stationed well to the rear of the battlefield.

battlefield. As a result, the medical evacuation plans were haphazard, being left mainly to the regimental bandsmen to organize. Unfortunately, under the circumstances, the majority of the medical officers were located well to the rear. It thus took a long time to get the wounded to them; and when they arrived (despite Guthrie's efforts) amputation remained the commonest treatment for gunshot wounds. It is hardly surprising that between 40,000 and 50,000 men were either killed or wounded at Waterloo. Somewhat late in the day a field hospital was set up near Wellington's headquarters, but this was largely as a result of the injuries suffered by his own staff.

Once there was a return to peace, all the lessons learnt and the efforts of Guthrie and McGrigor were forgotten. Successive cuts in military expenditure led to a continuing reduction in the medical services, as they were not thought to be necessary in peacetime. The result was the medical disaster of the Crimea.

The Crimean War

That the Crimean War was a turning-point in the provision of military medical services is now accepted. But the improvements only occurred after a disaster of gigantic proportions, caused by an almost total lack of medical administration and planning. There was no transport for the sick and wounded, for example: the Army set out with only two four-wheeled wagons, and these were left behind on the actual journey – in order to accommodate officers' horses. There were no trained stretcher bearers and as at Waterloo, it was left to the regimental bandsmen to bring the wounded out of the battle.

Conditions in the trenches of the Crimea were appalling. There was insufficient food and clothing, supplies of medical equipment were inadequate and sanitation was at best rudimentary. Cholera, dysentery and typhus were rife. For those who were ill or injured, there was the terrible journey from the battlefield to the base hospital at Scutari 300 miles (483km) away. But the hospital offered no respite, for there everything was chaos. Originally a Turkish barracks, it was now a series of rat-infested, unheated wards. There were stables next to the wards, prostitutes plied their trade in the cellars underneath and the wards were overflowing with people. With an official capacity of 1000, this number had soon been exceeded: casualties lay on the floors, not just in the wards but also in the corridors. Amputations were carried out in the wards with instruments that were rarely cleaned – and without the benefit of chloroform. For although chloroform had been in use for about seven years, little was available at Scutari. In two months, 2000 men died from illnesses and infection picked up after they entered the hospital itself. In the seven months after the landing in the Crimea, 10,000 men of the Army's total strength of 28,000 had died from disease, compared with only a small fraction from enemy action.

Above: A contemporary engraving of Queen Victoria, Prince Albert and two of their sons, talking to wounded soldiers from the Crimea, in a hospital ward at Fort Pitt, Chatham. The Queen supported Florence Nightingale (inset) in her efforts to improve the care of the wounded.

This appalling state of affairs was brought to the notice of the British public and Parliament by the dispatches of W. H. Russell of *The Times*. Action was needed and took the form of a nursing mission led by Florence Nightingale. The Lady of the Lamp, as she became known from her nightly rounds of the hospital, set about her task with determination and fortitude. She fought doctors, inspectors, the High Command and the War Office. The Chief of Medical Staff at Scutari, Dr John Hall, was also a target for her disapproval.

A fresh attempt was made to organize the evacuation of the wounded and the hospitals themselves were reorganized. In all her efforts Miss Nightingale had the support of the British people, thanks to the continuing flow of articles from Russell. Queen Victoria herself lent her authority to the cause, as did the Secretary of State for War, Sidney Herbert. Herbert supported Florence Nightingale in every way, and she drove him hard in the hope that he would bring order out of the chaos. Their partnership continued for five years until Herbert died, it is said, from overwork aggravated by the insanitary conditions at the War Office itself.

Following the war, the horrors of Scutari did yield something of value in the end: they provided the much-needed spur to transform the medical service from its disorganized, inefficient state into a cohesive and autonomous branch within the Army. In 1857, a Royal Commission was appointed to inquire into the sanitary conditions of troops, barracks and hospitals. It made many recommendations, among which were the establishment of an Army medical school, the introduction of a statistical branch, the formation of two hospitals, and better recruitment and pay for medical officers. It also recommended the establishment of a Hospital Corps and improvements in barracks.

A major deficiency, however, was not recognized by the Royal Commission: it still supported the existing system of regimental hospitals and doctors. It thus failed to invest the medical department with sufficient authority and postponed the creation of a unified medical service. The Army Hospital Corps and the Army Medical Department also remained separate, and thus there continued to be inadequacies in the provision of medical services to the Army. Despite the Commission's recommendations, medical services deteriorated once again. Some lessons were learned from the Franco-Prussian War, especially since the well organized German medical services were seen to produce results. In 1873 the regimental hospitals were, with the exception of the Guards and Household Cavalry, abolished, and the regimental medical officers brought within the Army Medical Department.

Despite all this the status of the medical officer deteriorated until the British Medical Association intervened. Their report bore fruit in that it helped to bring about the formation of the Royal Army Medical Corps in 1898. Yet, again, in practice change did not follow.

Above: A painting showing Surgeon A.J. Landon treating the wounded at Majuba Hill during the Boer War. Although more soldiers died from disease than from enemy action, progress was made in the treatment of gunshot wounds.

The Boer War

Despite these recurring disasters and reorganizations there were lessons still to be learnt. The Boer War (1899-1902) in South Africa brought home once again the vital importance of sanitation and hygiene. It was (as before) a desperately expensive lesson, but this time one that was to be remembered. A total of 22,000 troops were treated for injury, but 20 times that number were admitted to hospital for disease. The sickness rate rose to about 950 per 1000 troops a year. Disease killed 14,000 and enemy action only 6000. Attempts were made to prevent illness by inoculation, but the technique was still in its infancy: relatively few were inoculated against typhoid, and among those who were the incidence of the disease was only halved.

In contrast to this, the treatment of gunshot wounds and the like made progress. For the first time, the British Army was equipped with an early form of field dressing, consisting of a waterproof package containing two sterile dressings, each being made of a gauze pad with a bandage sewn on. Anaesthetics were now in common use and the principles of asepsis and sterility were well understood. Chest injuries were being treated with a high degree of success and surgery to the head was being carried out in field hospitals. An X-ray machine was reported to have been in use at the siege of Ladysmith in 1899.

Undoubtedly, local conditions helped in that the soil of South Africa was relatively clean: the organisms causing tetanus and gas gangrene were uncommon. Furthermore, the new high-velocity bullets produced clean wounds. These two factors combined, luckily, to prevent the incidence of infection and subsequent death from being even higher than it was.

The developments in treatment and the lessons relating to sanitation learned in South Africa were not forgotten and furthermore, following the war, important organizational changes were made. These were, for once, evolutionary rather than precipitated by crisis. There were changes in the senior staff, the nurses were formed into the Queen Alexandra's Imperial Military Nursing Service and the ranks of the medical corps were restructured.

On March 1, 1906, a further fundamental change of the field medical service took place with the introduction of the field ambulance. These were allocated three to each division and were a centre for the initial collection and treatment of casualties from the forward troops. The wounded then passed to the clearing hospitals before being sent to the static hospitals further back. The reserve medical forces were also reorganized and given better training to bring them more into line with the regular forces.

By 1914, therefore, the medical services were well-structured and well trained, with a better understanding of the requirements needed to support an army at war.

The Great War

Unfortunately, these preparations did not anticipate the scale of World War I (1914-18), which necessitated a huge expansion of the medical services. This was carried out under the direction of Sir Alfred Keogh. Keogh also brought in eminent senior civilian surgical advisers who oversaw a general rise in the standards of surgery. Overall, the clinical problems were made even more difficult by the sheer extent of the fighting, by the increasing diversity of the weaponry used, by the geographical spread of the war and, in Europe, by the contaminated nature of the soil.

Fortunately, inoculation against typhoid was by now established practice, and the incidence was only 2 per cent of the Boer War figure. Still, Europe's contaminated soil harboured the germs of tetanus and gas gangrene, and while large-scale use of anti-tetanus

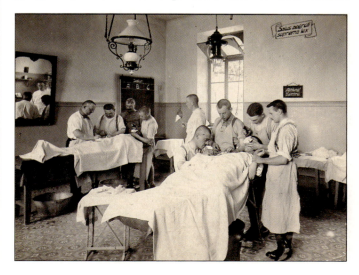

serum reduced the incidence of the former, amputation was still necessary for gas gangrene. Widespread use of antiseptics did not bring about the hoped-for reduction in infection and, indeed, over-reliance on them often worsened the problem.

Two specific diseases were associated with the war on the Western Front: trench foot and trench fever. Trench foot was caused by the prolonged immersion of the feet in water, often resulting in severe damage, with loss of toes and sometimes even the foot itself. Prevention rather than cure was the best way of solving the problem. Trench fever proved more difficult to treat, until it was realized that it was spread by the body louse. Again, prevention was the key.

The evacuation of casualties from the point of wounding was by stretcher-bearers to the Regimental Aid Posts, where the casualties were seen by the medical officer. From there they were taken to the Advanced Dressing Station and the Main Dressing Station of the Field Ambulance. The next stop was the Casualty Clearing Station, where the first surgery was carried out before transfer to the base hospital. Some of the latter were huge, with a capacity of 20,000 beds or more. All the armies involved in the War faced similar problems and used similar evacuation chains. The movement of casualties was often by handcart, horse-drawn cart and later by motorized ambulance.

World War I saw very significant advances being made in all branches of surgery. Abdominal wounds were treated consistently successfully for the first time, with sections of gut often being removed. There were developments in chest and orthopaedic surgery. Eye surgery and neuro-surgery made substantial strides.

The necessity for blood transfusion was also beginning to be recognized, but there were still uncertainties about the techniques of cross-matching blood and in the prevention of clotting. It was the US Army hospitals that led the way in this field and they developed the direct transfer of blood from donor to recipient.

In addition to the surgical advances there were two major new problems to be dealt with. These were poison gas and psychiatric casualties. The horrifying use of gas caused terrible injuries, although in fact the numbers involved were not all that great when compared to the overall figures for those killed or wounded. There was relatively little that could be done once the gas had produced its effects and most of the developments were in producing effective gas masks and protective clothing.

The occurrence of psychiatric casualties was also recognized for the first time. Initially, soldiers were shot for cowardice, when in reality they were suffering

Left: An operating theatre in a German army field hospital during World War I. British Regimental Aid Posts during the battles of Amiens (top right) and Somme (above right). Right: British soldiers whose legs have been amputated are taught to use their artificial limbs at Roehampton. World War I saw many amputations due to gas gangrene.

from psychiatric disorders brought on by the fighting. The existence of shell-shock and battle or combat fatigue was acknowledged, with the USA again playing a significant part in developing treatments.

The War ended with an appalling toll of casualties, but with major advances in surgery and medicine having been made. The years after World War I saw continuous developments, with advances in the techniques of blood transfusion on both sides of the Atlantic, techniques of blood cross-matching and storage becoming established and the separation of plasma being developed. The discovery of antibiotics which attacked specific infections was a very significant development. In Germany the sulpha group of antibiotic drugs was discovered in 1935 and further developed by 1939.

Above: RAMC personnel practise dealing with poison gas casualties at Millbank, London, in 1939.
Below: During the D-Day landings, German prisoners of war carry a wounded comrade to a landing craft for treatment.

World War II

World War II was much more widespread than World War I, both in terms of the participants and of geography. It was also a mobile, as opposed to a largely static, war: armoured and air warfare had come of age. Special forces, such as the commandos, long-range patrol groups, and the Special Operations Executive (SOE) and Special Air Service (SAS) had come into being. All these, clearly, necessitated changes in the way medical services were organized. For example, airborne forces were used for the first time, and these had to be accompanied by airborne medical support.

The surgical support was greatly enhanced by specialist teams which were deployed relatively far forward. Chest surgery was significantly improved and there were great advances in neuro-surgery and in maxillo-facial surgery. Blood transfusions had now become an established part of surgery and blood transfusion teams were an essential part of any medical force. In addition, dried plasma was introduced and became a very effective long-lasting blood substitute.

A major advance was the use of the antibiotic penicillin. Although discovered by Sir Alexander Fleming in 1928, it did not become feasible to make it in sizeable quantities until much later. In the early part of the war, the USA was responsible for the majority of its production but by 1943 it was also being made in Britain. It reduced the incidence of infection and thus ensured the survival of many casualties.

After undergoing operations in forward hospitals, casualties required evacuation to base hospitals and this was to be greatly speeded up by the introduction of air evacuation. This was first practised in the desert war in North Africa, where the huge distances could pose particular problems.

Back in Britain, major advances were made in restorative surgery, prompted by the increasing use of armoured fighting vehicles and aircraft which had resulted in a very large increase in casualties suffering from burns, particularly of the face. Such figures as Archibald McIndoe at East Grinstead carried out pioneering work in plastic and reconstructive surgery.

The widely dispersed theatres of war gave rise to a corresponding increase in the range of health and hygiene problems. It is a tribute both to the medical services and to field commanders that the incidence of disease was significantly reduced. The importance of preventive measures such as inoculation was well appreciated. In the Far East malaria was a problem that was brought under control by the use of the newly discovered dichloro-diphenyl-trichloro-ethane (DDT) to eradicate the mosquito and by the use of drugs, such as mepacrine, to prevent infection.

Following on from the experience gained in World War I the importance of psychiatric support was recognized with the introduction of field psychiatric teams. It was realized that, if treated early enough, many soldiers could return to battle quite rapidly.

Wounded American soldiers are evacuated by helicopter during the Vietnam War (above). In a Normandy foxhole in June 1944, US Army medics treat a wounded GI (below). The perfection of helicopter medevac techniques in Vietnam did not produce as great an increase in the survival rate of casualties as the US Army had expected.

Korea and Vietnam

The Korean and Vietnam Wars continued the trend set by World War II. The Korean War (1950-53) saw the first helicopter evacuation of casualties, a technique that was refined in Vietnam (1964-75). The rapid evacuation of wounded soldiers became commonplace, casualties at times finding themselves on the operating table as little as 20 minutes after being injured.

The ever-increasing levels of expertise coupled with improvements in the evacuation chain have led to corresponding improvements in the ability of casualties to survive, with one notable exception. In World War I 8 per cent of US casualties who entered the medical 'chain' subsequently died. This dropped to 4.5 per cent in World War II and to 2.5 per cent in Korea. In Vietnam the death rate within the chain rose to 3.6 per cent. There are two reasons for this. First, immediate evacuation of the casualties from the point of wounding by helicopter may not always be in their best interests: better results may be achieved by stabilizing the casualty's condition first. Second, people who might otherwise have died are now able to receive the attention of the medical services. Thus, more seriously injured patients are being dealt with and inevitably they have a correspondingly reduced chance of survival. In addition, those who do survive may be more severely handicapped.

The Falklands War again demonstrated the need for stabilization followed by rapid evacuation. It also demonstrated a need for an ability to look after injured soldiers at the point of wounding often for lengthy periods until evacuation was possible. As well as any special skills possessed by the medical services, it was essential that every soldier could administer first aid. Also, soldiers who were more highly medically trained were needed to sustain wounded men until battle conditions allowed them to be moved.

Below: While under heavy enemy fire on the outskirts of Saigon, Vietnam, in May 1968, US infantrymen, using the protection of an M113 armoured personnel carrier, carry a wounded comrade off to get medical treatment.

Military medicine today

Continual evolution of the organization of medical services, learning and relearning the lessons of history, coupled with medical advances, have led to very similar concepts of medical evacuation and treatment in the majority of forces today. Terminology and detail vary, but the overall concepts remain the same.

Initial treatment

If wounded, soldiers rely on their neighbours or 'buddies' to provide first aid. It is therefore especially important that all soldiers know enough first aid, particularly the main principles. The order in which injuries are treated is often crucial. Problems with breathing are dealt with first, as someone who cannot breathe obviously will die. Knowledge of airway management will therefore save lives, often with casualties who may have little else wrong with them. The next most important problem is bleeding. All external bleeding can be stopped; internal bleeding is often more difficult to control, but there are measures that will help. The next group of injuries to be considered are breaks or fractures. Simple fractures will cause relatively little trouble, but more serious ones such as multiple breaks, involving the skin and maybe adjoining blood vessels and nerves, may be very serious. Considerable quantities of blood may be lost into the tissues and thus correct treatment is vital. The fourth group of casualties are those who have been burnt. Whereas burns may be very severe and may ultimately prove fatal, they are, generally speaking, less of a first

Above: A medical orderly, during a US Army exercise in Korea in 1984, tends the 'wounded' before evacuation. Below: During the Falklands War, a survivor of the sinking of HMS *Sheffield* is helped across the deck of HMS *Hermes* to the sick-bay by medical staff wearing anti-flash hoods.

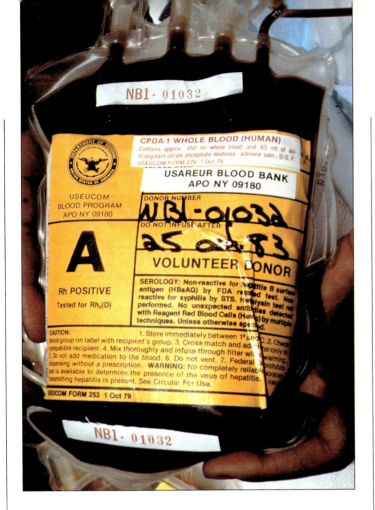

Above: Blood for transfusions was flown in as part of setting up a complete field hospital during US Army exercise Reforger in West Germany in 1983.
Above right: Tracked armoured vehicles, such as this West German M113, are used to evacuate casualties.

aid problem. From this stems the rule of the four 'B's – Breathing, Bleeding, Breaks and Burns – the order in which soldiers are taught to treat casualties. Obviously many casualties will have multiple injuries – but the same rule applies – breathing must be sorted out before bleeding, and so on.

If the casualties cannot be evacuated immediately, provision must be made for looking after them. This becomes especially important with special forces or with small isolated groups. Such forces require a more highly trained 'medic' who is able to look after a casualty, often for a considerable period. Again, the airway is of prime importance: it must be kept open at all times if the casualty is to survive.

The other important skill which the medic should possess is the ability to set up and manage an intravenous infusion. In the medical sense, shock is the result of a loss in the circulating blood volume and, to restore this, the fluid lost needs to be replaced. Ideally, if significant quantities of blood have been lost, then blood should be given. Unfortunately, whole blood has a shelf-life of only three to five weeks and if it is to be kept for that time it must be refrigerated. This, together with the requirement for cross-matching, means that it is not a practical proposition to transfuse blood forward of hospitals. Much research has been done in the USA and Britain on the deep-freezing of blood, but as yet no completely satisfactory solution has

been found. It is therefore necessary to infuse a substitute for blood. If only a relatively small loss has been sustained or the time before a higher level of medical support is available is short, then an electrolyte solution may be sufficient. Alternatively plasma expanders can be used, such as the Dextrans or gelatin-based compounds like Haemaccel. These are solutions that are made from large molecule compounds that draw fluid into the vascular system and keep it there, as opposed to the electrolyte solutions which slowly leak out. The skills needed to set up and manage such infusions are being increasingly taught to forward troops of all armies. Special forces have been trained in these techniques for some time.

The medical officer

Following the initial treatment, a casualty is evacuated as quickly as possible through the Company Aid Post to the Regimental Aid Post. This is normally the first place that the casualty would see a doctor. The main role of the medical officer is to assess the casualty and to decide on the priority for treatment and evacuation. This process, known as triage, is fundamental to the efficient management of large numbers of casualties. In essence, casualties are divided into priorities depending on the urgency of treatment necessary for survival over the next stage of their journey. For example, a casualty who is not breathing is obviously a Priority 1 for treatment. However, with respiration restored, the casualty may drop to Priority 3 for evacuation. If respiration remains a problem, then such a casualty could remain a Priority 1 for evacuation.

Having allocated priorities, the medical officer then directs treatment, including the management of chest and abdominal wounds, fractures and limb injuries. Antibiotics, analgesics and tetanus toxoid may be given. The initial documentation of casualties is started. There is an increasing tendency to adopt standard treatments for casualties. This assists the doctor and staff and means that those at subsequent levels of care will know what has been done, should the documents go missing. It also allows standardization of medical supplies.

Within the fighting area, the movement of casualties will be in vehicles similar to those of the fighting troops. Thus, in armoured warfare, ambulances would also be tracked armoured vehicles, whereas in an airmobile battle it is likely that either helicopters or wheeled ambulances would be used to move casualties. Behind the Regimental Aid Post wheeled vehicles would be more common, as casualties could then be moved more quickly and in greater numbers.

At the 'second line' medical facility casualties are reassessed and, where necessary, additional treatment is initiated or current treatment maintained and improved. A greater range of equipment is available and so a more sophisticated level of treatment can be given. In some special circumstances surgical teams can be established this far forward to carry out early surgery. This, however, presupposes that it will not be necessary to relocate the post, since, once operated on, a casualty should not be disturbed for several days. In a highly mobile battle or when in retreat, this is not possible. Such forward surgical teams, then, can only be used if the medical facility is to remain static.

Casualties are then once again triaged into priorities for treatment and evacuation to field hospitals. Evacuation from the 'second line' is by wheeled ambulances augmented by helicopters, which may be dedicated to the CASualty EVACuation (CASEVAC) role.

On entry to the field hospital, casualties are again assessed by triage and given a priority for surgery. Only those in most urgent need of surgery are likely to be operated on this far forward. Those who can survive a longer journey will be stabilized and further evacuated by road, rail or air.

Above: In the US military exercise codenamed Reforger which took place in West Germany in 1983, all the inflatable structures, equipment and supplies for a complete field hospital were packed in large crates and transported to the site by US Army CH47 Chinook helicopters.
Below: Once the structures have been inflated in position, the wards (inset) and operating theatres are made ready.

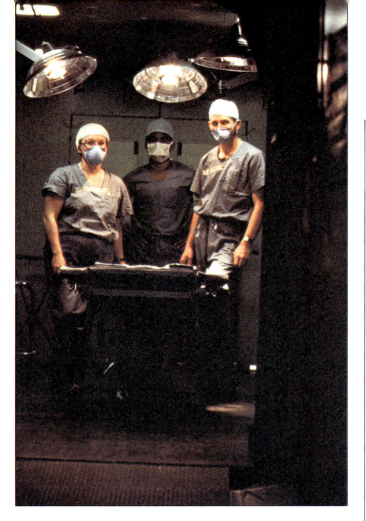

Above: In the fully equipped operating theatre of a US Army field hospital of the type set up for the Reforger exercise, all the early surgical procedures can be carried out before casualties are evacuated to 'fourth-line' hospitals.

Principles of war surgery

The principles of military surgery have been developed during the course of the major wars of this century and differ in some important respects from peacetime surgery. Surgeons from civilian life are often tempted to carry on as if they were working in a civilian hospital. Unfortunately, this often leads to unnecessary complications and loss of life. Battlefield medicine and surgery at this level is a low-technology affair and is directed solely towards saving life.

Every wound sustained in the course of action must be assumed to be contaminated. Infection does not set in for about six hours and it is therefore necessary to get the casualty to initial surgery within this time. This means that surgical facilities need to be fairly far forward, although this has to be balanced with the crucial requirement for post-operative rest and thus the stability of the medical facility.

The surgical treatment of wounds is a two-stage process. The first stage is concerned with 'wound toilet' – cleaning the wound and removing all dead and contaminated tissue. The ballistics of modern high-velocity rounds means that damage to tissue, particularly muscle, may be far more extensive than first realized, so it is vital to be firm about removing any doubtful tissue. In addition, great efforts must be made to stop all bleeding, as blood and dead tissue form ideal breeding grounds for the organisms of gas gangrene.

Gas gangrene organisms also thrive in the absence of oxygen, so war wounds are not closed initially, but are left open and covered with a light dressing. Only when the initial healing of the wound has started and infection is seen to be absent, is the wound closed.

There are, however, some circumstances when early closure is necessary, wounds to the face being an example. Delay in closing the wounds will lead to excessive scarring. With chest and abdominal wounds also, at least the deeper layers need to be closed in order to maintain the integrity of the chest or abdominal cavity.

After a casualty has been operated on, frequent inspections of the wound must be avoided, since continually exposing the injury increases the risk of infection. Antibiotics are often seen as a cure-all, but they are no substitute for proper surgery when dealing with the types of injury encountered in modern warfare.

Early surgery, then, is aimed at saving life mainly by reducing the risk of infection and lessening the chances of complications: in principle it is simple and straightforward. Having recovered from this initial surgery and often before the wounds are closed, the casualty will be evacuated to the 'fourth-line' hospitals. It is here that the definitive and specialist surgery is carried out.

Burns

One of the major injuries sustained in modern warfare, whether on land, sea or in the air, is the burn. A significant percentage of casualties today suffer from burns either on their own or in association with other injuries. The first aid for burns is relatively simple – clean dressings, preferably non-adherent, are applied, analgesics are administered, and any fluid lost is replaced. Superficial burns will heal readily without undue scarring, but deeper burns require surgical treatment in the form of skin grafts and subsequent plastic surgery.

Skin lost either as a result of burns or other trauma will need to be replaced in all but small wounds, and the skin used has to come from the individual's own body. Occasionally a defect can be temporarily covered using animal skins or synthetic substitutes, but for definitive cover a graft from another part of the body is required. A partial-thickness or split-skin graft is taken from one of the flatter parts of the body such as the thigh. This is done with a hand-held knife or, more commonly nowadays, with a powered reciprocating knife known as a dermatome, which can be adjusted to produce a slice of skin of the required thickness. The donor skin is then laid over the defect and stitched around the edge. The site to be covered must be completely clean with all dead tissue excised and all bleeding stopped. A pressure dressing is applied to discourage the collection of any fluid under the graft, as this would lift it and prevent it from 'taking'.

A more modern development is to mesh the graft in a meshing dermatome to produce a piece of skin that can be expanded rather in the manner of chicken wire. The meshing can be done in varying ratios so as to expand the skin by three or five times, for example. Such meshed skin can obviously cover much bigger defects but also has additional advantages: it will cover irregular surfaces better than an unmeshed graft and it will allow any fluids collecting underneath to leak out, so that if bleeding or infection occur the results will not be so damaging. Such mesh grafts cannot always be used. The face, for example, requires the complete skin, largely for cosmetic reasons, since the meshed graft heals with a fish-scale effect. Other sites may need other forms of full-thickness grafts with the formation of special flaps and multi-stage procedures.

Fractures

Another feature of modern warfare is the very large numbers of fractures caused by high-velocity missiles; more often than not these are complicated by coexistent open wounds. It is extremely difficult to treat such fractures by splintage and plaster of Paris, although these may well be suitable for the early stages. As a result, the practice of fixing fractures internally with plates, screws and nails inserted into or on to the bones, was extensively developed. Unfortunately a majority of war wounds are contaminated and the

Below: During the Falklands campaign, a Royal Marine commando with a broken leg is carried to a waiting helicopter to be evacuated. A high proportion of wounds are fractures caused by high-velocity missiles.

insertion of foreign bodies greatly increases the risks of infection. To get round this problem in turn, methods of fixing the fractures externally have recently been developed. Pins are inserted into the bones and bone fragments and their protruding ends are held together with a series of rods, clamps and screws which are all outside the skin. This framework can then be adjusted, under X-ray control, to produce an accurate alignment of the bony pieces. When the bones have united, the structure is dismantled and the pins removed. During the healing period mobility can be maintained at the joints on either side of the fracture, thus aiding the rehabilitation process.

Forward hospitals, however, are not the place for these more advanced surgical procedures. Their job is simply and primarily to carry out emergency life-saving surgery. For the types of advanced surgery described above, the casualty would have to be evacuated.

Nuclear and chemical war

In any future major war the surgical problems of the wounded may well be compounded by the effects of Nuclear, Chemical and Biological (NBC) warfare. Nuclear war produces huge numbers of casualties of all types, with a high preponderance of burns. In addition, many casualties will suffer from the effects of radiation. The numbers of casualties produced could well alter the triage process by making an additional priority necessary: those who are most severely injured with little chance of ultimate survival may only be offered palliative treatment. Thus those who in other circumstances would be the first to receive treatment will go to the end of the queue. It may be possible to recover from radiation sickness but many of those affected, although appearing unharmed, will succumb.

Chemical warfare is also a distinct possibility today, as the Iran-Iraq conflict shows. Much work has been done in developing effective protective equipment to allow soldiers to continue to fight in a chemical environment. For those who have already been affected, prophylactic drugs are available which alleviate the effects of nerve agents. Those contaminated by chemical agents may need prolonged artificial respiration, for which portable resuscitators have been developed. Of great importance to the medical services is the need for an environment proof against chemicals in which treatment, including surgery, can be carried out. Collective protection equipments are now in use. These vary, but consist basically of a positive-pressure environment with air locks for entry and exit. Because of their complexity and expense, they are used only for those areas in which treatment is to take place.

The implications of biological warfare are more difficult to assess. Good hygiene will go some way towards minimizing the effects of whatever pathogens are used. Vaccination against suspected potential hazards, meanwhile, will play a significant part in maintaining the health of troops.

Today, troops may have to fight wearing special NBC suits (above), but as in the Falklands, it is still vital to provide basic medical services on the battlefield to ensure that the wounded survive evacuation (below and inset).

The lessons of history

Whatever the nature of any future war, the lessons of history must be remembered, for all too often in the past they have been forgotten – with disastrous results. The importance of good sanitation and hygiene is now well appreciated but, again, it is all too easy to forget the essential principles. In a nuclear or chemical war such principles will be even more important if hostilities are not to be followed by wholesale disease.

The triage of casualties into priorities for treatment and then evacuation has been proved to be the best basis on which to organize the medical services. Casualties should receive sufficient treatment to sustain them through to the next stage of their journey along the medical chain, and should have initial surgery within six hours of being wounded. These are the guiding principles of war surgery, and to forget them, even in today's 'high-tech' wars, will result in unnecessary loss of life. Above all, the soldiers themselves need to be well trained in first aid. The medical services as a whole need to continue to train effectively in peacetime if they are to provide an efficient service in war. This need for training is not just the responsibility of the medical services, it is encumbent on all commanders at all levels to ensure that the lessons of history, which have already been learned, are never forgotten.

Chapter 5

AIR WAR:
THE RAF'S
70TH ANNIVERSARY

Seventy years ago the pilots of the embryo Royal Air Force took to the air above the World War I trenches. Poorly funded and ill-equipped, the airmen were at first met with derision from the other two services. But every year since then has seen the RAF grow in importance and – from the Battle of Britain to its role as a vital component of the NATO alliance today – the RAF now has a service record which would fill those early pilots with pride.

In 1940 the Royal Air Force came of age. Throughout the summer the young pilots in their Hurricanes and Spitfires, supported by the unremitting labours of those on the ground, defeated the Luftwaffe and averted Hitler's threatened invasion.

On April 1, 1988, the Royal Air Force celebrated its 70th anniversary. But on April 1, 1918, tens of thousands of people joined the RAF without even noticing. They were far too busy fighting a war.

Indeed, until World War I was over most of those who fought in it as members of the RAF never wore RAF uniform. Ground crew usually wore the khaki uniform of the Royal Flying Corps (RFC) or the naval uniform of the Royal Naval Air Service (RNAS). Officers or pilots, meanwhile, wore a bewildering variety of uniforms – anything from a Royal Navy uniform to that of a Scottish Highland regiment.

British 'air power' perhaps dated from 1885, when the Army took balloon detachments into active service in the Sudan and Bechuanaland. A balloon factory was set up at South Farnborough, an air battalion came into

being on April 1, 1911, and at last an interest began to be shown in heavier-than-air machines. Out of this, on May 13, 1912, was born the Royal Flying Corps, while the rival 'dark blues' created the Royal Naval Air Service. The fact that it was the RNAS that first ordered the Handley Page heavy bombers resulted largely from the personality and foresight of individual Royal Navy officers.

World War I

In World War I the British air services tended to learn 'the hard way' – by their mistakes – although nobody could criticize the skill and courage of the men involved or deny their accomplishments. But air warfare, with its whole technology and techniques, was in its infancy. An example of 'learning the hard way' was the defence of Britain against air attack, something that a mere five years earlier would have been dismissed as pure fantasy. At first airships – the Zeppelins of the Imperial German Navy and the Schutte-Lanz ships of the army –

Left: Handley Page 0/400 heavy bomber on patrol near Bonn, May 1919. Along with the 0/100 it was used for strategic bombing from 1917 by the RNAS and RFC. Above: Cover of *The War Budget Illustrated*, June 1915, depicting the aerial bombing of a Zeppelin, which earned Flt Sub-Lt R.A.J. Warneford, RN, the Victoria Cross.

were regarded as the chief menace. But from 1916 German bombers too became a threat, and at the end of that year the Gothas and Staaken 'Giants' penetrated to London. A damaging raid on Folkestone in May 1917 provoked a simmering public discontent which boiled over on June 13, 1917, when, in broad daylight, 20 Gothas released 72 heavy bombs simultaneously over a large area of London, from Aldgate to Poplar. A further raid on July 7 resulted in riots in London, triggered mainly by the apparent impotence of the defences. A *Times* leader thundered 'One great defect in the present system is that the air defences are under the dual control of the Army and the Navy . . .'

Even had there been a unified command things might not have been much better, but the upshot was typically British: a committee was appointed, to be chaired by former Boer enemy, General Smuts. He unequivocally recommended that the RFC and RNAS should be amalgamated into one 'air force'. At the time, this was a completely novel idea. Even though the admirals and generals took it for granted that this upstart would be the most junior service, most were antipathetic towards it.

What in peacetime might take years, can in wartime be accomplished in days or even hours. Thus, by May 19, 1918, the whole of south-east England was covered by a coherent defence system. As German bombers approached the coast, their engines were heard by forward observers who would telephone via local control centres and alert the London Defence HQ, where a large plotting-board would be used to chart their course. On that night in May the Germans sent 43 bombers against Britain. Only 13 reached London, and 6 were shot down over England by fighters and Anti-Aircraft (AA) guns, others being lost in accidents.

After the war was over this defence system constructed with such urgency fell into decay. The only nation that appeared to have any capability of bombing

Above: A German Gotha G IV bomber being prepared for a raid against England.
Above right: No. 1 Flying Training School at Netheravon, from a painting by Wilfred Hardy, GAvA. A Bristol Fighter F.2B (foreground) and an Avro 504K (centre) are taxiing before take off.

Britain was France, a close ally. From April 1920 until September 1922, Britain's air defence consisted only of a handful of stored guns and a single squadron (No. 25) of Sopwith Snipes, based at Hawkinge in Kent.

Inter-service jealousies continued after World War I, and both the Army and Navy strove to have the now tiny RAF killed off. In just one area was there a true conflict of interest. All shipborne aircraft, whether catapulted from surface warships or operated from carriers, remained RAF aircraft, with RAF pilots and observers. In the early '20s the Royal Navy won back agreement that observers should be naval officers and that 70 per cent of pilots should be naval officers with dual RN and RAF rank. But the RAF continued to handle all procurement of aircraft until, in May 1939, the Fleet Air Arm became a totally separate service.

Peace-keeping duties

Relations with the Army could have remained equally strained, had it not been for conflicts far from Britain. During the war there had been prolonged skirmishing along India's North-West Frontier, and the warlike Mohmand and Mahsud tribes had sued for peace because they were powerless to defend themselves against air attacks, even by such primitive machines as the B.E.2c. Immediately after the Armistice, the RAF was by chance able to contain a potentially explosive situation in Turkey. Thus, at a conference in Cairo in March 1921, the RAF was charged with peace-keeping duties throughout the troubled parts of the Empire. During the 1920s it was the RAF that bore the brunt of the long campaign against Sheik Mahmud, the Kurdish nationalist leader, mainly in Iraq. In many other parts of the world RAF aircraft were often called upon to preserve the peace. They were always successful and, since they did not require the deployment of massive ground forces, proved a cost-effective solution.

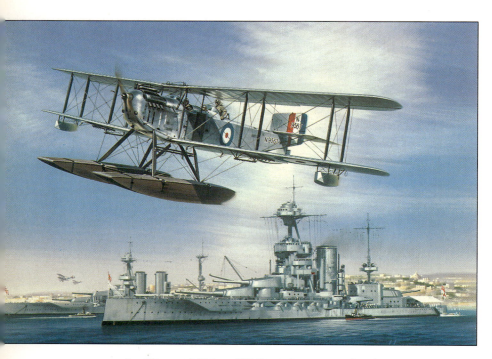

Above: A Fairey IIID floatplane operating from Malta with No. 481 Flight of the Fleet Air Arm (later to become No. 202 RAF Squadron), from a painting by Wilfred Hardy, GAvA. Below: Crashed R.E.8, Egypt, towards the end of World War I.

The need for better equipment could not be ignored, however, and from 1923 modest funds became available for aircraft with more powerful engines and with an airframe made not from wood but from metal. Further expenditure was required on special racing seaplanes to compete in the biennial Schneider Trophy race. The RAF High-Speed Flight won what had become the most famous air race in the world in 1927, 1929 and 1931, thereby retaining the trophy in perpetuity and ending the Schneider series. The 1931 team was funded by a private citizen, Lady Houston, the government declining to do so. What she was funding, in effect, was the development of Supermarine Aviation's ability to build stressed-skin airframes, and Rolls-Royce's ability to develop engines of unprecedented power.

The RAF also participated in many important attempts to set records for distance or altitude at this time. Yet these achievements, and what was learned from them, very rarely happened to have any influence on RAF equipment procurement policy decisions. For example, very little was done subsequently to develop high-altitude engines, with either two-stage or turbo superchargers. In World War II, RAF aircraft almost invariably had shorter ranges than their US counterparts, especially in the case of fighters.

A further serious shortcoming of British aircraft was the reluctance of British industry – and, indeed, of its chief customers, the RAF and Imperial Airways – to exploit new technological developments. While the Royal Aircraft Establishment (RAE) at Farnborough often led the world in research, the aircraft manufacturers clung to the wire-braced, fabric-covered biplane, with a carved wooden propeller and fixed landing gear. The only area where British products remained competitive was engines, partly because of the dynamic drive of Roy Fedden at the Bristol Aeroplane Company, who campaigned ceaselessly for variable-pitch propellers and higher-octane petrol, and partly because of the Schneider Trophy experience of Rolls-Royce. But when Rolls-Royce wanted a modern streamlined aircraft in which to test their engines they were forced to buy one from abroad, the final choice being a German Heinkel He 70.

Developing the fighter

From the closing days of World War I many eminent officers had theorized about the near-invincibility of offensive air power. Trenchard, Mitchell, Douhet and others had campaigned on behalf of bombers and, in particular, of strategic bombers able to strike at the enemy's heartlands and both sap their will to fight and ability to do so by destroying industry. It became fashionable for politicians to preach that 'the bomber will always get through', and such developments as the USA's Martin bomber, put into service by the US Army as the B-10, appeared to bear this out. The Martin had all-round defensive firepower, yet was faster than any fighter of its day. However, such aerodynamically 'clean' aircraft were not ordered by the RAF, and the lumbering Heyford biplane bomber remained in production until July 1936; the Gladiator, a biplane fighter, meanwhile, did not even reach the RAF until 1937.

Big changes were, however, being planned. One of the most significant concerned the armament of fighters. In July 1934 a conference held at the Air Ministry considered that, if certain speeds were assumed for future fighters and bombers, the fighter could not count on having a bomber in its sights for longer than two seconds. With guns firing at 1000 rounds per minute, it was calculated that to destroy a bomber in that time would require 'at least eight guns'. This was a revolutionary idea, campaigned for by a young but influential squadron leader, Ralph Sorely, and it was written into fighter specification F.5/34.

Hurricanes and Spitfires

Two British designers, Sydney Camm of Hawker and Reginald Mitchell of Supermarine, had already begun designing monoplane fighters with two or four machine guns and a 600-hp (447-kW) engine. Had these gone into mass-production they would have been obsolete by 1940, and it is extremely unlikely that a successor would have been ready. It proved to be of the utmost importance that both fighters were abandoned and replaced on the drawing board by completely fresh designs powered by the new Rolls-Royce PV.12 engine, later named the Merlin, in the 1000-hp (746-kW) class. The new fighters had retractable landing gear, flaps, enclosed cockpits and other new features, and were planned to carry eight machine guns, all mounted in the wings outboard of the propeller disc. Despite prolonged difficulties, the new engine became available just in time for the Hawker F.36/34, later named the Hurricane, to fly on November 6, 1935, and for the Supermarine 300, later named the Spitfire, to follow on March 5, 1936.

**Below: The prototype Spitfire, designed by R.J. Mitchell and built by Vickers, just before its test flight in 1936.
Bottom: Sidney Camm (second from left), a model aircraft enthusiast, became Hawker's chief designer.**

Above: Vickers-Supermarine Spitfire Mk IXs of No. 602 (City of Glasgow) Squadron on patrol in early 1944, from a painting by Wilfred Hardy, GAvA. This squadron was among the first to land in Normandy after D-Day.

Few aircraft have ever been so important to the nation that produced them. The Hurricane was a traditional braced tubular structure with fabric covering. From the start it was an excellent aircraft. As early as March 1936, sensing that their decision could be of immense importance, the Hawker board took the gamble of tooling up their factory to build 1000 Hurricanes. The first order, for 600, followed just over three months later. This order was to prove crucial in the summer of 1940, for, with 500 fewer Hurricanes the Battle of Britain, and thus the war, would almost certainly have been lost.

As for the Spitfire, this was a smaller, faster and more modern aircraft, with a stressed-skin structure. It took longer to get into production and was more difficult than the Hurricane to look after and repair, but its potential was much greater. The combination of the stressed-skin structure and the Merlin engine (and its more powerful twin, the Griffon), made the Spitfire a formidable fighter and it was to remain in production throughout World War II. Both the Hurricane and Spitfire were later fitted with cannon, equipped to carry bombs or rockets and developed in naval carrier-based versions. However, nothing can conceal the fact that there was a large element of luck in the fact that they became available in adequate quantities just in time for the crucial summer of 1940.

Other important developments came about just in time for the RAF to win the Battle of Britain. One was 100-octane petrol. Here most of the progress was made by the USA, although the important difference in behaviour between engines run on weak or rich fuel mixtures was discovered in Britain. Changing from earlier fuel, typically of 87 octane (a measure of the fuel's resistance to detonation or 'knocking'), to the new fuel meant that boost pressure could be significantly increased. For example, in the early Merlin engines it changed from 6lb/sq. in. (0.42kg/cm^2) to 12lb/sq. in. (0.84kg/cm^2), resulting in an increase in power from 1000hp (746kW) to 1300hp (969kW). This just tipped the balance in favour of the British fighters. German and British fighters were otherwise so evenly matched that even a small advantage to either side could exert a very large influence on the overall result.

Invention of radar

Another important development was the invention of radar. In 1934, A.P. Rowe at the Air Ministry, perturbed at the sudden emergence of the menacing power of Hitler's Germany, searched for information on how science could help air defence. He found virtually nothing. The national defence system was in a much worse state than it had been in 1918, and with the prospect of swarms of newly built bombers joining the Luftwaffe, he felt something should be done. A radio expert, Robert Watson Watt, was asked whether the popular idea of a 'death ray' could ever be realized in practice. He proved that it was not feasible but added that such a device would have needed some method of aiming it and that here radio methods could offer some help. With remarkable speed he demonstrated how even a fabric-covered Heyford reflected radio waves. In February 1935, Watson Watt submitted the most important document in the history of scientific air power. His report, 'Detection of Aircraft by Radio Methods', explained how powerful radio transmitters and receivers could be set up to protect the country against air attack.

Previously, there had been hardly any warning of an air raid on Britain. The only aids had been binoculars and crude devices for focusing the sound of the bombers' engines. Both, of course, had to be pointed at the bombers to be effective. The new invention of radar promised, with development, to be able to detect enemy aircraft while they were still over the Continent as well as indicating their speed, course, altitude and approximate numerical strength. After various trials at Biggin Hill in August 1936, all the sceptics and opponents were overcome.

This revolutionized the defence of Britain. Previously, fighters had had to mount 'standing patrols', flying to and fro on boring patrol missions in areas where it was thought enemy bombers might appear. This was tiring for the pilots, wore out engines, and burned large amounts of fuel to no purpose. With radar, the whole country could be protected by an invisible electronic 'screen' which could unfailingly detect even single aircraft. Fighters could wait at readiness, secure in the knowledge that they would be 'scrambled' in time and then directed to intercept each enemy formation.

Above: Among the heavy bombers brought into service by the RAF around 1940 was the four-engined Short Stirling. Before the switch to night operations by Bomber Command, daylight raids were carried out early in the war.

Reorganization and expansion

The mid-1930s saw the complete reorganization of the Home RAF. No longer was it divided into 'areas' according to a complex geographical carve-up of England, with bomber and fighter squadrons disposed so as to counter a hypothetical attack by France. Instead the RAF was divided into Fighter Command, Bomber Command and Coastal Command. The Commands were later backed up by other groups such as Army Cooperation Command and Transport, Flying Training, Technical Training, Maintenance and Balloon Commands. The new arrangement did tend to polarize the RAF in operational terms making it, for example, more difficult for fighters and bombers to work closely together. Overall, however, it was generally to prove to be an excellent arrangement for fighting a major war.

In the provision of bombers much time was lost in trying to comply with rules and restrictions decreed by the futile 1932 Geneva Disarmament Conference. From late 1934 such handicaps were removed, but just how the RAF bomber force could best expand was very uncertain. Such important specifications as B.9/32, P.27/32, B.3/34, P.4/34, B.1/35 and P.13/36 all led to important prototypes of modern design, but in order to increase numbers quickly and train crews the main production was of the 600-hp (447-kW) Hawker Hind, a tiny biplane in all basic respects similar to the single-engined bombers of 1916. The 528 Hinds built between 1935 and 1938 did at least enable pilots and back-seat gunners to gain experience, and they suited the small grass aerodromes. Meanwhile, new designs were prepared and vast new factories were built – some by the aircraft industry and others at public expense as part of a Shadow scheme in which new types were mass-produced along car-industry lines, under car-industry management. Large airfields were constructed and, from 1937, were equipped with paved runways.

In terms of numbers the most important new bombers were two light bombers, the Fairey Battle and Bristol Blenheim, intended for use in low-level operations against army units in the field. It was not appreciated that, although modern in conception and a vast advance over the Hind, they would be sitting ducks for the Bf 109E and even highly vulnerable to the massed 20mm and 37mm flak of the German army. A little later came the bigger Handley Page Hampden, Vickers Wellington and Armstrong Whitworth Whitley. A little later still came the mighty Short Stirling and Handley Page Halifax four-engined heavy bombers and the twin-engined Avro Manchester. The latter was redesigned, with four engines, as the Lancaster – the best RAF bomber of World War II. Unfortunately, the Spanish Civil War and other experiences, including exercises, all suggested that bombers could operate with virtual impunity by day, if necessary defended against fighters by the massed firepower of their power-driven gun turrets.

World War II

World War II opened on September 3, 1939. Seven months of so-called 'phoney war' followed before Hitler first took over Denmark and Norway and then struck with overwhelming force in the west. RAF operations with fighters and bombers during this period were on a very limited scale, but they showed that Blenheims or Wellingtons used against German targets in daylight would suffer totally unacceptable casualties. Suddenly,

Below: A prototype Armstrong Whitworth Albemarle. Intended to be a bomber, it was later used as a transport. Right: World War II recruiting poster for the Women's Auxiliary Air Force which was formed in June 1939.

the RAF realized that it had to learn how to operate at night. Although the new bombers carried specialist navigators, a new trade only introduced with the new bombers in 1938, most crews had the greatest difficulty in finding allotted targets, and a large proportion of each raiding force became lost soon after leaving base. While the Luftwaffe followed specially devised radio beams, the RAF bombers had to rely on astro-navigation and dead reckoning, and very occasional sightings of major rivers or other identifiable ground features.

During the early part of the war there was a vast and sustained expansion of manufacturing industry under the dynamic Lord Beaverbrook. This inevitably tended to favour established types of aircraft (even those already proved unsatisfactory) and tended to discourage and even kill off anything new. Thus, supporters of the de Havilland Mosquito had to fight for its existence before and after its first flight on November 25, 1940. Only gradually was it appreciated that it was an extremely effective, war-winning aircraft. On the other hand, great efforts were put into the production of such aircraft as the Botha, Albermarle, Warwick and Buckingham, which were eventually found employment in roles other than those for which they were designed.

SERVE IN THE WAAF
WITH THE MEN WHO FLY

An equally dramatic expansion took place in all forms of training at this time. The huge demand for aircrew was met partly by schools in Britain, but the network of schools built up in Canada, Southern Rhodesia, Australia and New Zealand played an increasingly important role. Later, large numbers of British pilots were trained in the USA. Such training could proceed without interference from enemy action, and the weather was invariably much better than in Britain. Many other supporting actions were taken. In June 1939, a large Women's Auxiliary Air Force (WAAF) was formed to handle a vast range of ground duties and release able-bodied men for other duties. An RAF Regiment was created in January 1942, primarily to defend airfields. In September 1939, the Air Transport Auxiliary, a civilian organization responsible for delivering new or repaired aircraft and repositioning aircraft throughout Britain, was set up.

The Battle of Britain and after

Perhaps the most crucial time, for the RAF at least, was the six months following the unleashing of the Blitzkrieg in the west on May 10, 1940. Sir Hugh Dowding, Air Officer Commanding (AOC) Fighter Command, could see that the terrible drain on his command as squadrons were sent on seemingly hopeless missions to France would be bound to result, sooner or later, in the total defeat of Britain. He had the courage to stand firm, and the result was that, for the first time, the huge and effective Luftwaffe found itself

Below: The navigator of an RAF Lancaster bomber operates a Gee set. This radio navigation aid was first used successfully by No. 115 (Bomber) Squadron during a raid on Mönchen Gladback in August 1941.

Above: RAF ground crew prepare a Typhoon Mk IB of No. 175 Squadron for a mission; two 500-lb (227-kg) bombs are about to be loaded. This aircraft was formidable in the close-support and ground-attack role.

up against an enemy it could not defeat. Reichsmarschall Goering turned instead to a night 'blitz' on London and other cities and Fighter Command licked its wounds and quickly regained its strength. The RAF as a whole entered a period of sustained expansion and increasingly took the war to the enemy.

The two main factors contributing to the increasing effectiveness of Bomber Command were electronic. 'Gee' was a radio navigation aid which, for the first time, enabled crews to locate their position precisely, even on the darkest or cloudiest night. 'Oboe' was an even more accurate navigation aid (navaid), though usable only out to a radius of about 250 miles (400km), and only by one aircraft at a time. The answer was to use special aircraft, formed into a PathFinder Force (PFF), with Oboe guidance, in order to put down markers on which the main force would bomb. Gradually Bomber Command, although suffering terrible losses, learned how to put down great tonnages accurately on target in highly concentrated raids lasting 30 minutes or less. Traditional bombs of (for example) 250lb (113kg) or 500lb (227kg) size gave way almost completely to millions of incendiaries mixed with a few 'blockbusters' of 4000lb (1814kg) and upwards. B. N. Wallis developed special weapons for use against dams, U-boat pens and, by creating a local earthquake, such structures as viaducts. In these huge and sustained operations Bomber Command brought the new art of electronic warfare to a pitch of excellence. It was odd, therefore, that the 'heavies' broadcast their presence with H_2S ground-mapping radar and Monica tail-warning radar, and bristled with guns firing ahead, upwards and to the rear, yet there was not even a small window in the defenceless belly from which the crew could see the deadly upward-firing German night fighters.

Apart from the Battle of Britain in the summer of 1940, the most crucial conflict of the war was the Battle of the Atlantic. The vast U-boat fleets of Admiral Dönitz almost brought Britain to her knees, but at the climax in April and May 1943 it was the Anti-Submarine Warfare (ASW) forces that emerged victorious. Coastal Command played a major part in this grim battle. Thanks to such aircraft as the Catalina and Liberator – both made by the US Consolidated company – the previous gap in the North Atlantic defences, unreachable by shore-based aircraft, was closed. Coastal aircraft fought with radar and Leigh lights (a powerful form of searchlight) to find their targets and increasingly had to contend with U-boats in surface battles.

In other theatres the RAF's role was chiefly to support land, or land-and-sea, campaigns. Fighters carried bombs or rockets, and the stalwart Hurricane appeared with twin 40mm guns in the role of tank-buster. Its successor, the Typhoon, was a disappointment as a high-altitude fighter, but in the close-support and attack role, carrying four 20mm guns and either two 1000lb (454kg) bombs or eight rockets, it was formidable. On many occasions in north-west Europe Typhoons completely destroyed large Panzer formations, even blowing the turrets off Tiger tanks. Often squadrons would form a 'cab rank' in the sky, ready to strike at points designated by the local ground-force commander. They made many precision attacks on individual buildings, such as the headquarters of the German 15th Army, emulating similar precision attacks by Mosquitoes on such targets as Amiens prison and various city-centre Gestapo headquarters.

In the final year of the war the RAF could do little against the A4 ('V2') rocket, but made a giant contribution to shooting down Fi-103 ('V1') flying bombs, a single Tempest wing destroying 638. Tempests also destroyed 20 of the formidable Me-262 twin-jets, and the Allies never lost complete command of the sky, even over the heart of Germany.

Post-war developments

In the aftermath of World War II Britain, faced by severe financial and industrial problems, was forced to reduce defence expenditure. The RAF inevitably had to concentrate on essentials and research and development suffered. No attempt was made to apply captured German data on swept wings, rocket engines and other advanced technologies, and a programme to build a supersonic aircraft, the Miles M.52, was cancelled. The RAF's first jet fighters, the Meteor and Vampire, were essentially airframes of traditional type powered by turbo-jet engines of Whittle derivation. Although both were later modified as radar-equipped night fighters, no attempt was made to match the potential of their engines with transonic aerodynamics. Specifications were written for advanced new fighters and bombers, but their development proceeded slowly taking in each case more than ten years.

Top: One of the RAF's first jet fighters, the de Havilland Vampire F.Mk1 was produced in 1945 and served with No. 247 Squadron at RAF Chilbolton and Odiham.
Above: The B.Mk 1 prototype of the English Electric Canberra jet bomber, on its maiden flight, May 13, 1949.

In June 1948, the USSR began a blockade of Berlin aimed at starving out the occupation forces of its former allies. An airlift was quickly organized, which by the time the Soviet blockade was lifted, in May 1949, had flown in almost 1.6 million tons of supplies, of which RAF aircraft contributed 281,727 tons.

In March 1950 the Air League expressed 'deep anxiety regarding the air defences of the United Kingdom . . .', but the decline was suddenly arrested with the outbreak of war in Korea three months later when attempts were made to make up for the lost years. A super-priority scheme was started giving certain aircraft projects first claim on scarce materials, tools and labour. The Canberra jet bomber was rushed into production not only at the parent English Electric factory but also at Avro, Short and Handley Page, while its Rolls-Royce Avon engine was also manufactured by Bristol, Napier and Standard Motors.

Above: An Avro Vulcan B.Mk 2 carrying a Blue Steel missile
takes off bound for Woomera in November 1960.
Inset right: Blue Steel missiles in production, 1963.
Below right: A Thor rocket is deployed by No. 77 Squadron
at RAF Feltwell in February 1960.

The V-force

For the more distant future, development proceeded on
two advanced jet bombers, later to become the Avro
Vulcan and Handley Page Victor. Oddly, not only were
both put into production, entering service in 1956–57,
but a third type, the Vickers-Armstrong Valiant, was
also ordered and rushed into service in 1955. All were
designed to carry nuclear bombs, known as Blue
Danube. A guided bomb, Blue Boar, was cancelled, but
a stand-off bomb (in effect an air-launched cruise
missile) was developed under the name Blue Steel.
Small numbers of the Blue Steel bombs were deployed
by the Mk. 2 versions of the Vulcan and Victor in the
early 1960s, but by this time it was reluctantly being
recognized that, in future, hostile airspace would have
to be penetrated at the lowest possible altitude to
minimize detection and tracking by defending radar and
other surveillance systems.

These changes struck at the heart of the RAF's
policy of placing most emphasis on its ability to carry out
strategic bombing missions. In the mid-1950s, the
development in the USA of Intercontinental Ballistic
Missiles (ICBMs), paralleled by even bigger missiles in
the USSR, was hardly something Britain could ignore.
An all-British Long-Range Ballistic Missile (LRBM),
Blue Streak, was put into urgent development for
deployment by RAF Bomber Command. While this was

being made ready, an American Intermediate-Range Ballistic Missile (IRBM), the Douglas Thor, was supplied to Bomber Command.

The mid-1950s were a time of rapid technological change. In an attempt to modernize at least some squadrons of Fighter Command and of the RAF units in the 2nd Tactical Air Force in Germany, Britain purchased 430 North American Sabres. Built by Canadair, they were paid for by Mutual Defense Assistance Program Funds and delivered in 1952 and 1953. For the same purpose Bomber Command received 88 Boeing B-29 heavy bombers, and Coastal Command 52 Lockheed P2V–5 Neptunes, while the North American RB-45C Tornado four-jet reconnaissance aircraft was supplied to a joint USAF/RAF unit which, between 1951 and 1954 made clandestine nightflights over the USSR.

Fighter developments

While the squadrons were being equipped with Sabres, British industry strove to develop new fighters. The Swift proved unacceptable, although two squadrons equipped with them served in the tactical reconnaissance role. The Hawker Hunter, however, very gradually matured to become an excellent aircraft, which served in the day-fighter and ground-attack roles in all theatres. From 1956 the Gloster Javelin served as an all-weather interceptor, initially with 30mm guns and later with Firestreak infra-red homing Air-to-Air Missiles (AAMs), but it performed inadequately. Fortunately English Electric, having developed the Canberra

into a valued bomber and reconnaissance aircraft, then set about designing a fighter able to shoot it down. The result was the P.1B, later named the Lightning.

The Lightning first flew on April 4, 1957, and on the very same day the Ministry of Defence published its *Outline of Future Policy*. The policies it recommended were seen at the time as being highly controversial – the cancellation of work on new fighters and bombers, and their replacement by missiles. The document can be seen to have been misguided at the very least. Britain never deployed its network of Surface-to-Air Missiles (SAMs), although the RAF did receive a limited number of Bloodhounds. These are still ready to be fired in the UK, although as they approach the age of 30 their refurbishment becomes an increasing problem. As for the great force of ballistic missiles, Blue Streak was cancelled in 1960 and Thor withdrawn in 1963. This left only the Vulcan and Victor bombers capable of taking on a nuclear deterrent role until this was assumed by the Royal Navy's Polaris missile submarines in 1969.

Cancellation of the TSR.2

Fortunately, the Lightning proved to be such an excellent aircraft that, with great reluctance, the Treasury did sanction modest expenditure on updating it with new weapons, more power, better avionics and, above all, a greater internal and external fuel capacity. Contrary to the 1957 prediction, the last Lightning was not withdrawn until 1988. Nevertheless, the *Outline*

Left: A Bloodhound Mk 2 blasts off from the launching pad. These surface-to-air missiles, although now almost 30 years old, are still in service with the RAF.
Below: RAF pilots are de-briefed in front of their Lightning fighters, which entered service in June 1960.

Above: The British Aircraft Corporation's TSR.2 prototype on the tarmac at RAF Duxford. This was the only prototype of this tactical strike/reconnaissance aircraft to fly before the project was cancelled because of government cuts.

had a traumatic effect on RAF morale – and on recruiting – and an equally shattering effect on manufacturing industry. While such aircraft as the F-104 and Mirage captured huge world markets, the British aircraft industry was subjected to a succession of politically enforced 'shotgun weddings', the emergent groups then being promised state orders for aircraft. Only one of the latter was military: the TSR.2, an extremely advanced long-range strike and reconnaissance aircraft, to be built by the newly formed British Aircraft Corporation and powered by Bristol Siddeley engines. The need for an aircraft which would find out in any future war what was happening and carry out surgically precise attacks on moving targets was obvious. However, the media was full of self-appointed experts who (to quote a typical comment) believed that 'Britain has no need of so costly an aircraft now we are getting Polaris'. (Polaris is a submarine-launched missile unable to fly reconnaissance missions or hit moving targets.) Unfortunately, the Labour Party, too, saw the TSR.2 as an example of unnecessary expenditure, and when they were returned to office they cancelled it.

In January 1965 the Labour Government also cancelled the only other new RAF aircraft, the Hawker Siddeley 1154 supersonic Short Take-Off, Vertical-Landing (STOVL) strike fighter and its supporting HS.681 STOVL jet transport. The alternative seemed simple: to buy American aircraft. The replacement for TSR.2 was the swing-wing F-111K, but this was soon cancelled. In its place came the Anglo-French Variable-Geometry (AFVG) aircraft, and when this was cancelled it was replaced by the tripartite Multi-Role Combat Aircraft (MRCA), the Tornado, developed by Britain, West Germany and Italy. Somehow, despite attempts to cancel this, it survived.

Purchase of the Phantom

The replacement for the HS.1154 was the McDonnell Douglas Phantom. Although its cost was enormously increased and its performance degraded by fitting British engines, it has proved a valuable aircraft which has brought a lot of refurbishment and rectification work to British industry. To meet a sudden shortage of fighters in 1982 – caused by the Falklands campaign – 15 extra F-4Js were ordered second-hand from the US Navy, and these retain their J79 engines. With no deficiencies other than overall obsolescence, the Phantom remains an important RAF aircraft, able to intercept 'Zombies', the probing Soviet aircraft engaged in ELectronic INTelligence (ELINT) missions, and also if necessary to carry out ground-attack missions (although this appears unlikely).

The replacement for the HS.681 was the Lockheed C-130K Hercules, a wholly conventional runway-based

Below: Phantoms of No. 29 (Fighter) Squadron over Port Stanley, October 1982, from a painting by Wilfred Hardy, GAvA. The squadron arrived after hostilities had ended to provide air defence against possible further attacks.

'airlifter'. First flown in 1954, it is such a good aircraft that it remains in production, with almost 2000 having been built for some 60 air forces. The 66 supplied to the RAF from 1966 to 1968 were basically similar to the C-130H, but with British avionics. Subsequently 30 of them were stretched to L-100-30 standard. Other 'Herky birds' have in-flight refuelling probes, while a few are equipped for EW missions (one is a specialized meteorological research aircraft).

Taking the broadest view of the RAF's development in the middle part of the century, the most profound changes occurred in the period between 1956 and 1963. In 1956 there were 23 major aircraft companies, over 60 projects for new military aircraft and helicopters, no manpower problem (because of compulsory national service) and RAF units all over the world. In 1963 there were only four aircraft manufacturers, only five projects for new military aircraft (three of which were soon to be cancelled), no national service, poor morale in the service due to its uncertain future, and RAF bases were being abandoned all over the world.

Another important factor, though one common to almost all countries, was that manpower was becoming very expensive. Without national service, personnel had to be enticed into the armed forces, and with civilian pay often rising at 20 per cent or (in 1974) even 30 per cent per year, the cost of personnel was tending to double in five or six years. Instead of having perhaps 1000 'erks' spending much of their time on pointless or menial tasks, the average RAF station was fast becoming the ultra-hi-tech employer of highly trained and highly skilled professional men and women whose accomplishments, of course, automatically qualified them for high civilian salaries. The hundreds of tons of handwritten and typewritten forms were gone, to be replaced by computer print-outs and colourful graphic displays. Instead of having thousands of aircraft, each with an active life of anything from a few months to three years, the RAF counted its aircraft in mere dozens, but had to keep them in excellent condition for 20 or 30 years.

Preparing for a European War

Britain's shrinking defence commitments over the years have inevitably influenced the RAF's requirements of its aircraft, which have progressively been designed to meet the conditions of a supposed European conflict. Thus the Tornado, cornerstone of RAF air power from 1980 to 2020, has a generally shorter radius of action than its predecessor the Vulcan (or the TSR.2 or F-111K). The primary mission of the basic version of the Tornado is interdiction, or attack on surface targets well behind a battlefront. This is strange, for the RAF had already purchased the Jaguar, Buccaneer and Harrier for the same mission.

The Jaguar began life as a light attack and training aircraft, developed jointly by Britain and France. It was mainly British influence that made it into a far more

Above: A Jaguar GR. Mk 1 of No. 2 Squadron and a Buccaneer S.Mk 2 of No. 15 Squadron fly in formation, 1983. Below: A Panavia Tornado GR.Mk 1 in low-level flight, 1984. The RAF plans to use Tornados for interdiction until 2020.

formidable aircraft, able to carry an external weapons load of 10500lb (4763kg). Among its excellent features are two fuel-efficient engines, small overall size, great agility, and landing gear with such long-stroke legs and such low tyre-pressure that operations could be sustained from any reasonably flat strip about 4000ft (1250m) long. It is surprising, then, that RAF Jaguar units are not trained to operate from short strips. Two Jaguar units, 2 and 41 Squadrons, can operate in the reconnaissance role using an external camera pod. The Buccaneer was designed as a carrier-based naval attack aircraft far ahead of its time, in being built for full-throttle attacks at sea level. It was ordered for the RAF in 1968, following cancellation of the F-111K and AFVG.

When the government cancelled the HS.1154 in January 1965, it permitted some of that aircraft's avionics to be put into a development of the much smaller Kestrel, and the Harrier was the result. Entering service in early 1969, it gave the RAF the unique ability to have a few aircraft that could never be caught on an airfield because they do not need one (in reality they probably *would* be caught on an airfield, unless there had been sufficient warning for them to disperse). The original Harrier was limited in capability, although it could fly attack and reconnaissance missions and proved tough and simple to service. Retro-fitted with a more powerful Pegasus engine, the GR.3 version proved that it could carry an 8000lb (3629kg) weapon load. With a 5000lb (2268kg) load it has a greater combat radius than a Hunter. It has also proved itself to be a tough air-combat opponent, able to vector its total engine thrust to make 'impossible' manoeuvres.

Below: V/STOL Harrier GR. Mk 3s of No. 1 Squadron, RAF Wittering, in Arctic camouflage, take part in an exercise in Norway. Able to take off from roads and clearings, Harriers can operate independently of airfields.

Above: The Hawker Siddeley Nimrod AEW.Mk3 with an Avro Shackleton AEW.Mk 2 (foreground), which it was to replace. The Nimrod was cancelled and the Shackletons are now being replaced by Boeing AWACS aircraft.

Maritime and ASW aircraft

For the all-important maritime and ASW role, the venerable Lancaster was developed, via the Lincoln, into the Shackleton, which entered service in February 1951. What nobody expected at the outset was that on withdrawal from service in 1971, a total of 12 Shackleton MR.2s should be converted into temporary Airborne Early Warning (AEW) platforms by fitting them with APS-20F(I) surveillance radars. These were updated sets designed in 1946, but fitted with Doppler stabilization. The RAF is all too used to relying on the skill of its airmen to make up for deficiencies in its equipment, but the story of Britain's AEW force is a particularly outrageous example.

It had long been planned to replace the Shackletons with the Nimrod AEW.3. The original Maritime Reconnaissance (MR) Nimrod had been developed in the mid-1960s as a replacement for the original Shackletons. Using an airframe derived from the civil Comet 4C, the Nimrod combined turbo fan propulsion with comprehensive navigation, communications and ASW sensors and weapons. It entered service in 1969, the year in which, on November 27, all RAF operational aircraft other than those in RAF Germany (part of the 2nd Allied Tactical Air Force) became part of a single integrated force called Strike Command.

The Nimrod has performed excellently in the MR role, especially after a mid-life update to MR.2 standard. The AEW.3 project, however, became a typically British fiasco – by trying to do everything on the cheap, by repeatedly upgrading the requirement and by failing in the vital task of programme management, the project soon collapsed. After expenditure of approximately £1 billion it was cancelled in December 1986. Instead, the RAF will receive 12 Boeing Airborne Warning And Control System (AWACS) aircraft, with CFM56 engines and some British avionics. Delivered in the 1990s, these will take over from the AEW Shackletons.

UKADGE

Also in the early 1990s most of the elements of the UK Air Defence Ground Environment (UKADGE) system will become operational. In the early 1960s, Britain declined to participate in the NATO Air Defence Ground Environment (NADGE) system, which was the first, and so far only, successful attempt by all the NATO nations to construct something on a common basis. NADGE, implemented in the 1970s, comprises a computer-controlled and totally integrated air-defence system of radars, displays and secure communications stretching from northern Norway to eastern Turkey. Britain sadly committed herself to a combined civil–military air traffic control and defence system which, overall, proved to be a failure. The setting-up of UKADGE was a recognition of the problem, and in the 1990s Britain should have a comprehensive air defence system for the first time since 1945.

In supporting roles, the superiority of American transport aircraft was highlighted by the Berlin Airlift. The situation has improved only slightly, successive RAF transports over the years being mere adaptations of civil machines. A large sum was spent between 1958 and 1964 developing the Shorts Belfast strategic freighter, but only ten were built. Another curious feature was that, although the RAF pioneered air

Right: RAF bases in Britain and Germany, including all operational squadrons and training units, but not RAF Regiment Rapier SAM or University Air Squadrons, Air Experience Flights or Air Cadet Gliding facilities.

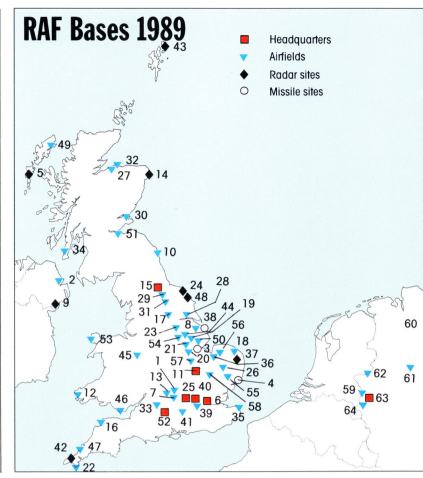

RAF Bases 1989

- ■ Headquarters
- ▼ Airfields
- ◆ Radar sites
- ○ Missile sites

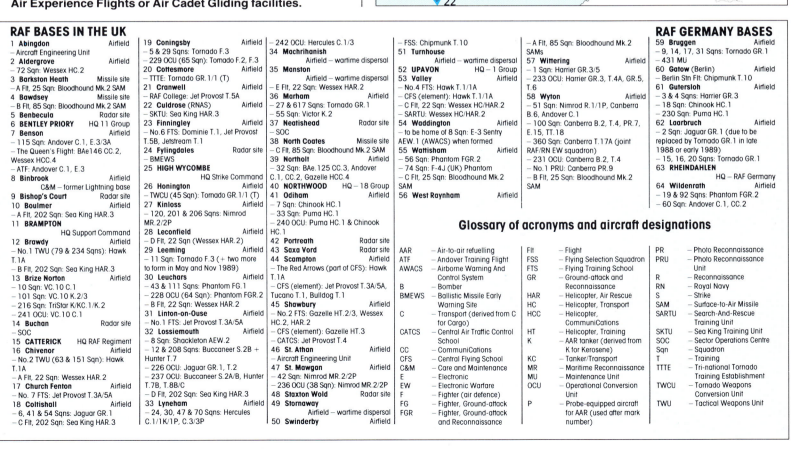

RAF BASES IN THE UK

1 **Abingdon** — Airfield
– Aircraft Engineering Unit
2 **Aldergrove** — Airfield
– 72 Sqn: Wessex HC.2
3 **Barkston Heath** — Missile site
– A Flt, 25 Sqn: Bloodhound Mk.2 SAM
4 **Bawdsey** — Missile site
– B Flt, 85 Sqn: Bloodhound Mk.2 SAM
5 **Benbecula** — Radar site
6 **BENTLEY PRIORY** — HQ 11 Group
7 **Benson** — Airfield
– 115 Sqn: Andover C.1, E.3/3A
– The Queen's Flight: BAe146 CC.2, Wessex HCC.4
– ATF: Andover C.1, E.3
8 **Binbrook** — Airfield
C&M – former Lightning base
9 **Bishop's Court** — Radar site
10 **Boulmer** — Airfield
– A Flt, 202 Sqn: Sea King HAR.3
11 **BRAMPTON** — HQ Support Command
12 **Brawdy** — Airfield
– No.1 TWU (79 & 234 Sqns): Hawk T.1A
– B Flt, 202 Sqn: Sea King HAR.3
13 **Brize Norton** — Airfield
– 10 Sqn: VC.10 C.1
– 101 Sqn: VC.10 K.2/3
– 216 Sqn: TriStar K/KC.1/K.2
– 241 OCU: VC.10 C.1
14 **Buchan** — Radar site
– SOC
15 **CATTERICK** — HQ RAF Regiment
16 **Chivenor** — Airfield
– No.2 TWU (63 & 151 Sqn): Hawk T.1A
– A Flt, 22 Sqn: Wessex HAR.2
17 **Church Fenton** — Airfield
– No. 7 FTS: Jet Provost T.3A/5A
18 **Coltishall** — Airfield
– 6, 41 & 54 Sqns: Jaguar GR.1
– C Flt, 202 Sqn: Sea King HAR.3

19 **Coningsby** — Airfield
– 5 & 29 Sqns: Tornado F.3
– 229 OCU (65 Sqn): Tornado F.2, F.3
20 **Cottesmore** — Airfield
– TTTE: Tornado GR.1/1 (T)
21 **Cranwell** — Airfield
– RAF College: Jet Provost T.5A
22 **Culdrose** (RNAS) — Airfield
– SKTU: Sea King HAR.3
23 **Finningley** — Airfield
– No.6 FTS: Dominie T.1, Jet Provost T.5B, Jetstream T.1
24 **Fylingdales** — Radar site
– BMEWS
25 **HIGH WYCOMBE** — HQ Strike Command
26 **Honington** — Airfield
– TWCU (45 Sqn): Tornado GR.1/1 (T)
27 **Kinloss** — Airfield
– 120, 201 & 206 Sqns: Nimrod MR.2/2P
28 **Leconfield** — Airfield
– D Flt, 22 Sqn (Wessex HAR.2)
29 **Leeming** — Airfield
– 11 Sqn: Tornado F.3 (+ two more to form in May and Nov 1989)
30 **Leuchars** — Airfield
– 43 & 111 Sqns: Phantom FG.1
– 228 OCU (64 Sqn): Phantom FGR.2
– B Flt, 22 Sqn: Wessex HAR.2
31 **Linton-on-Ouse** — Airfield
– No.1 FTS: Jet Provost T.3A/5A
32 **Lossiemouth** — Airfield
– 8 Sqn: Shackleton AEW.2
– 12 & 208 Sqns: Buccaneer S.2B + Hunter T.7
– 226 OCU: Jaguar GR.1, T.2
– 237 OCU: Buccaneer S.2A/B, Hunter T.7B, T.8B/C
– D Flt, 22 Sqn: Sea King HAR.3
33 **Lyneham** — Airfield
– 24, 30, 47 & 70 Sqns: Hercules C.1/1K/1P, C.3/3P

– 242 OCU: Hercules C.1/3
34 **Machrihanish** — Airfield – wartime dispersal
35 **Manston** — Airfield – wartime dispersal
– E Flt, 22 Sqn: Wessex HAR.2
36 **Marham** — Airfield
– 27 & 617 Sqns: Tornado GR.1
– 55 Sqn: Victor K.2
37 **Neatishead** — Radar site
– SOC
38 **North Coates** — Missile site
– C Flt, 85 Sqn: Bloodhound Mk.2 SAM
39 **Northolt** — Airfield
– 32 Sqn: BAe.125 CC.3, Andover C.1, CC.2, Gazelle HCC.4
40 **NORTHWOOD** — HQ – 18 Group
41 **Odiham** — Airfield
– 7 Sqn: Chinook HC.1
– 33 Sqn: Puma HC.1
– 240 OCU: Puma HC.1 & Chinook HC.1
42 **Portreath** — Radar site
43 **Saxa Vord** — Radar site
44 **Scampton** — Airfield
– The Red Arrows (part of CFS): Hawk T.1A
– CFS (element): Jet Provost T.3A/5A, Tucano T.1, Bulldog T.1
45 **Shawbury** — Airfield
– No.2 FTS: Gazelle HT.2/3, Wessex HC.2, HAR.2
– CFS (element): Gazelle HT.3
– CATCS: Jet Provost T.4
46 **St. Athan** — Airfield
– Aircraft Engineering Unit
47 **St. Mawgan** — Airfield
– 42 Sqn: Nimrod MR.2/2P
– 236 OCU (38 Sqn): Nimrod MR.2/2P
48 **Staxton Wold** — Radar site
49 **Stornoway** — Airfield – wartime dispersal
50 **Swinderby** — Airfield

– FSS: Chipmunk T.10
51 **Turnhouse** — Airfield – wartime dispersal
52 **UPAVON** — HQ – 1 Group
53 **Valley** — Airfield
– No.4 FTS: Hawk T.1/1A
– CFS (element): Hawk T.1/1A
– C Flt, 22 Sqn: Wessex HC/HAR.2
– SARTU: Wessex HC/HAR.2
54 **Waddington** — Airfield
– to be home of 8 Sqn: E-3 Sentry AEW.1 (AWACS) when formed
55 **Wattisham** — Airfield
– 56 Sqn: Phantom FGR.2
– 74 Sqn: F-4J (UK) Phantom
– C Flt, 25 Sqn: Bloodhound Mk.2 SAM
56 **West Raynham** — Airfield

– A Flt, 85 Sqn: Bloodhound Mk.2 SAMs
57 **Wittering** — Airfield
– 1 Sqn: Harrier GR.3/5
– 233 OCU: Harrier GR.3, T.4A, GR.5, T.6
58 **Wyton** — Airfield
– 51 Sqn: Nimrod R.1/1P, Canberra B.6, Andover C.1
– 100 Sqn: Canberra B.2, T.4, PR.7, E.15, TT.18
– 360 Sqn: Canberra T.17A (joint RAF/RN EW squadron)
– 231 OCU: Canberra B.2, T.4
– No.1 PRU: Canberra PR.9
– B Flt, 25 Sqn: Bloodhound Mk.2 SAM

RAF GERMANY BASES

59 **Bruggen** — Airfield
– 9, 14, 17, 31 Sqns: Tornado GR.1
– 431 MU
60 **Gatow** (Berlin) — Airfield
– Berlin Stn Flt: Chipmunk T.10
61 **Gutersloh** — Airfield
– 3 & 4 Sqns: Harrier GR.3
– 18 Sqn: Chinook HC.1
– 230 Sqn: Puma HC.1
62 **Laarbruch** — Airfield
– 2 Sqn: Jaguar GR.1 (due to be replaced by Tornado GR.1 in late 1988 or early 1989)
– 15, 16, 20 Sqns: Tornado GR.1
63 **RHEINDAHLEN** — HQ – RAF Germany
64 **Wildenrath** — Airfield
– 19 & 92 Sqns: Phantom FGR.2
– 60 Sqn: Andover C.1, CC.2

Glossary of acronyms and aircraft designations

AAR	– Air-to-air refuelling	Flt	– Flight	PR	– Photo Reconnaissance
ATF	– Andover Training Flight	FSS	– Flying Selection Squadron	PRU	– Photo Reconnaissance Unit
AWACS	– Airborne Warning And Control System	FTS	– Flying Training School		
		GR	– Ground-attack and Reconnaissance	R	– Reconnaissance
B	– Bomber			RN	– Royal Navy
BMEWS	– Ballistic Missile Early Warning Site	HAR	– Helicopter, Air Rescue	S	– Strike
		HC	– Helicopter, Transport	SAM	– Surface-to-Air Missile
C	– Transport (derived from C for Cargo)	HCC	– Helicopter, CommuniCations	SARTU	– Search-And-Rescue Training Unit
CATCS	– Central Air Traffic Control School	HT	– Helicopter, Training	SKTU	– Sea King Training Unit
CC	– CommuniCations	K	– AAR tanker (derived from K for Kerosene)	SOC	– Sector Operations Centre
CFS	– Central Flying School			Sqn	– Squadron
C&M	– Care and Maintenance	KC	– Tanker/Transport	T	– Training
E	– Electronic	MR	– Maritime Reconnaissance	TTTE	– Tri-national Tornado Training Establishment
EW	– Electronic Warfare	MU	– Maintenance Unit	TWCU	– Tornado Weapons Conversion Unit
F	– Fighter (air defence)	OCU	– Operational Conversion Unit	TWU	– Tactical Weapons Unit
FG	– Fighter, Ground-attack				
FGR	– Fighter, Ground-attack and Reconnaissance	P	– Probe-equipped aircraft for AAR (used after mark number)		

refuelling, it failed to utilize its skills in this area until ten years after the USAF, and then had to modify the V-bombers.

As for helicopters, the RAF has invariably had to buy whatever happened to be available. The only helicopter designed specially for the RAF, the Belvedere, was not a success. The RAF versions of the Wessex, with two turbo-shaft power sections, have had a long and useful career, but with the withdrawal of Britain from the NH-90 project there is no sign of a replacement for it. The more modern Puma was designed in France but made partly in Britain as the result of an inter-governmental agreement (which also covered the small Gazelle, used for training and communications). The vital task of Search And Rescue (SAR) is performed by the Sea King HAR.3s of 202 Squadron. The biggest RAF helicopter, the Boeing Chinook, provides an essential heavy-lift capability.

The Falklands War

The Chinook played a vital role in Operation Corporate, which was mounted to recover the Falkland Islands from the invading Argentinian forces in April 1982. For a country which had chosen to eliminate its conventional sea-going airpower, a sudden armed conflict some 8000 miles (12900km) from Britain posed almost insuperable problems. The whole operation was only made possible by the Harrier. Although the key role was played by Sea Harriers, the GR.3 version of No. 1 Squadron soon assumed responsibility for all attack and reconnaissance missions which, incidentally, it began by flying 3700 miles (6000km) to RAF Wideawake, the base on Ascension Island. Vulcans, Hercules and other aircraft were subjected to various modifications, designed and

Below: Panavia Tornado GR.1s (interdictor/strike variant) over England. At about £14m each (1,000 times more expensive than a Spitfire), each of the RAF's Tornados must be used intensively to justify the massive cost.

effected in hours instead of the years that would normally have been needed. One of the key features, for obvious geographical reasons, was the urgent requirement for more tankers and for the fitting of an air-refuelling capability to most of the aircraft. Even the Hercules was pressed into service as a tanker but, for the longer-term, a decision was taken to buy six L-1011-500 TriStars from British Airways. These have been rebuilt by Marshall as versatile transport/tankers. Bigger and longer-ranged than any other RAF aircraft, their acquisition emphasizes a change in procurement policy. As a former head of Rolls-Royce commented, 'We will never sell an engine to the airlines until it has military experience' – yet the RAF never had an RB.211 until it bought some second-hand from an airline!

The Falklands campaign dramatically proved the value of the little Harrier. Fortunately, in the late 1970s British Aerospace and McDonnell Douglas collaborated on a second-generation Harrier II, and 96 of these are now being delivered to the RAF as the Harrier GR.5 or after upgrading, as the GR.7.

The RAF today

The Tornado GR.1 will remain the RAF's main attack aircraft until well into the next century. An update programme will be required in the 1990s, which Buccaneers are already going through now. Another odd feature about the RAF is that from having been the world leader in EW in 1944 it has in recent years become very much a follower, for example being glad to buy second-hand ALQ-101 jammer pods from the USAF. The Harrier GR.5/7 at last has a first-class internal EW system, but the RAF still has no dedicated aircraft for the Suppression of Enemy Air Defences (SEAD) or Electronic Countermeasures (ECM) missions. Prolonged talks were held with the other Tornado partners, but the Tornado Electronic Combat and Reconnaissance (ECR) version is in production for the Luftwaffe only.

The increasing deficiency in conventional air defence, which was marginally improved by equipping 88 Hawk trainers to carry two AIM-9L Sidewinder Anti-Aircraft Missiles (AAMs) for local defence, is now being made good by the building of a large force of Tornado F.3 interceptors. These are now supplied to No. 229 OCU, Nos. 65 and 29 squadrons and parts of two further squadons and will later replace the Phantom in three further squadrons. For the more distant future, No. 11 Group and units of RAF Germany may be equipped with an even more specialized 'dogfighter', the European Fighter Aircraft (EFA). This, however, has several basic deficiencies. For instance, it needs an airfield and it is not a stealth design, but it should be dramatically superior to anything in today's fighter generation. However, a period of 12 years elapses between the Outline Staff Target and the delivery of the first aircraft.

The fundamental problem faced by the RAF is a crippling shortage of money. Britain's defence budget

Above: British Aerospace Hawk T.Mk 1 XX192, bearing the markings of No. 234 Squadron, fires a salvo of unguided rockets from the Matra SNEB rocket pod fixed under the wing. Some Hawks now carry Sidewinder AAMs.

does not permit more than the tiniest fraction of the provisions for the future that are really needed. To highlight the deficiency one has only to look at what is happening in the USA. The USAF has invested many thousands of millions of dollars in acquiring the basic new technologies which are being incorporated in the Advanced Tactical Fighter (Lockheed YF-22A or Northrop YUF-23A) and Advanced Technology Bomber (Northrop B-2). The US Navy's Advanced Tactical Aircraft (McDonnell Douglas A-12A) will also be a whole generation in advance of anything flying today. With each year that passes, Britain probably falls about 11 months behind in the race.

British defence expenditure, 1987-1988

Total expenditure on RAF excluding the cost of training, reserves and support facilities was £2729 million

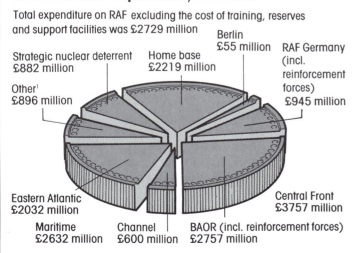

Strategic nuclear deterrent £882 million

Home base £2219 million

Berlin £55 million

RAF Germany (incl. reinforcement forces) £945 million

Other[1] £896 million

Eastern Atlantic £2032 million

Maritime £2632 million

Channel £600 million

BAOR (incl. reinforcement forces) £2757 million

Central Front £3757 million

[1] 'Other' includes the costs of amphibious capability, the Allied Command Europe Mobile Force (air and land), the United Kingdom Mobile Force, and out-of-area commitments

The future

The only way that the RAF will be able to remain in touch with the leaders in terms of advanced equipment in the future is by participating in such multinational programmes as ASTOVL and FIMA. The former, the Advanced Short Take-Off, Vertical Landing aircraft, is planned as a totally different successor to the Harrier. For five years design teams from leading companies in Britain, the USA and Canada have been trying to develop a combat aircraft that does not need to be parked on vulnerable airfields. The RAF will be lucky if it gets a squadron of whatever ASTOVL is picked by 2006! The development of the Future International Military/Civil Airlifter (FIMA) ought to proceed quickly because it is a more conventional replacement for the C-130.

For the more distant future the RAF is wistfully eyeing the Horizontal Take-Off and Landing (HOTOL) project. This would look rather like a slightly smaller Concorde and is the brainchild of British Aerospace and Rolls-Royce. No other nation has conceived of a vehicle which can take off from an ordinary airfield runway, fly off into space and then return to land at an ordinary airfield. Calculations show that the overall costs of space flight would be slashed to one-fifth of their present levels. HOTOL could be of tremendous importance to Britain, and to the RAF, if only there was the national will to commit the large funds needed for its full development. For example, by 2015, failure to exploit the concept now can only be to the RAF's detriment.

Below: The HOTOL space transport project is being undertaken by British Aerospace in conjunction with Rolls Royce. This artist's impression shows the launch of a satellite from the payload bay of the vehicle.

Chapter 6
HARDWARE:
THE ARMOURED PERSONNEL CARRIER

The story of the development of the APC is in many ways the story of the development of modern warfare itself. For as war has become increasingly mobile – from Hitler's blitzkrieg philosophy to NATO's Follow-On-Forces-Attack (FOFA) doctrine of today – so the simple APC 'taxi' of yesteryear has been up-graded and developed into the armoured, mobile Mechanized Infantry Combat Vehicle (MICV) – a formidable fighting vehicle in its own right on the modern battlefield.

An early version of the MCV-80 platoon vehicle shows its paces on trials. Claimed by its manufacturer GKN-Sankey to be the most advanced vehicle of its type, it is now in service with the British Army as the 'Warrior'.

World War I ended in November 1918, and in March 1919 the Commander-in-Chief of the British Armies in France, Field Marshal Sir Douglas Haig, wrote in his final dispatch that a decisive Allied victory had been won 'by the rifle and bayonet of the infantryman'. Field Marshal Haig's comment represented the prevailing opinion, yet the truth was that casualties on the Western Front had been high because of the infantry's vulnerability.

Post-war, the military authorities turned much more of their attention to this problem, and two ways of overcoming it were suggested. One was to give the infantry even more support – in the form of artillery, aeroplanes and tanks – and for the infantry to advance only when this support had neutralized enemy resistance. This solution was adopted by the French army immediately after the War. The other suggestion was that the infantry's mobility should be enhanced and that it should advance using a skilful combination of fire and manoeuvre. This solution was favoured by the British Army, and as a direct consequence the War Office announced, in April 1927, that an Experimental Mechanized Force was to be formed.

Nevertheless, the next year, one of Britain's most original military thinkers of the time – J.F.C. Fuller – felt it necessary to remind the Annual Staff Conference that while armouring ships had rendered ramming and boarding obsolete, the Army had not yet shown the same vision and scrapped the tactic of assaulting with men. Fuller insisted that the answer was 'half an inch of steel' and that, while foot soldiers were acceptable in the mountains, the only way to render them effective in open country was to place them in machines.

Fuller's comment pointed to a real failing in Army equipment planning, for while the new Vickers Medium Mark III tank, with its 47mm gun, was a considerable improvement on its predecessor, there was still no vehicle in existence in which the infantry could accompany the tanks of the Experimental Mechanized Force into battle.

Developments in the 1920s and 1930s

In the 1920s, however, the British did pioneer what were, in effect, prototypes of the small infantry carrier and the latter, in turn, was to become a most important type of vehicle in World War II. Post-World War II, the troop carrier was to evolve further to become the Armoured Personnel Carrier (APC).

The forebears of the infantry carrier, such as the Martel 'tankette' of the 1920s, were used by the Mechanized Force for reconnaissance purposes rather

Bottom left: A British Army Vickers Medium Mark III tank of 1928, together with early examples of the infantry carrier – (clockwise from top left) a Crossley half-track, a Morris-Martel two-man tank of 1926 and a Loyd tankette, which developed into the Bren-gun carrier.

Above left: The Schützenpanzerwagen Sd Kfz 251, the most famous of the German armoured half-track infantry carriers used in World War II, negotiates a river crossing. The larger Sd Kfz 7 half-track (above right), made by Kraus-Maffei, was used as an artillery tractor.

than as machine-gun carriers. The first successful carrier, the Carden-Loyd Mk VI, was powered by a Ford Model T engine, but was only lightly armoured; and, unlike the 'tankette', it only ran on tracks. The two-man crew – a driver and a gunner – sat on each side of the engine, with a Vickers machine gun arranged to fire forward. In 1934 Vickers improved on the Carden-Loyd design by developing a larger chassis with the stronger Horstmann suspension, and this formed the basis of a much sturdier, bigger infantry carrier. The new Carrier Machine Gun Mk 1 could carry two men in addition to the crew of two. But the most famous development in the Vickers carrier series was the well known Bren-gun carrier, which came into service with the British Army in 1937. Designed to provide infantry batallions with a carrying vehicle for the Bren light machine gun – which was then being issued as an infantry platoon weapon – the Bren carrier had a three-man crew, a Ford 65-hp (48-kW) engine and a top speed of 30mph (48km/h). A variant of this vehicle developed in the period from 1937 to 1940 could be described as an early example of a Mechanized Infantry Combat Vehicle (MICV). Known as the Scout Carrier, this variant was equipped with a Boys anti-tank rifle, a Bren-gun on an Anti-Aircraft (AA) mount, a three-inch smoke projector, and a radio.

While the British had progressed from the 'tankette' to the Bren-gun carrier in the decade before World War II, the Germans were also busy mechanizing their infantry. The half-tracks developed in France, Britain, and the USA were simple affairs, being little more than trucks with the rear wheels replaced by tracked

suspension units. The tracks were usually made of rubber or simple steel links, and steering was by the front wheels. By contrast, the German half-tracks were engineered to the same high quality as tanks, with manganese webbed steel track shoes, interleaved torsion-bar suspension and a brake system that helped the tracks to steer the vehicle as the front wheels turned. A complete range of vehicles was designed and prototypes were ready in 1934 and early production vehicles appeared in 1938. Vast numbers continued to be manufactured throughout World War II.

Armoured versions of the 1-ton (1016-kg) and 3-ton (3048-kg) class of half-tracks were developed in 1939 specifically to equip the infantry of the Panzer Grenadiers. These vehicles had the same chassis as the normal models but were fitted with a well shaped and angled armoured body. The most famous of all these was the Sd Kfz 251, built by Hanomag on the 3-ton (3048-kg) chassis. The armour was 0.5in. (12mm) thick, the vehicle weighed 8.37 tons (8504kg) and it carried a squad of ten infantrymen with their machine gun. Another machine gun was fitted behind a shield at the front of the vehicle. The squad machine gun could be pintle-mounted at the rear in the AA role. One of the three infantry battalions in each Panzer division was equipped with these armoured half-tracks, the other battalions having trucks or unarmoured half-tracks. The Sd Kfz 251 was a true APC and years ahead of its time. It was to provide the main equipment for the German motorized infantry regiments throughout World War II.

US interest in half-tracks dates back to 1925, when the US Ordnance Department purchased two French Citroën-Kegresse vehicles for evaluation. In 1931, the US firm of Cunningham built some military half-tracks, the TI series, derived from the Citroëns. Other makers also contributed a variety of designs, culminating in the T9 built by Marmon-Herrington in 1937.

Post-war developments

The early British carriers, the German armoured half-tracks and, to a lesser extent, the US half-tracks were the precursors of the post-war APC. Nevertheless, after the war it was the Soviets who were to be the first to recognize in their planning that future warfare would be highly mobile. Their BTR-152 is one of the best known of all APCs. Introduced in 1946, the BTR-152 was built on the chassis of the Zil-157 truck. The body is remarkably similar in style to the German half-tracks of the war years. It is 22ft (6.83m) long, weighs 9.6 tons (9750kg), has 0.5in. (14mm) of armour and carries 12 men.

The BTR-152 was replaced in 1961 by the BTR-60P, an eight-wheeled vehicle weighing 10 tons (10,160kg) and capable of carrying an infantry squad. Like all Soviet APCs it was designed to enable its crew to fight, if necessary, from the vehicle: firing ports allowed infantrymen to fire their personal weapons from the vehicle and a later model, the BTR-60PK, was provided with a small turret in which a machine gun was mounted. An amphibious vehicle, the BTR-60PK was also able to drive straight on to, or through, an objective. Thus, from the beginning of the APC era, the Soviets saw APCs as fighting vehicles that accompanied tanks into battle. The perception in the West was different.

In Britain, US half-tracks of World War II vintage were finally replaced in 1952 by the Alvis Saracen. Design work on the Saracen had started shortly after the end of the War, and it met the British Army's requirement for a rugged, uncomplicated armoured vehicle. The Saracen transported an infantry section around the battlefield in relative safety, but it was not designed – and herein lies the essential difference between British and Soviet design philosophy – to fight its way on to, or through, the objective. Its task was to transport its infantrymen to a position short of the objective, from where an attack could be launched on foot: this meant that its cross-country mobility was not comparable with that of a tank. It also meant that the Saracen was not equipped with firing ports. The Saracen was, nevertheless, a sturdy machine that provided valuable service as an APC with the British Army of the Rhine (BAOR) and as an Internal Security (IS) vehicle in many parts of the world, including Northern Ireland.

In the early 1950s the standard US Army APC was the M75; the M75 was followed in 1954 by the M59. Both were tracked, with a crew of two, and capable of carrying a further ten infantrymen. The M75 was not amphibious. Both were basic vehicles with a limited performance, and neither was really satisfactory. In 1954 plans were thus made for a new series of vehicles. In 1958 prototypes of the T113 (with an aluminium hull) and T117 (with a steel hull) were built, and in mid-1959 a modified version of the T113 was cleared for production; the M113 entered service with the US Army in 1960.

Top: The most widely used US APC of the 1960s and 1970s was the M113, seen here in Vietnam, May 1968, carrying a wounded NVA soldier guarded by US troops.
Above: A Soviet army APC of this period was the BTR-60P.

In 1964, the original petrol-engined M113 was replaced by the M113-A1 diesel-powered version and this was to become the most widely used APC of the 1960s and 1970s. The M113-A1 saw action in Vietnam, and has been used by other armies in countless conflicts all over the world. It represented the culmination of the post-World War II trend towards the tracked armoured 'taxi', and was the direct descendant of the pre-World War II carriers, the German armoured half-track APCs of World War II, the US half-tracks and the post-war wheeled APCs. The M113-A1's design specification also revealed the contemporary Western perception of the limited role of the APC – for it was, again, capable only of taking infantrymen to the battle, but not into it. It carried a crew of two plus 11 infantrymen in the rear, and it was fully amphibious (being propelled in the water by its tracks); however, its sole armament was a pintle-mounted 0.5in. Browning machine gun controlled by the vehicle commander from his cupola. Instead of doors a ramp was lowered at the rear of the crew compartment for quick egress.

The M113 spawned a whole range of variants, and also a number of less successful competitors from other Western nations. Notable among these were the British FV 432 series, introduced into the British Army in the

BMP-1 APC

73mm 2A20 smoothbore gun

'Sagger' anti-tank missile

Gunner

Fuel-filled doors

V6 6-cylinder diesel engine

Front armour

Commander

Driver-mechanic

Infantry squad

Firing ports

Dead space

Above: The Soviet army's BMP-1 APC carries a crew of three and eight infantrymen. These BMP-1s taking part in a Moscow May Day parade in 1976 (right) are armed with 73mm main guns and Sagger anti-tank guided weapons.

early 1960s, the French AMX VTP troop carrier, which was adapted from the chassis of the successful AMX-13 light tank, the Swedish STR 60 APC, the German HS30 and the wheeled Dutch DAF-YP 308. More obscure vehicles were also developed during the same period.

The MICV concept

It was in the late 1960s that the concept of the Mechanized Infantry Combat Vehicle, or MICV, was developed – although Soviet APCs such as the BTR-50 and the BMP-1 were, in effect, already hybrid APCs/MICVs, as they had greater integral firepower and were capable of taking on tanks if necessary. The development of the MICV concept was followed by NATO's shift away from a strategy of positional defence to one of 'manoeuvre warfare' in the late 1970s. For manoeuvre warfare made it essential to provide the infantry with greater mobility and more firepower, and it was recognized that the 'armoured taxi' type of vehicle was inadequate for the task. NATO began to think in terms of mobile defence involving counter-moves and deep strikes, ideas that were encapsulated in the new Air-Land Battle (ALB) and Follow-on-Forces-Attack (FOFA) policy ideas, which became official NATO doctrine in 1982 and 1984 respectively.

To some extent, the development of the MICV preceded this new thinking, but for the most part the new strategies and the MICV evolved together. Certainly, NATO's new thinking confirmed the place of the MICV in the NATO order of battle.

Under NATO's new thinking, the infantry would no longer plod along behind heavy tanks, but would have to keep up with fast-moving armoured spearheads and be able to survive and fight in the midst of a high-intensity battlefield. Infantry would have to learn to fight within, as well as outside, its transport and should be equipped to take on enemy Main Battle Tanks (MBTs) as well as infantry fighting vehicles. The vehicle required for such a task was the MICV. A much more formidable vehicle than the old APC, the MICV was distinguished from it by the fact that it carried its own tactical weapons system rather than a simple defensive machine gun or two – and it allowed troops to fight from inside the vehicle if necessary.

Milan ATGW missile and launcher

7.62mm coaxial machine gun

Electrically operated smoke dischargers

20mm Rheinmetall Mk 20 RH202 cannon

Marder MICV

Commander

Two-man turret (designed by Keller and Knappich)

Troop compartment contains six infantrymen

Gunner

Driver

Above and left: The West German army's Marder MICV carries six infantrymen plus crew. It is armed with a 20mm cannon and two 7.62mm machine guns, one in the turret and the other, remote-controlled, at the rear.

The Soviet army was the pioneer in the development of the MICV. The Bronevaya Maschina Piekhota (BMP-1), or armoured vehicle infantry, was deployed in the early 1960s to equip its motor-rifle regiments for the demands of offensive operations on the nuclear battlefield. The original model was armed with six Sagger Anti-Tank Guided Weapons (ATGW) fired from a single launcher located above the main armament. The latter consisted of a 73mm smooth-bore, low-pressure gun firing fin-stabilized, rocket-assisted High Explosive Anti-Tank (HEAT) projectiles. Later models were fitted with laser-homing Spandrel ATGWs and a new turret mounting a 30mm cannon.

In spite of its advanced design, the BMP's debut (with the Syrian army on the Golan Heights in 1973) was a disaster. A Syrian attack on the Israeli defences resulted in literally hundreds of burned-out BMP hulls littering the Valley of Tears. Although the armoured protection afforded by these earlier models was not

adequate (and has since been uprated), it was chiefly the clumsy handling and tactical inflexibility of a poorly trained Syrian army that was the cause of these losses.

The first Western MICV entered service with the West German army in 1969. The Marder carries six infantrymen in an all-welded armoured hull and, in its original version, was armed with a 20mm cannon in a two-man turret. The West German army's sizeable inventory of this excellent vehicle is being reworked to mount a harder-hitting 25mm cannon and to carry the Milan ATGW. The Marder is well armoured and, with an impressive power-to-weight ratio, is highly mobile. This allows it to work with the Leopard 2 MBT as a combined arms team in the Panzer Grenadier regiments of the West German army. It has a road speed of 47mph (75km/h), and is fitted with a rearward-firing remotely operated machine gun, and with firing ports.

The French AMX-10P, which entered service with the French army in 1973, was another step forward in Western MICV development with its all-welded alloy hull, Nuclear, Biological, Chemical warfare (NBC) protection, a 20mm dual-feed cannon and space for a nine-man infantry squad. Later variants have been equipped with the Franco-German HOT and Milan ATGWs. The failure to provide firing ports in the AMX-10P probably resulted from the French army's

M2 Bradley MICV

7.62mm M240C coaxial machine gun

McDonnell Douglas Helicopter Company M242 25mm chain gun

M257 smoke discharger

Engine compartment

Vehicle commander

Gunner

TOW anti-tank guided missile launcher

Turret, part steel and part aluminium-armoured

Firing port

Above and right: The US Army's M2 Bradley MICV carries six infantrymen and three crew and is armed with a 25mm Hughes chain gun, a coaxial 7.62mm machine gun and a twin launcher for seven TOW anti-tank guided weapons.

demand for complete NBC protection. Although this is a problem that has since been overcome, the integrity of a MICV's NBC protection was to some extent compromised by the requirement for firing ports.

The US Army took a very long time to bring MICVs into service, which could be seen as a tribute to the M113 and the valuable service it had provided for so many years. Although the original requirement for a MICV was drafted in the early 1960s, the first prototype XM2 Infantry Fighting Vehicle was not accepted by the US Army until 1978. Issue of the vehicle to the US Army in Europe did not commence until 1983 and was still only 50 per cent complete in 1988. The M2, now named the Bradley, is very expensive to produce and its introduction, as with many other NATO equipment programmes, is being phased over a period of years. The US Army has a total requirement for some 6882 M2 and M3 vehicles, the latter being an M2 derivative intended for use as a Cavalry Fighting Vehicle (CFV).

The M2 Bradley has an all-welded aluminium-armour hull with a layer of steel armour welded to the hull front, upper sides and rear for added protection. In addition, the hull sides have a thin layer of steel armour, the space between the aluminium and steel being filled with foam to increase the buoyancy of the vehicle in water.

The armoured protection of the M2 is claimed to be effective against Soviet 14.5mm armour-piercing rounds and 155mm air-burst shell splinters.

The M2's spaced armour also has the effect of diminishing the penetrating power of HEAT projectiles by detonating the warhead further away from the main vehicle hull. The vehicle is armed with a 25mm Hughes chain gun and a coaxial 7.62mm machine gun. A twin launcher for the TOW ATGW is mounted on the left side of the turret. A total of 900 rounds of 25mm, 2340 rounds of 7.62mm and seven TOW missiles is carried. The troop compartment is provided with a total of six firing ports, with two on each side and two at the rear for the M231 weapon. The latter is a specially developed version of the M16 rifle, cut down and sealed in a ball mount. The M2 is fully amphibious, although a flotation screen is required. The crew compartment is fitted with an NBC system and the vehicle has a full range of night-vision equipment.

MCV-80 Warrior MICV

30mm Rarden cannon

Commander in two-man turret

Gunner

Driver

Troop compartment

Infantryman armed with SA-80 rifle

Single rear door

Above and left: The British Army's MCV-80 MICV carries eight infantrymen and two crew and is armed with a 30mm Rarden cannon and a 7.62mm chain gun. It can travel fast even over rough and difficult terrain.

The M2 Bradley may be superbly equipped, but the penalties for this are the high cost and a small crew compartment. The effective size of the squad that disembarks to fight from the vehicle is only six men, a further three men remaining in the vehicle to operate it and provide fire support. Nevertheless, despite these limitations, in the M2 the US Army has undoubtedly acquired the most effective MICV in service on the central front today. The chain gun – the same weapon that is fitted to the Apache AH-64A attack helicopter – is a formidable weapon. The gunner can select single shots, or rates of fire of 100 or 200 rounds per minute. The General Electric turret drive and stabilization system allow the armament to be laid and fired while the Bradley moves across rough terrain. While the chain gun is designed to take on MICVs and APCs, the M2 can engage MBTs with its TOW missiles out to a range of 12,300ft (3750m).

The latest MICV to enter service is the British

MCV-80, now known as the Warrior by the British Army. The Warrior was designed to accommodate eight fully equipped infantrymen and two crew, and to sustain them for 48 hours on the battlefield. Thus it can be said that the vehicle was built around the British infantry section of eight men (consisting of two fire teams, each of four men), something which cannot be said of the Bradley. Mobility and protection were judged to be of equal importance after the basic accommodation requirement. Provision of firepower was the last priority, additional ATGW firepower being rejected as a distraction from the vehicle's primary role.

The Warrior has an impressive performance. The Rolls Royce 550-hp (412-kW) 8-cylinder diesel engine gives a maximum road speed of 47mph (75km/h) and an impressive cross-country performance. The rear compartment holds seven infantrymen with the section commander, who must dismount with his section, being accommodated in the turret with his gunner. Offensive firepower is provided by the 30mm Rarden cannon and the 7.62mm chain gun. Warrior does not have the ability to take on MBTs, and whether this is a wise decision remains to be seen. Since it will always be working as part of an all-arms battlegroup, the theory is that accompanying tanks will deal with enemy tanks – leaving Warrior to provide infantry support.

Tactical use of the MICV

All the Warsaw Pact and NATO armies are now equipped, or in the process of being equipped, with MICVs; the interesting question now is how different armies imagine they can be most effectively deployed on the battlefield. For example, all tacticians agree that the role of the MICV is to fight as an integral part of an all-arms battlegroup – but there are differing views on how they should be used within that battlegroup. The two main areas of debate are, first, whether or not the MICV should 'mix it' with tanks and, second, to what degree the infantry should fight from within the MICV.

As regards the first question, the Soviets, Germans and US have given their MICVs an ATGW capability, but the British have not. While the British may be sensible in discouraging the infantry in Warrior from perceiving the vehicle as a tank, it would also seem to have been sensible to provide it with some defence against tanks. In the open at ranges under 9800ft (3000m) an MICV would stand little or no chance in a confrontation with a tank. An MBT could fire two or three rounds from its main armament in the time it would take an ATGW to fly the same distance – and contemporary tank fire-control systems should ensure a hit with the first round. But from a hull-down, static position an MICV could engage an MBT successfully. An ATGW capability could be added to Warrior

relatively easily. It may well be that the £1000 million development costs precluded any further expenditure on the vehicle at this stage.

While it is probably an advantage for infantry to be able to fight from their MICV, it would be a mistake to assume that they will always be most effective when fighting from within the vehicle. For MICVs do not have the same degree of protection as tanks. There will be occasions, particularly in defence, when the infantry will be more effective operating dismounted – and Warrior is optimized to support dismounted infantry. Nevertheless, it would appear to be unnecessary to forgo the additional flexibility afforded by firing ports.

The MICV has evolved as a fundamentally more advanced vehicle than the APC. Correspondingly, it is able to play a more important part in the manoeuvre warfare tactics which form the basis of NATO's defence strategy today. Until the early 1970s NATO's defensive tactics were largely positional in nature, involving the holding of ground around so-called 'killing areas'. Troops would fight from well-prepared defensive positions and APCs were required simply to get the troops

Below: A US M60 tank and M113 carrier (left) and M163 Vulcan ADS (right) during an exercise in 1984.
Right: A British Army Challenger MBT on field manoeuvres with a Saxon APC and an MCV-80 (foreground).

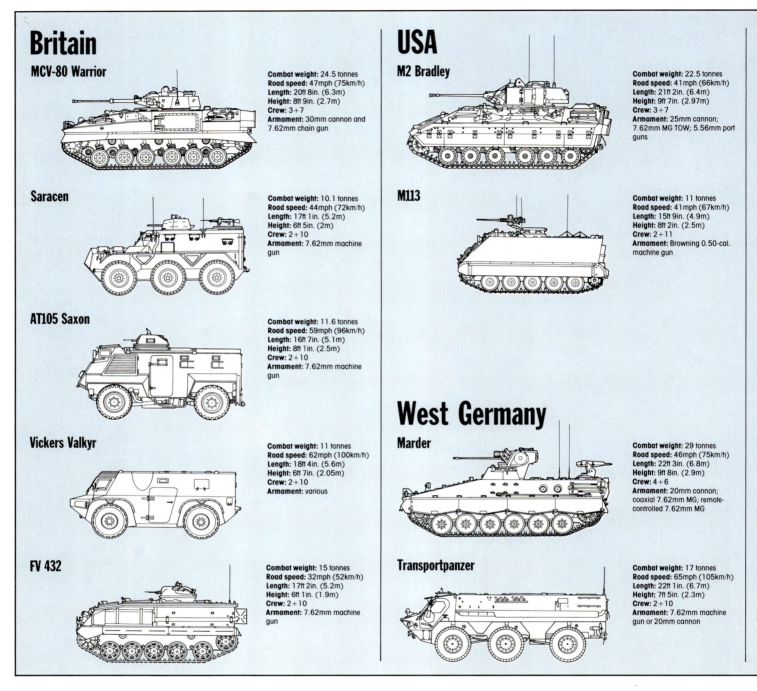

Britain

MCV-80 Warrior

Combat weight: 24.5 tonnes
Road speed: 47mph (75km/h)
Length: 20ft 8in. (6.3m)
Height: 8ft 9in. (2.7m)
Crew: 3+7
Armament: 30mm cannon and 7.62mm chain gun

Saracen

Combat weight: 10.1 tonnes
Road speed: 44mph (72km/h)
Length: 17ft 1in. (5.2m)
Height: 6ft 5in. (2m)
Crew: 2+10
Armament: 7.62mm machine gun

AT105 Saxon

Combat weight: 11.6 tonnes
Road speed: 59mph (96km/h)
Length: 16ft 7in. (5.1m)
Height: 8ft 1in. (2.5m)
Crew: 2+10
Armament: 7.62mm machine gun

Vickers Valkyr

Combat weight: 11 tonnes
Road speed: 62mph (100km/h)
Length: 18ft 4in. (5.6m)
Height: 6ft 9in. (2.05m)
Crew: 2+10
Armament: various

FV 432

Combat weight: 15 tonnes
Road speed: 32mph (52km/h)
Length: 17ft 2in. (5.2m)
Height: 6ft 1in. (1.9m)
Crew: 2+10
Armament: 7.62mm machine gun

USA

M2 Bradley

Combat weight: 22.5 tonnes
Road speed: 41mph (66km/h)
Length: 21ft 2in. (6.4m)
Height: 9ft 7in. (2.97m)
Crew: 3+7
Armament: 25mm cannon; 7.62mm MG TOW; 5.56mm port guns

M113

Combat weight: 11 tonnes
Road speed: 41mph (67km/h)
Length: 15ft 9in. (4.9m)
Height: 8ft 2in. (2.5m)
Crew: 2+11
Armament: Browning 0.50-cal. machine gun

West Germany

Marder

Combat weight: 29 tonnes
Road speed: 46mph (75km/h)
Length: 22ft 3in. (6.8m)
Height: 9ft 8in. (2.9m)
Crew: 4+6
Armament: 20mm cannon; coaxial 7.62mm MG; remote-controlled 7.62mm MG

Transportpanzer

Combat weight: 17 tonnes
Road speed: 65mph (105km/h)
Length: 22ft 1in. (6.7m)
Height: 7ft 5in. (2.3m)
Crew: 2+10
Armament: 7.62mm machine gun or 20mm cannon

to those positions in safety, and then to transport them to their next position in the event of a withdrawal. Tactics today involve close cooperation between armour and mechanized infantry in a fast-moving, constantly changing and highly mobile battlefield; NATO's tactics involve accepting penetration by enemy forces. Since the enemy can achieve a superiority in terms of numbers of troops of up to ten to one at the point of their main effort by concentrating their forces for a breakthrough (although their superiority overall may only be three to one), so NATO tactics logically assume that the enemy will achieve sizeable penetrations with large armoured formations. It follows that the defence must be mobile and flexible in response.

Above: The Armoured Personnel Carriers and Mechanized Infantry Combat Vehicles currently in service with Britain, the USA, West Germany, France and the Warsaw Pact countries, together with their specifications.

Design criteria

Offensive defence, or manoeuvre warfare of the type represented by the action described above, clearly depends upon the ability of NATO's armour, infantry, artillery, engineers and attack helicopters (as well as their logistic support) to operate flexibly over wide frontages and in depth. The APC was not designed for this sort of warfare, whereas the MICV is. Its most important characteristics are mobility, firepower and protection, though a different emphasis may be put on

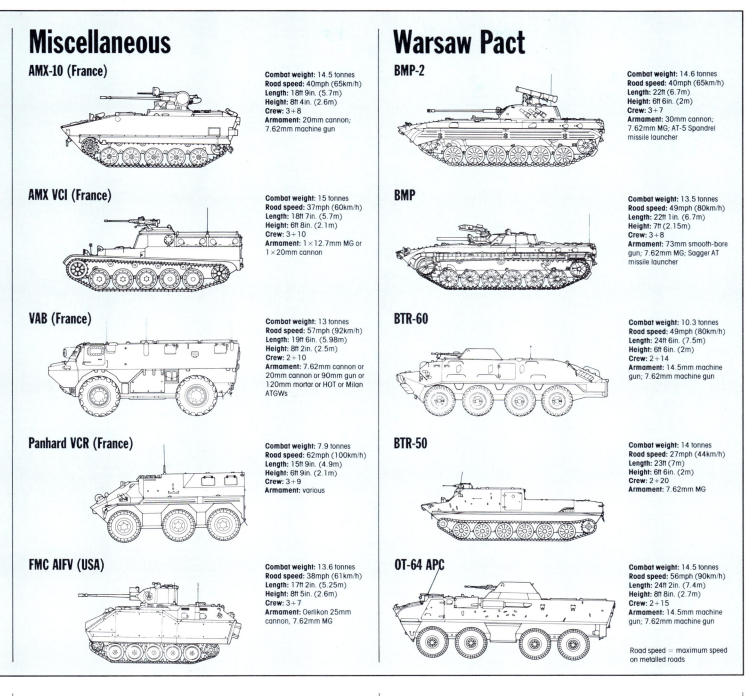

Miscellaneous

AMX-10 (France)
Combat weight: 14.5 tonnes
Road speed: 40mph (65km/h)
Length: 18ft 9in. (5.7m)
Height: 8ft 4in. (2.6m)
Crew: 3+8
Armament: 20mm cannon;
7.62mm machine gun

AMX VCI (France)
Combat weight: 15 tonnes
Road speed: 37mph (60km/h)
Length: 18ft 7in. (5.7m)
Height: 6ft 8in. (2.1m)
Crew: 3+10
Armament: 1×12.7mm MG or
1×20mm cannon

VAB (France)
Combat weight: 13 tonnes
Road speed: 57mph (92km/h)
Length: 19ft 6in. (5.98m)
Height: 8ft 2in. (2.5m)
Crew: 2+10
Armament: 7.62mm cannon or
20mm cannon or 90mm gun or
120mm mortar or HOT or Milan
ATGWs

Panhard VCR (France)
Combat weight: 7.9 tonnes
Road speed: 62mph (100km/h)
Length: 15ft 9in. (4.9m)
Height: 6ft 9in. (2.1m)
Crew: 3+9
Armament: various

FMC AIFV (USA)
Combat weight: 13.6 tonnes
Road speed: 38mph (61km/h)
Length: 17ft 2in. (5.25m)
Height: 8ft 8in. (2.6m)
Crew: 3+7
Armament: Oerlikon 25mm
cannon, 7.62mm MG

Warsaw Pact

BMP-2
Combat weight: 14.6 tonnes
Road speed: 40mph (65km/h)
Length: 22ft (6.7m)
Height: 6ft 6in. (2m)
Crew: 3+7
Armament: 30mm cannon;
7.62mm MG; AT-5 Spandrel
missile launcher

BMP
Combat weight: 13.5 tonnes
Road speed: 49mph (80km/h)
Length: 22ft 1in. (6.7m)
Height: 7ft (2.15m)
Crew: 3+8
Armament: 73mm smooth-bore
gun; 7.62mm MG; Sagger AT
missile launcher

BTR-60
Combat weight: 10.3 tonnes
Road speed: 49mph (80km/h)
Length: 24ft 6in. (7.5m)
Height: 6ft 6in. (2m)
Crew: 2+14
Armament: 14.5mm machine
gun; 7.62mm machine gun

BTR-50
Combat weight: 14 tonnes
Road speed: 27mph (44km/h)
Length: 23ft (7m)
Height: 6ft 6in. (2m)
Crew: 2+20
Armament: 7.62mm MG

OT-64 APC
Combat weight: 14.5 tonnes
Road speed: 56mph (90km/h)
Length: 24ft 2in. (7.4m)
Height: 8ft 8in. (2.7m)
Crew: 2+15
Armament: 14.5mm machine
gun; 7.62mm machine gun

Road speed = maximum speed
on metalled roads

each by different designers. Some MICVs are amphibious, though MCV-80 is not. In theory, it will generally be quicker to cross a river using an existing bridge, or bridging supplied by engineers and, anyway, preparing armoured vehicles for 'swimming' is time-consuming, complicated, and always hazardous. Even the Soviet Union, whose armoured vehicles invariably have an amphibious capability, would cross a major water obstacle by means of military bridging or ferries, although their reconnaissance vehicles may have to swim. Although most MICVs are airportable, it is no longer really necessary for them to be so. Lighter, less complex APCs have now been designed for out-of-area operations. Finally, MICVs must be tracked to ensure

that they are able to travel over all kinds of terrain.

Other factors have to be taken into consideration when designing MICVs. For example, the ever more rapid increase in the cost of defence equipment has forced NATO governments to examine the possibility of standardizing equipment. In other cases, collaboration over a project has been possible. Two examples are the Timoney BDX and Vickers Valkyr Internal Security (IS) vehicles. There are other examples of jointly developed APCs, though national considerations have ensured that major MICV projects have to date been single-nation projects. It makes little sense for NATO to be equipped with different MICV types. The way ahead must be for standardization and collaboration.

Above: Nicknamed the 'Pig' by the soldiers who man it, the armoured 4 × 4 Humber has been extensively adapted and is being used by the British Army in Northern Ireland for internal security duties. The sides of this example have been equipped with defensive screens.

Internal Security (IS) vehicles

The last 30 years have seen an unprecedented number of revolutionary, or so-called 'brush-fire' wars, ranging from Vietnam at one end of the scale to urban Internal Security (IS) situations, such as that in Northern Ireland, at the other end. This has led to the emergence of a separate breed of armoured IS vehicles. Whereas most APCs and MICVs designed for general warfare are tracked in order to fulfil their primary cross-country role as efficiently as possible, tracked vehicles are not suited to the IS role for a number of reasons. They are often difficult and expensive to operate and maintain; they are noisier than wheeled vehicles; they can cause damage to road surfaces and, most important of all, they are classified as tanks by the layman and the media. Use of tanks for crowd or riot control is usually deemed to be politically unacceptable. The majority of IS vehicles are required to operate on roads and in an urban environment, for which wheels are more suitable.

IS vehicles are generally four-wheel drive and are designed to afford the occupants protection from small arms fire from weapons of calibres up to and including 7.62mm. They must be provided with observation 'blocks' (armoured glass windows) so that the crew can see what is happening around them. In a conventional war in a rural environment, an APC or MICV is likely to be operating in wide-open spaces in conjunction with many other vehicles and infantry on the ground, so it is not vital that a vehicle crew has a comprehensive all-round view. However, for IS work, good all-round

vision is essential – for example to spot a petrol-bomber's approach. Similarly, firing ports must be provided so that the crew can, if required, use small arms from within the vehicle. Vulnerable points on the vehicle, such as the fuel tank or the radiator, should be given special protection – particularly from bomb attack. The other main threat is from attack by anti-tank grenades. In Northern Ireland, for instance, the IRA has used RPG-7 rocket launchers against IS vehicles, but with limited success. Although IS vehicles are insufficiently armoured to prevent penetration by projectiles from rocket launchers, in an urban environment in which a terrorist is forced to engage a target at very close range during a limited exposure time, it is in fact very difficult to achieve a hit. The few seconds during which an armoured vehicle passes a fixed point means that the firer has very little time to recognize the target, prepare to fire, acquire the target, aim and engage. Often RPG-7 projectiles have passed behind the target, on some occasions completely unnoticed by the occupants of the IS vehicle.

An IS vehicle must be designed so as to allow rapid access and egress by crew and passengers. In a confused situation, which would probably involve large and disorderly crowds, it is practical for the vehicle to have multiple doors. In a conventional war, the enemy is normally expected from a single direction, whereas in a riot, for example, attack may come from any quarter. The occupants must therefore be able to leave the vehicle from the opposite side to the direction of attack. Side-doors dictate that there should be only four wheels; this arrangement is also advisable in the interests of simplicity and mechanical reliability.

IS armoured vehicles may have a variety of armaments installed, including water cannon, tear-gas launchers and machine guns. The hulls of some can even be electrified to prevent rioters climbing on to the vehicle. Weapons systems have been designed so as to achieve

Below: Italy's Fiat 6614 APC has the wedge-shaped hull which is designed to deflect blast from land mines.

the greatest protection for the vehicle itself and its occupants against a terrorist threat: there is no need for sophisticated 'vehicle-killing' systems such as the Rarden 30mm cannon or Hughes chain gun. A common threat to the IS vehicle, however, is the land mine, particularly in a rural environment. The hull should therefore be designed so as to deflect as much of the blast as possible: an upwardly sloping hull structure should achieve this, while a strong monocoque structure should provide maximum protection for the crew inside, so long as they are strapped firmly into their seats. Examples of a wedge-shaped hull are the South African Hippo IS vehicle, the British GKN-Sankey Saxon, and Italy's Fiat 6614 APC.

IS vehicles should be of simple and rugged construction, as they are usually deployed in less developed countries with limited maintenance resources. The GKN-Sankey Saxon, for example, was designed with ease of maintenance specifically in mind. The Saxon is powered by the widely available Bedford Type 500 6-cylinder diesel truck engine, and the use of commercially available automotive parts means that anyone who can maintain a truck can also maintain the Saxon. This vehicle is in service not only with the British Army, but also with the armed forces or police in Bahrain, Kuwait, Malaysia, Nigeria and Oman. The French Berliet VXB anti-riot vehicle also uses off-the-shelf Berliet truck spare parts, and again it is both simple and cost-effective to maintain.

Design details

With IS vehicles, seemingly minor design details are disproportionately important. For example, with the Belgian Beherman Demoen BDX, the engine air intake is located below the generous canopy over the driving position; the intake also has a moving shutter. All this is designed to provide protection against Molotov cocktails. The twin exhaust pipes, meanwhile, run along two sides of the roof – to make it more difficult for rioters to climb on to the vehicle. So-called 'top cover' is also particularly important for urban IS work, where terrorists may drop Molotov cocktails or even armour-piercing shaped charges from the roofs of buildings. The South African Armscor AC 200 is typical of IS

Below: The British Army's GKN-Sankey Saxon AT-105 is designed for conventional warfare and internal security duties. It can be fully equipped with a television surveillance system (inset) to enable the crew to monitor what is happening all around the vehicle.

vehicles in being provided with individual hatches in the roof to allow riflemen to look outwards and upwards. In addition, this vehicle has both side and rear exits, armoured windows, and firing ports – which allow the crew to engage targets from within the vehicle.

Older APCs can be adapted successfully for IS purposes. In Northern Ireland, for example, the British Army has adapted the long-serving armoured 4 × 4 Humber, commonly known as the 'Pig', by attaching unfolding fenders to each side of the vehicle. Thus, when parked in the middle of a relatively narrow road flanked by buildings, the 'Flying Pig' – as the adapted vehicle is known – can block most of the road by extending its 'wings' to provide protection for dismounted soldiers against missiles thrown by rioters. Other possible attachments are roof- or turret-mounted searchlights, loudspeaker systems, surveillance devices, a hostile fire detection device, an air-conditioning system providing a slightly higher interior atmospheric pressure (to prevent the entry of noxious fumes or smoke), and a blue flashing light. A 'cowcatcher' is also frequently added for the removal of street barricades.

Many IS APCs are adapted from standard-wheeled APCs. But there is one type of IS vehicle which could only be used for IS work: the small, fast, light armoured IS vehicle. Examples are the Hotspur Hussar, the Shorts Shorland armoured patrol vehicle (both Land Rover derivatives), the USA's Commando Ranger and the French Panhard VBL high-speed IS intervention vehicle. These are all based on Land Rover or Land Rover-equivalent chassis. They are smaller, lighter, faster and cheaper, and can carry five riot police. They are ideal for such organizations as the French riot police (the CRS), or the Royal Ulster Constabulary.

Below: Japanese police quell a demonstration in 1971 using an armoured anti-riot vehicle equipped with watercannon and searchlights.

Above: The Shorts Shorland S55 APC is a small, fast, light-armoured Internal Security vehicle which is derived from the Land Rover. Similar versions of Land Rover-derived vehicles are being used by the Royal Ulster Constabulary.

MICVs and IS vehicles today

In view of the fact that large amounts of money are now being spent developing increasingly sophisticated MICVs, it is ironic that there is probably a greater market potential for simple and rugged APCs suitable for counter-revolutionary warfare and IS operations. The situation now is such that even NATO armies cannot always afford to equip all their formations with MICVs. For example, the US Army will retain the M113 in service alongside the M2 Bradley for the foreseeable future, and the British Army is retaining a proportion of its FV 432 vehicles in service alongside the Warrior.

Wheeled APCs, meanwhile, are cheaper and less complex technically than their tracked counterparts, and will thus remain in service for less demanding and more closely defined battlefield roles, such as operations in rear or urban areas. Behind the front lines in Germany lie the vital lines of communication, headquarters locations, logistics installations, the crucial 'Hawk Belt' (the main NATO air-defence belt based on the USA's Hawk missile), Harrier sites, key bridges and many other strategically important installations. Sizeable numbers of troops are allocated by the NATO armies to the defence of these areas against Special Forces attack or airborne landings or both. As, for the most part, the sites are permanent (or semi-permanent), and are located on or near arterial roads, there is no need to equip rear-area troops with expensive and sophisticated MICVs.

Above: The FV 432 APC continues to be used by the British Army alongside the Warrior. GKN-Sankey have now developed the Warrior weapons platform with the Oerlikon Air Defence Anti-tank System (right).

The future

The European battlefield of the future will be more automated: there will be an increase in the number and sophistication of 'smart' weapons as NATO carries its new FOFA doctrine to its logical conclusion; and more 'top attack' weapons will be deployed as the relevant technology becomes available. The latter could be air-delivered or sub-munitions via a Multi-Launcher Rocket System (MLRS) rocket, or even delivered from an infantry mortar.

The tank, meanwhile, has consistently defied all attempts to consign it to the history books and is likely to be around on the battlefield for some time yet. However, there is no doubt that emerging technology will make its survival more difficult. The forthcoming third-generation ATGW, TRIGAT, which is being developed by Germany, France and Britain, is likely to be a fire-and-forget-system which will have increased accuracy, range and lethality against the MBT. Even more important, the pace at which modern attack helicopters are developing will make them an increasing threat to the tank on the battlefield. Of course, what is a threat to the tank is also a threat to the MICV.

While the future is likely to see a greater emphasis on air-mobile operations and thus on the use of attack helicopters, it will still be necessary for the infantry to hold ground once it has been gained. This task would be difficult if the infantry were deposited on the territory by helicopter. For, while air-mobile infantry can be highly effective in, for example, a counter-attack, they

can only hold ground against prolonged attack by armoured vehicles if they have the fire support, mobility and NBC protection which can only be provided by an MICV. Moreover, helicopters will always, to some extent, be vulnerable to adverse weather conditions. Irrespective of the future of the tank, therefore, ground-holding infantry is likely to continue to require the support of MICVs.

The MICV's development will, then, continue. Its essential characteristics are likely to remain unchanged for the foreseeable future: the improvements will come in cross-country performance, in weapon lethalities and in crew facilities. However, as the issuing of the M2 Bradley and Warrior to the US and British Armies respectively will not be completed until the early 1990s, replacements incorporating the latest technology will not be seen until well after the year 2000. Broadly speaking, the same can be said for the IS vehicle as for the MICV – the continued threat of terrorism will ensure that it continues to evolve and improve. The basic vehicle will change very little, though increasingly sophisticated attachments are likely to be specially developed and installed.

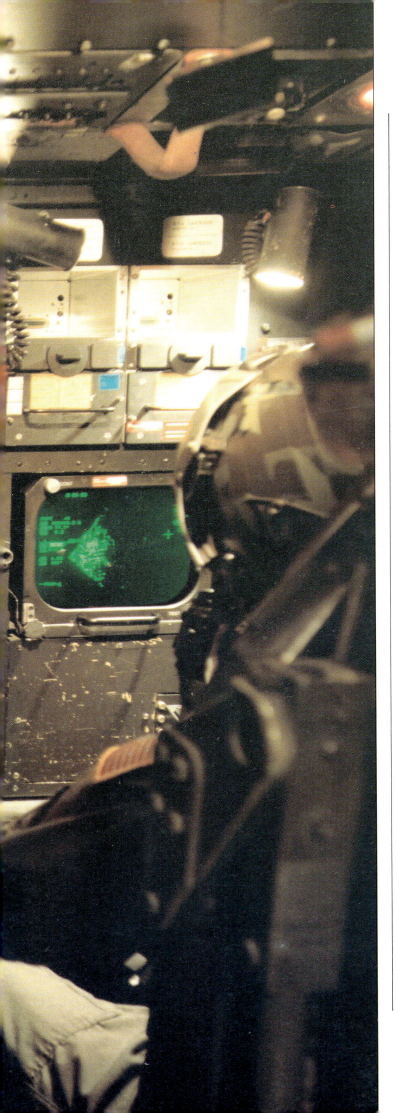

Chapter 7

SPY WAR:
THE INTELLIGENCE-GATHERERS

Most people still think of spying in terms of networks of agents, working undercover in foreign countries. But although the human spy still plays a part in intelligence-gathering operations today, in the last three decades increasingly sophisticated equipment has largely usurped the human's role. From equipment which 'hoovers' the radio frequencies in random searches for information of technical or strategic value, to spy satellites and networks of listening posts, today's 'spies' are capable of gathering an unprecedented amount of information – and in previously undreamed-of detail.

Operators at a radar console on board a USAF Boeing E-4 advanced Airborne Command Post – from which the President would order retaliatory strikes if the USA were to come under nuclear attack. In such an event, the President would rely at all times on information supplied by a network of SIGINT satellites and listening posts.

When future historians come to assess superpower relations post-1945, it may well be that what is found to have been the most influential factor on them was not that obvious symbol of mutually assured destruction, the ICBM, but rather the shadowy workings of the intelligence agencies. For it is they who, on the one hand, have worked assiduously to intensify the chill of the Cold War; on the other, they have been a major factor in preventing a nuclear Armageddon. Contradictory as this may seem, it does illustrate the paradoxical nature of the intelligence-gatherers' work, seamlessly serving various masters as the requirements of the day dictate.

Intelligence gathering – spying – is as old as recorded history. Until World War I, the primary means of obtaining information was the agent, working on the ground in the target country. He or she might be a diplomat, a paid informant or a trained operative who could live and work in the country without arousing suspicion. In all cases, the aim was the same: in peace, to gather economic, political, military and technological information on rival states; in war, to obtain data on the military capabilities and intentions of an enemy.

Reliance on technical means

While the traditional spy retains an important role today, a number of factors have led today's intelligence agencies to rely more and more on 'technical means' rather than field agents. The reasons for this are not hard to find. As noted earlier, World War I marked a watershed in the development of espionage which relied heavily on technology. In intelligence gathering, the most important aspect of this development was the first

Below: One of the earliest applications of technology to the gathering of intelligence was the use of photography for aerial reconnaissance in World War I. Here a French camera is being placed in a biplane in August 1918.

widespread use of radio communications. Although radio revolutionized battlefield communications, it had a flaw in that it was and is easily accessible to eavesdroppers. Recognizing this possibility, the 1914–18 combatants coded their messages so that, even if a transmission was intercepted, it would be unintelligible. This in turn led to the rise of the code breakers who, for this period, are best exemplified by the staff of the Admiralty's 'Room 40'. Early on in the hostilities, the British had established a chain of radio receiver stations along Britain's east coast to intercept the German navy's radio traffic. The signals received allowed the Admiralty both to locate the position of the transmission source (by triangulation) and to decipher the content of the messages.

Room 40's activities showed just how effective technical means of intelligence gathering could be. This said, the advantage gained was considerably reduced by a lack of understanding on the part of the military in the field about how best to use the acquired data. Thus, on the eve of the Battle of Jutland in 1916, the British Fleet commander asked his intelligence staff for the call-sign of the German flagship rather than explicitly requesting the enemy commander's precise location. While Admiral Jellico was well aware of the value of radio intelligence, he was not familiar with the German navy's practice of using false call-signs to deceive the British. His intelligence staff knew this but were, apparently, too frightened of his rank to inform him of his mistake. Jutland was but an early example of the misuse, deliberate or through ignorance, of intelligence data by the military, a trend which still continues.

Enigma and World War II

If technically acquired intelligence proved to be important in World War I, it was crucial in World War II. If nothing else, Hitler's Germany was virtually a closed state to the outside world even before the hostilities began. Such totalitarian states are extremely difficult for agents to penetrate, and throughout the war Allied agents had limited success in bringing information out of the Reich and Occupied Europe. Fortunately for the Allies, however, Germany was also extremely imaginative in its application of technology to warfare. Thus, although the German Army's blitzkrieg style of mobile land warfare proved so effective, its Achilles' heel lay in its need for excellent communications to direct and control the flow of battle. With typical Germanic thoroughness, this need was met by the provision of a highly effective radio communications system backed up by the Enigma encoder. So certain were the Germans of the effectiveness of the device that they made it the foundation of the secure communications until the collapse in 1945. What they never realized was that the system had been under attack for at least a decade before the outbreak of hostilities and that from the summer of 1940 the British were regularly reading significant portions of their signals traffic.

The story of the attack on Enigma is as fascinating as the way in which the Allies came to use the intelligence gained during the conflict. By way of background, the Enigma unit itself was an electro-mechanical wired encyphering machine which used a typewriter-style keyboard to enter messages and a series of encoding wheels to scramble the message before transmission. The device was first marketed during the 1920s and between 1926 and 1934 was adopted by all three German armed services. The secret services of a number of European countries began to take a particular interest in the device at this time. During 1932, the French secret service began to receive high-grade information concerning it from a German source. During the following year, the French began collaborating with the Polish authorities, who had also been investigating the equipment since 1928. By 1934, the Poles were building their own copies of Enigma and, in 1937, they began development of the 'cryptographic Bombe', a mechanism designed to find the encryption keys used with a particular Enigma machine by a rapid automatic testing of thousands of possible combinations.

The French appear to have shared some of their knowledge of Enigma with the British Government Code and Cypher School (GCCS) cryptanalysis organization at a relatively early stage in the game, but the British showed little interest in collaboration at the time. The increasing likelihood of war changed this, and a series of meetings between the French, the Poles and GCCS during 1939 culminated in the Poles' offer to both the French and the British of an example of a Polish-built Enigma machine and technical drawings of the Bombe. This was the situation at the outbreak of war. It is believed that the first wartime reading of an Enigma transmission took place in Paris late in 1939. In the UK, GCCS had made some progress with decipherment by means of a laborious manual method, but really got into its stride in May 1940 following the delivery of the first British-built Bombe.

For the remainder of the war, GCCS, from its base at Bletchley Park in Buckinghamshire, refined the technology, grew enormously in size and poured out a constant stream of high-grade strategic and tactical

Above: German wireless operators in General Guderian's command car in 1940, using Enigma encoding machines. Below: A reconnaissance photograph shot before D-Day shows an improvement on World War I pictures.

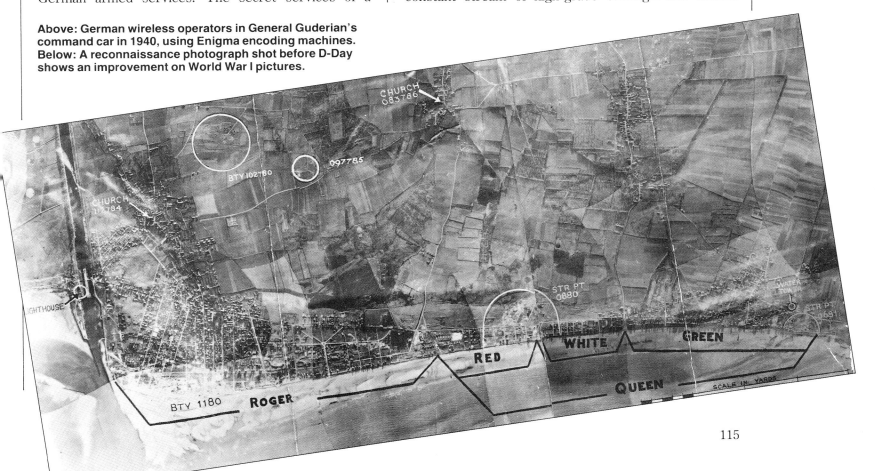

intelligence which went under the umbrella term of 'Ultra'. It should not be thought that Ultra, one of the war's best kept secrets, allowed the Allies to read all of Germany's communications: even at the end of the war there were variant Enigma codes which still could not be effectively deciphered. Equally, the GCCS Ultra was only one, if the most important, element in the overall Allied SIGnals INTelligence (SIGINT) effort. For its part, the USA broke the high-grade Japanese 'Purple' code which had profound implications for the conduct of the Pacific campaign. Both Britain and the USA made great strides in the actual collection of raw transmission data, with the British 'Y' service eventually operating a vast network of SIGINT stations feeding material into Bletchley and other agencies. On the tactical level, the RAF pioneered what are today known as ELectronic INTelligence (ELINT) operations, using aircraft fitted out with reception gear to chart the growth of the German radar network throughout Europe in support of the bomber offensive.

The Cold War

When hostilities ceased in 1945, Britain and the USA had under their control an enormous web of intelligence-gathering stations dotted around the world together with proven and advanced technical means of data collection. This was perhaps fortunate, as it had become apparent that even before the fall of the Axis powers, the uneasy alliance between the USSR and Britain and the USA was coming unglued. If this cooling of relations did not result in open warfare, it did nothing to make the peace easier and within two years, post-war Europe was in the grip of the superpower stand-off known as the Cold War. The speed of events meant that, unlike many of the other bureaucracies created during the recent war, the Anglo-American

intelligence organizations were not stood down but simply deployed against the new 'enemy', the Soviet Union. Indeed, there is reasonable circumstantial evidence to suggest that the USAAF, as it was then termed, was flying photo-reconnaissance sorties over Soviet-held territory even *before* the war with Germany ended.

The smooth transition from one set of targets to another had other profound, if subtle, effects on the nature of post-war operations. The closeness of the working relationships between the British and American personnel built up during the war years continued and remains even today, despite the setbacks caused by the discovery of the Soviet moles (Burgess, Maclean and Philby) working within British intelligence during the 1950s and the senior-partner stance taken by the USA. The closeness of this relationship was further strengthened during 1947 by the UKUSA or UK–USA Security Agreement, which divided SIGINT collection responsibilities between the 'first party', the USA, and the 'second parties', Australia, Britain, Canada and New Zealand. Under UKUSA, the world was divided into areas of responsibility, with each nation undertaking collection in a particular area. It also covered access to the overall 'take', methods of handling data, the standardization of codewords used to classify material and the standardization of security agreements which personnel had to sign prior to their employment.

UKUSA illustrates the importance attached to technical methods of intelligence gathering post-war. Even more importantly, the Agreement has encouraged the gradual build-up among intelligence personnel of an ethos of loyalty to a multi-national 'brotherhood', which at times may even transcend that owed to the mother country. Indeed, it would not be too far-fetched to suggest that the brotherhood even extends to the enemy. In the stressful, amoral and highly secretive world of the spy, where the only people a particular operative can relate to are other operatives, it is perhaps understandable that it can cease to matter which side the 'colleague' is working for, the psychological imperative being for contact with someone who understands the pressures involved in the job.

The rapid transition from 'hot' to 'cold' war has left today's intelligence agencies with other legacies. The men who ran them throughout the 1950s and 1960s predominantly learnt their trade in wartime. Consequently, the ethos of war operations was carried over into the 'peace' and in some ways has not altered since. Consequently, the watchword has been 'whatever it takes'. Such an outlook, combined with charters which in many cases put the agencies if not actually above the law then at least well beyond the effective scrutiny of any outside regulatory body, has led to excesses.

Left: The discovery in the 1950's of Soviet moles (clockwise from the left, Donald Maclean, Guy Burgess, Anthony Blunt and Kim Philby) in British Intelligence was a severe blow to relations with its US counterpart.

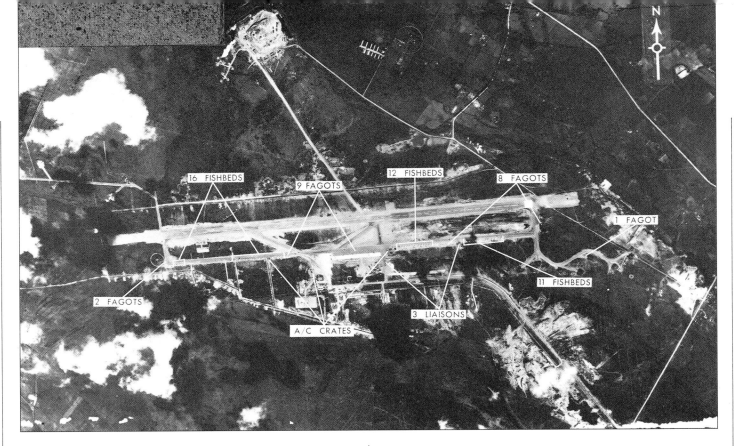

Above: This photograph of Soviet fighters deployed on a Cuban airfield was one of a series which precipitated the missile crisis of October 1962. The pictures were taken by cameras on a USAF Lockheed high-altitude aircraft.
Below: Reinhard Gehlen, once Hitler's spymaster, became head of West Germany's Intelligence Service.

Developing networks

In the immediate aftermath of the war, when US policy was to eradicate Nazism from Germany, Hitler's spy master, Reinhard Gehlen, was welcomed with open arms despite his associations with the SS, simply because he knew a great deal about the Soviet Union and was thought still to have agents in place in Eastern Europe. Although Gehlen's recording of all the aspects of Soviet society that the Germans had experienced in

the war was of value to the West, his agents and recruiting policy were, to say the least, suspect. Indeed, his fall from grace as head of the Bundes-nachrichtendienst (BDN), West Germany's federal intelligence service, was as much to do with the ex-SS men he recruited as for any other reason.

Mention of Gehlen's supposed network of agents in Eastern Europe leads neatly to one of the primary reasons for the West's current heavy reliance on technical means of intelligence gathering rather than the traditional agent on the ground. As with Germany in the 1930s, the post-war USSR and its satellites in Eastern Europe have proved remarkably resistant to penetration. This, together with the proven record of the technologies deployed to overcome it, has led the West almost to abandon the traditional methods of espionage. This is not to say that agents are not still recruited and defectors welcomed, but rather that the technical means have proved to be far more effective, especially in the monitoring of Soviet weapons development. The nature of the Western democracies has, on the other hand, allowed the Soviet Union the best of both worlds. Today, not only does the USSR have excellent technical means but also appears well able to continue to recruit or coerce agents throughout Europe and America. The list of such recruits is long and includes Philby, Burgess, Maclean, Blunt, Prime and Hambleton in Britain, together with Johnson, Boyce and Lee in the USA. Motivation appears to vary, with the British traitors professing theirs to be ideological, whereas the Americans seem, for the most part, to have no good reason for their activities other than money and the sense of power they bring. The excellence and frankness of the West's trade and technical press also make life much easier for the Soviet intelligence gatherers. All they need to do is visit the news-stands and send the relevant cuttings back to Moscow!

Above: A US AC-130H gunship, carrying the AN/ASD-5 Black Crow RINT sensor which was used to detect trucks on the Ho Chi Minh trail into South Vietnam from the north.

Technical definitions

The Anglo-American effort during World War II centred on SIGINT data derived from radio intercepts and in the intervening years, SIGINT, and its related disciplines of ELINT, COMmunications INTelligence (COMINT), TELemetry INTelligence (TELINT) and Radiation INTelligence (RINT) grew in importance.

SIGINT is the umbrella term for the various aspects

of material gathered from the Radio Frequency (RF) portion of the electromagnetic spectrum. ELINT describes those operations aimed at 'non-communicative' emitters such as radars. By examining the electronic 'fingerprint' of a radar emission (its frequency, wavelength, pulse-repetition frequency, antenna scan rate and form, among other characteristics), its purpose can be deduced. Equally, triangulation of its transmissions can be used to find its location. ELINT data is used to establish what is known as an electronic order of battle which allows air force planners to determine how to deal with a particular air defence network. ELINT data also plays an important part in the development of electronic countermeasures – electronic methods of blinding radars and radio-control links. Equally, it is useful in identifying new weapons systems as they appear and establishing whether they are still in development or have entered service.

COMINT is concerned with the interception of radio communications, whether by voice or data link, which provides early warning of an opponent's intentions. Even when a particular transmission cannot be understood, its interception can be of the greatest value. One aspect of COMINT data is 'traffic analysis' in which the

1 **Eielson AFB,** Alaska. USAF, RC-135S/X aircraft.
2 **Inuvik,** New Territories, Canada. Canadian Armed Forces' SIGINT station.
3 **Whitehorse,** Canada. Canadian Armed Forces' SIGINT station.
4 **Beale AFB,** California. USAF, SR-71/U-2R/TR-1 aircraft.
5 **Palmerola,** Honduras. US Army, RU-21 ELINT aircraft.
6 **Guantanamo Bay,** Cuba. USN SIGINT station.
7 **Eglin AFB,** Florida. 'Forward Operating Location' FOL for USAF SIGINT aircraft.
8 **FORT GEORGE C. MEADE,** Maryland. NSA headquarters.
9 **Offutt AFB,** Nebraska. USAF, RC-135U/V/W aircraft.
10 **Menwith Hill.** NSA telecoms monitoring station.
11 **RAF Alconbury/RAF Mildenhall/RAF Wyton:** Alconbury – USAF, U-2R/TR-1 aircraft; Mildenhall

– FOL for USAF RC/135U/V/W aircraft; Wyton – RAF Nimrod R.1 SIGINT aircraft.
12 **RAF Chicksands.** US COMINT station.
13 **CHELTENHAM.** GCHQ.
14 **Schleswig,** West Germany. USAF SIGINT station.
15 **Fauske,** Norway. Norwegian VHF SIGINT station.
16 **Vadso,** Norway. Norwegian HF/VHF SIGINT station.
17 **Kirkenes,** Norway. NSA SIGINT station.
18 **Nordholz,** West Germany. Bundesmarine 'Peace Peek' Atlantique SIGINT aircraft.
19 **Berlin,** Major US/UK SIGINT facilities.
20 **Luchow,** West Germany. Luftwaffe SIGINT station.
21 **Braunschweig,** West Germany. German Intelligence Service SIGINT station.
22 **Augsburg,** West Germany. US COMINT station.
23 **Echterdingen,** West Germany. US Army, RV-1 ELINT aircraft.
24 **Zweibrucken,** West Germany. US Army, RC-12

SIGINT aircraft.
25 **Rota,** Spain. USN, EP-3E/EA-3B aircraft.
26 **Kenitra,** Morocco. Possible US SIGINT station.
27 **Brindisi,** Italy. US SIGINT station.
28 **Hellenikon,** Greece. FOL for USAF RC-135 aircraft.
29 **Mount Olympus,** Cyprus. UK SIGINT station.
30 **RAF Akrotiri,** Cyprus. FOL for USAF SR-71/U-2 aircraft.
31 **Istanbul,** Turkey. USN ELINT station.
32 **Sinop,** Turkey. US SIGINT station.
33 **Incirlik,** Turkey. One time FOL for USAF RC-135/ CIA U-2 aircraft.
34 **Iraklion,** Crete. US SIGINT/TELINT station.
35 **Masirah Island,** Oman. UK/US SIGINT station.
36 **Diego Garcia,** UK/US SIGINT station.
37 **Bada Bier,** Pakistan. USAF SIGINT station.
38 **Peshawar,** Pakistan. One time FOL for CIA U-2 aircraft.
39 **Qitai,** Northern China. US/Chinese SIGINT station.

40 **Korla,** Northern China. US/Chinese SIGINT station.
41 **Stanley Fort/Chung Hom Kok/Tai Mo Shan,** Hong Kong. UK SIGINT stations.
42 **Clark AFB,** Philippines. US SIGINT station.
43 **Cubi Point,** Philippines. FOL for USN EP-3E/EA-3B aircraft.
44 **North West Cape,** Australia. USN SIGINT station.
45 **Nurrungar,** Australia. US early warning satellite terminal.
46 **Pine Gap,** Australia. US SIGINT satellite terminal.
47 **Agana,** Guam. USN, EP-3E/EA-3B aircraft.
48 **Kadena AFB,** Okinawa. FOL for USAF SR-71/U-2/ RC/135 aircraft.
49 **Atsugi AFB,** Japan. FOL for USN EP-3E/EA/3B aircraft.
50 **Misawa AFB,** Japan. US SIGINT station.
51 **Wakkanai,** Japan. Japanese/US SIGINT station.
52 **Shemya AFB,** Aleutian Islands. FOL for USAF RC-135S/X aircraft.

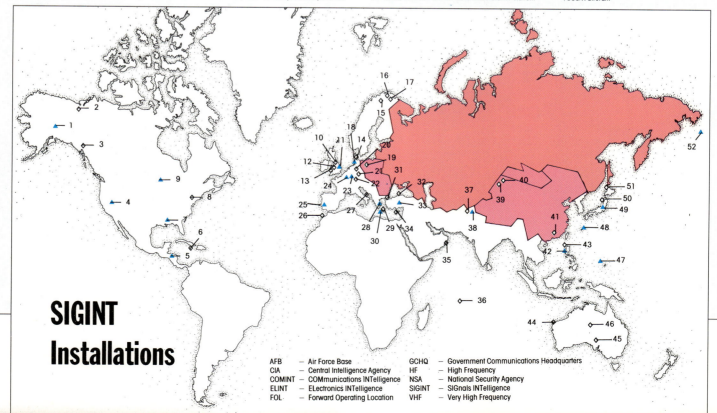

SIGINT Installations

AFB	– Air Force Base		GCHQ	– Government Communications Headquarters
CIA	– Central Intelligence Agency		HF	– High Frequency
COMINT	– COMmunications INTelligence		NSA	– National Security Agency
ELINT	– ELectronics INTelligence		SIGINT	– SIGnals INTelligence
FOL	– Forward Operating Location		VHF	– Very High Frequency

operator examines the frequency of transmissions, at whom they are aimed, call signs, etc. Once a pattern has been established, it is relatively easy to spot the unusual, even if the particular signal is not fully understood. Thus, for instance, if operators detect an increase in signals traffic from an identified Soviet tank division in East Germany, they know something is afoot, even if the nature of that 'something' is not clear. Equally, a new call sign or signal in a particular area signifies a new formation or piece of equipment.

TELINT is the interception of the real-time data (pressure, velocity, surface angular position, etc.) transmitted from systems such as missiles to a ground station during tests. TELINT has taken on a special significance in Western intelligence gathering in that it is one of the best ways of evaluating the performance and capabilities of the Soviet Union's successive generations of nuclear missile-delivery systems. Indeed, there has been the suggestion that in the various periods of détente, the Russians have not been averse to this monitoring, seeing it as an informal way of maintaining the nuclear balance through confidence-building.

The final item in the SIGINT fold, RINT, is perhaps the most interesting. It makes use of the fact that active items such as power lines, generators and unshielded vehicle spark plugs transmit a receivable RF signal. Much can be gleaned from these rather curious signals. In the strategic context, the monitoring of the electric power going into, say, a tank factory allows estimates to be made of its power requirements. This in turn can give some idea of what equipment is being used in the manufacturing process by comparison with known production techniques. At the tactical level, RINT sensors can form a useful adjunct to the normal range of attack sensors on aircraft. An example of such an application is the American AN/ASD-5 Black Crow system which was deployed operationally on AC-130H gunships used in Vietnam. By the late 1960s, the northern parts of the famous Ho Chi Minh logistics trail into South Vietnam were developed enough to carry trucks. Because of American air superiority, the North Vietnamese moved supplies mainly at night when the thick jungle canopy which covered the trail in parts of Laos and Cambodia, shielded movement from patrolling aircraft. The Russian GAZ trucks used in the operation were fitted with unshielded spark plugs and Black Crow was used to pick up their emissions, handing-off the location to other onboard sensors for the attack run. Operational experience showed that ASD-5 was effective and there are reports that the equipment has also been used for reconnaissance in Central America.

SIGINT operations

Clearly, SIGINT is one of the most important intelligence-gathering tools available today. In the strategic context, that is, the gathering of intelligence for use in formulating military and political policies in peacetime, France, Israel, Britain, the USA, the USSR and West Germany appear to be the major players. A mixture of land-based, seaborne, airborne and space platforms is used to gather the necessary information.

Taking these countries in order, French SIGINT activity is based on the Direction Générale de la Sécurité Extérieure (DGSE), which, despite its name, is responsible for the collection of foreign intelligence, counter-intelligence inside France and 'covert' action (such as the mining of Greenpeace's ship, the *Rainbow Warrior* in Auckland harbour, New Zealand). While its SIGINT activities are well attested, the only clearly visible outward sign of this work is the specially modified DC-8 airliner operated on its behalf by the French Air Force's EE.51 stationed at Bretigny. This aeroplane carries an ELINT/COMINT suite developed by the French electronics company Thomson-CSF and is primarily a strategic system which has been used frequently to monitor activity in the Baltic region. France also operates a small number of Transall transports modified to carry Thomson's Gabriel SIGINT equipment.

Even more well camouflaged are the activities of Israel's Aman military intelligence organization. While firm details are hard to come by, no observant visitor to Israel can fail to notice the various SIGINT-orientated antenna fields spread along the country's coast. Again like the French, the Israeli Air Force operates at least two heavily modified Boeing 707 airliners packed with locally produced (the ELTA L-8300 or Tadiran TACDES suite) and US SIGINT equipment. In addition, the Israelis are thought to have supplied three IAI Arava Short Take-Off and Landing (STOL) aircraft fitted with SIGINT gear to Thailand, two SIGINT suites

Below: A Phantom FG.Mk 1 from RAF Leuchars intercepts a Soviet TU-95, Bear-D in 1973. The large radome (inset) houses a 'Big Bulge' radar; the other protruberances are antennas for ECM and SIGINT purposes.

Above: A Boeing RC-135V, a SIGINT aircraft which is currently in service with the USAF Strategic Air Command's 55th SRW, at Offutt, Nebraska.

to Argentina for use in its navy's Orion aircraft and four tanker/SIGINT Boeing 707s to South Africa.

SIGINT activity in the UK centres upon the Government Communications Headquarters (GCHQ) at Cheltenham in Gloucestershire. GCHQ is the lineal descendant of the wartime GCCS organization which was moved from Bletchley to London and then to Cheltenham in the late 1940s. GCHQ's current role is primarily SIGINT collection and analysis and the protection of government communications by means of encryption development. The centre's SIGINT activities are conducted in concert with those of the armed forces and authoritative sources suggest that it is involved with (or has been involved with) 38 listening posts overseas as well as 26 sites in Britain. In addition to these various ground-based locations, the RAF's 51 Squadron (Wyton) flies three SIGINT-equipped Nimrod R.1 aircraft on behalf of the organization. Of great importance to the work done at Cheltenham is the close relationship with the USA which has resulted in a US presence within GCHQ and its dovetailing with the USA's collection system. Thus GCHQ is a major recipient of US satellite intelligence although its own attempts to produce a national SIGINT satellite, Zircon, have foundered.

As might be expected, the USA runs the largest

Below: Britain's GCHQ, at two sites, Oakley and Benhall, in Cheltenham, is responsible for SIGINT collection and analysis in close collaboration with the USA.

SIGINT network of any of the free-world countries. Authoritative sources have established that the country's National Security Agency (NSA, the equivalent of the UK's GCHQ) and the intelligence departments of its three armed services have operated or are operating no less than 318 SIGINT stations and related facilities around the world. Of this number, 108 are located in North America, 10 in South Korea, 18 in Turkey, 23 in Japan, 14 in Britain and 66 in West Germany. The actual collection of material makes use of ground receivers, aircraft and space-based 'ferret' satellites. Between 1960 and 1971, this triad was supported by a fourth arm, ships. Under the auspices of the NSA, this progamme began in 1960 and eventually involved ten dedicated vessels together with electronics vans stowed on the decks of standard warships on an 'as and when needed' basis. Both these elements of the programme ran into trouble. Of the dedicated platforms, the USS *Liberty* was all but sunk off the Sinai coast on June 7, 1967, while the USS *Pueblo* was captured by North Korea off their coast on January 23, 1968. These losses put an end to the NSA/USN's 'spy fleet' and by 1971 the remaining ships had been quietly decommissioned. The use of SIGINT vans mounted on standard warships also had its share of troubles, with the 1964 North Vietnamese attack on the destroyers USS *Maddox* and USS *C. Turner Joy* during a SIGINT mission in the Gulf of Tonkin on August 4, 1964. More recently, the USA has again started using its warships for SIGINT operations off the coasts of Central America, relying on the vessel's own electronic 'fit' or suite to provide the necessary data.

Collecting data

Of the other systems noted, both the USAF and the USN have specialized SIGINT aircraft available. Within the USAF, the main type is the Boeing RC-135. Derived from the KC/C-135 family of jet tankers and transports, the RC-135 entered service with Strategic Air Command's 55th Strategic Reconnaissance Wing (SRW) during January 1967. Until now, some 12 operational and one training variant of the type have appeared, with 20 RC-135S, U, V, W, X and TC/135S aircraft currently operational. The two Cobra Ball RC-135S aircraft are assigned to the Alaskan-based 6th Strategic Wing (SW) but are crewed from the 55th SRW. Their job is to scramble when a Soviet ballistic missile test is taking place to photograph the re-entry as the weapon splashes down in the Sea of Okhotsk and to gather TELINT data. These aeroplanes are supported by the TC-135S trainer and are soon to be joined by the RC-135X aircraft which is currently being fitted out by E-Systems for the Cobra Eye programme. Sadly, it is probable that the Russians thought that the Korean Airlines Boeing 747 which they shot down over Sakhalin Island in September 1983, was a Cobra Ball RC-135.

The main RC-135 SIGINT effort is undertaken by the 55th SRW's two RC-135U, eight RC-135V and six

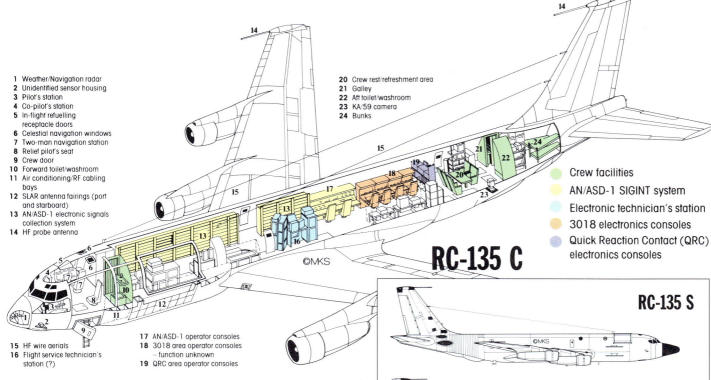

1. Weather/Navigation radar
2. Unidentified sensor housing
3. Pilot's station
4. Co-pilot's station
5. In-flight refuelling receptacle doors
6. Celestial navigation windows
7. Two-man navigation station
8. Relief pilot's seat
9. Crew door
10. Forward toilet/washroom
11. Air conditioning/RF cabling bays
12. SLAR antenna fairings (port and starboard)
13. AN/ASD-1 electronic signals collection system
14. HF probe antenna

15. HF wire aerials
16. Flight service technician's station (?)

17. AN/ASD-1 operator consoles
18. 3018 area operator consoles – function unknown
19. QRC area operator consoles

20. Crew rest/refreshment area
21. Galley
22. Aft toilet/washroom
23. KA/59 camera
24. Bunks

● Crew facilities
● AN/ASD-1 SIGINT system
● Electronic technician's station
● 3018 electronics consoles
● Quick Reaction Contact (QRC) electronics consoles

RC-135 C

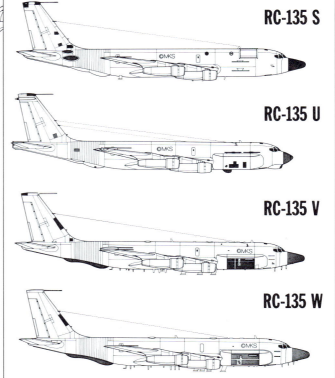

RC-135 S

RC-135 U

RC-135 V

RC-135 W

Above: Diagram of the general layout of the USAF's Boeing RC-135C SIGINT aircraft with the main variant configurations (right). Some details of the equipment are speculative since little information has been released. Below: The Israeli air force operates the Arava STOL and Boeing 707, using ELTA L-8300 electronic suites.

RC-135W aircraft. Based at Offutt Air Force Base in Nebraska, the Vs and the Ws are assigned to the Rivet Joint programme which provides electronic intelligence material against specifically assigned targets. A typical Rivet Joint mission starts off with an RC-135 lumbering off Offutt's runway and embarking on a flight of up to 24 hours' duration to one of the 55th's Forward Operating Locations (FOLs – presently at Mildenhall in Britain, Hellenikon in Greece and Kadena on Okinawa). To achieve this, all the Rivet Joint aircraft are equipped for in-flight refuelling, carry a relief flight crew and have dining and resting facilities for the systems crew. The transit flight to the FOL will be routed in such a way as

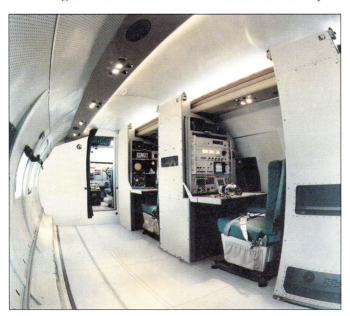

to take in an operational task. Once at the FOL, the aircraft will be used to undertake one or two local sorties of anything up to 15 or 20 hours' duration. With these completed, the plane heads back to Offutt, collecting more data on the way. There is reason to believe that the transit systems crew may be replaced by FOL personnel for the local missions. The remaining 55th aircraft, the two RC-135Us, are some of the most heavily modified members of the family and are reputed to be the most difficult to fly. The U is associated with the Combat Pink and Combat Scent programmes. While no clear indication of just what the equipment carried by these aircraft can do has ever been forthcoming, they are obviously extremely sophisticated, sucking up signals right across the RF spectrum from the ether.

US SIGINT ground facilities range from relatively simple wire-and-mast listening posts, to the futuristic satellite down-link stations, such as Pine Gap in Australia, to the truly spectacular 'elephant cage' aerials

Below: An Atlas-Agena B blasts off from Cape Kennedy in 1965. The Agena series of rocket stages were the standard carriers for all of the USA's early ferret satellites.

associated with the AN/FLR-9 HF/VHF COMINT and direction-finding system. More correctly known as a Circularly Disposed Antenna Array (CDAA), the 'elephant cage' consists of four concentric rings of reception elements. The outermost, comprising 120 equally spaced antenna elements, is approximately 875ft (267m) in diameter. Inside this is a second, higher ring which acts as a Very High Frequency (VHF) band reflector screen. Inside this is the High Frequency (HF) band reception array which is made up of 40 equally spaced 'folded monopole' elements. The whole is completed by a central ring which acts as an HF reflector screen.

The final element in the SIGINT triad, the space-based platform, is without doubt the most spectacular. The first known US SIGINT or 'ferret' satellite appears to have been launched on May 15, 1962. Using an Agena-B vehicle as a basis, this satellite was placed in a near-Polar orbit with a perigee (nearest point from the earth) of 180 miles (290km) and apogee (furthest point) of 401 miles (645km). By 1964, dedicated ferrets were growing larger and more expensive to launch, so the National Reconnaissance Office (NRO – the co-ordinating and control authority for all types of US reconnaissance satellites) instigated a second series of platforms which could ride into space piggyback on boosters carrying other payloads. One of the first was the 130lb (59kg) vehicle launched in tandem with a KH-6 photo-reconnaissance satellite on July 6, 1964.

Success and failure

Between 1962 and 1971, the USA launched 17 large ferret vehicles. On March 6, 1973, the first fully operational Rhyolite electronic reconnaissance vehicle sponsored by the Central Intelligence Agency (CIA) was launched. Rhyolite 1 was followed by three others (the last being orbited on April 7, 1978). Positioned in a geo-stationary orbit some 22,175 miles (35,686km) above Borneo, the Rhyolite cluster's main task was the monitoring of Soviet missile telemetry emanating from the Tyuratum and Plesetsk test centres. As a system, Rhylite proved highly effective until its secrets were betrayed by Boyce and Lee in the mid-1970s. After their arrest and trial, the Russians started to encode their missile telementry so that, although Rhyolite continued to intercept it, the data was unintelligible.

In an attempt to salvage something from this disaster, Rhyolite was renamed Aquacade in an effort to persuade the Russians that Rhyolite had been super-seded by a newer system so that they would let their guard fall. Whether this happened is not known, but, as far as can be ascertained, the Rhyolite cluster continues to circle over Borneo to this day. Rhyolite was followed in June 1978 by a second major system called Chalet. It is believed that three such satellites have been launched and, like Rhyolite, its name has been changed to Vortex following mention in the press of its original designation. The latest addition to this growing fleet of ferrets was

Above: A Soviet Mayak-class spy trawler tails HMS _Ark Royal._ Unlike the USSR, the USA no longer makes extensive use of spy ships.

launched aboard Shuttle mission 51-C on January 24, 1985. Called Magnum, this probably represents the ultimate in US SIGINT hardware currently in orbit.

The Soviet SIGINT network

Like that of its Western counterpart, the USSR's SIGINT effort is based on a range of options which includes ground stations, aircraft and satellites. Unlike the Americans, however, the Russians maintain a large fleet of SIGINT-dedicated ships, known in the West by their US designation Auxiliary Vessels, miscellaneous type, Intelligence (AGIs) or more popularly as spy trawlers. Such vessels, festooned with antennas, dog all NATO exercises and can be found lurking off the West's major SSBN, nuclear-powered, ballistic-missile submarine bases, missile test sites and any other interesting location. In the early 1980s the total AGI fleet stood at 57 vessels of 11 types (1 Balzam class, 6 Primorye, 3 Nikolai Zubov, 2 Pamir, 8 Moma, 4 Mirny, 8 Mayak, 15 Okean, 7 Lentra, 1 T-58 and 2 Dnepr).

Equally dogged are the USSR's ELINT aircraft which regularly monitor Western naval activity and probe the air defence regions of the North Atlantic Treaty Organization (NATO). Currently operational Soviet SIGINT aircraft include the Antonov An-12 Cub-B, the Ilyushin Il-20 Coot-A, the Mikoyan MiG-25 Foxbat-D, the Tupolev Tu-16 Badger-D, -F and -K, together with the ubiquitous Tupolev TU-142 Bear-D. All of these aircraft, with the exception of the Foxbat-D are flown by the Soviet naval air arm.

Again like the USA, Soviet Russia makes great use of SIGINT satellites. The first vehicle of this type, Cosmos 148, was launched into space on March 16, 1976, some five years after the first US ferret had been placed in orbit. Weighing about 900lb (408kg), Cosmos

148 was followed into orbit by a second-generation system (starting with Cosmos 189) in October of the same year. Since then, some 40 189-type vehicles have been launched, all of which have operated in clusters of four to improve the accuracy of emitter location. In February 1977, the first third-generation Soviet SIGINT satellite (Cosmos 895) was placed in an orbit 372 miles (599km) high around the earth. Much larger than its predecessors – 16ft (5m) long and weighing between 5000lb (2268kg) and 8000lb (3629kg) – the 895 class has consistently been deployed to provide global coverage. It is believed that the latest Soviet SIGINT space vehicle is the manoeuvrable Cosmos 1603 class. Launched into a parking orbit 115 miles (185km) up on September 28, 1984, 1603 went through a multiple manoeuvre until it had reached its operational altitude of 530 miles (853km) above the earth.

The remaining big-league SIGINT player is West Germany. Coming under the auspices of the BDN, the federal intelligence service, West Germany's political and strategic SIGINT operations are a highly centralized affair to which various agencies (such as the military) second personnel for specific purposes. Apart from the US listening posts situated on German soil which have already been mentioned, the Amt für Fernmeldewesen Bundeswehr (AFmBW – the federal armed forces telecommunications general office), the BDN itself, the Luftwaffe, the Heer (army) and the Bundesmarine (navy) operate 13 ground sites within the Republic. In addition, it is highly likely that the Luftwaffe maintains a SIGINT capability alongside the Bundesmarine's four Peace Peek electronic-surveillance Atlantique aircraft operated by MFG 3 from Nordholz.

The other major aspect of the current technical means of intelligence gathering is the use of optical and non-visible-radiation sensors. The development of really high performance aerial cameras is closely tied to the CIA's most famous piece of intelligence hardware, the Lockheed U-2. Developed in the mid-1940s, this jet-powered sailplane, with its phenomenal ability to fly

Below: The USAF Lockheed TR-1, based in Britain, provides a major photo-reconnaissance, SIGINT and emitter-location capability.

1960. Although the Powers' incident put a stop to the CIA's overflights of the USSR, in USAF hands the type went on to do sterling service during the Cuban missile crisis of 1962 and later on in the South-east Asian conflict of the late 1960s and early 1970s. Even today, the U-2's lineal successor, the TR-1, forms an important part of NATO European surveillance capability, with British-based aircraft providing a major part of the photo-reconnaissance, SIGINT and emitter-location capability.

Excellent though the Dragon Lady's performance was and is, it pales beside Lockheed's follow-on reconnaissance vehicle, the SR-71 Blackbird. Developed from the earlier A-11 aircraft, the 1960s-vintage SR-71 remains probably the fastest aircraft in the world. Perhaps more importantly, this speed is matched by a battery of sensors which include a pair of 48in. (1219mm) focal length technical-objective cameras which can cover a swath of the aircraft's flight path between 833 and 1619 nautical miles (1543 and 2998km) wide depending on the camera setting and the platform's altitude. The quality of the lens and film used enable an object resolution of *nine inches* to be achieved. Supporting these units, the Blackbird can also carry a nose-mounted optical bar camera with a 30in. (762mm) focal length which can photograph terrain between 1478 and 2930 nautical miles (2737 and 5426km) long in visible light or infra-red parts of the spectrum.

at high altitudes and specially developed, state-of-the-art cameras, revolutionized the USA's gathering of intelligence concerning Russia. Making its first overflight of the USSR on July 4, 1956, the U-2 brought back hundreds of priceless photographs of military installations and equipment over the next four years until operations were suspended following the shooting down of Powers' Dragon Lady over Sverdlovsk on May 1,

The most telling example of the dangers inherent in the superpowers' intelligence-gathering operations post-1945 must be the loss of an American U-2 spyplane over Sverdlovsk in the USSR on May 1, 1960. Developed and operated by the CIA, U-2 overflights of the USSR had begun in July 1956 and had provided an enormous increase in the quality of Soviet intelligence available to the USA in the years that followed.

Gary Powers' mission over Sverdlovsk on that fateful May Day was prompted by the discovery, during the preceding April, of major advances in the USSR's ICBM programme being undertaken at Sverdlovsk and Plesetsk. Powers' mission was in fact follow-up to an overflight on April 9.

Bad weather prevented the launch of the mission until May 1. Powers launched from the airfield at Peshawar in Pakistan. The flight was normal in every way until Powers began his photographic run over Sverdlovsk. He later recalled that the sky suddenly lit up, and then there was the noise of an explosion below and behind his aircraft. The U-2's right wing dropped and the nose pitched downwards.

At this point, Powers realized that his aircraft had broken in half. With the wrecked remains of his U-2 in a

flat spin, Powers evacuated the aircraft by parachute at 34,000ft (11,587m).

At first the Americans tried circulating the story that the U-2 had strayed off course during a test flight, but the pretence could not be maintained. The Russian leader, Khrushchev, cancelled a summit meeting and the Americans were forced into humiliating admissions concerning their spy flights over the Soviet Union. Powers was put on trial and incarcerated until he was swapped for the agent Rudolf Abel in February 1962.

US spy satellites

With sensor capabilities of this magnitude mounted in aircraft flying on the edge of space, it is not surprising that the USA rapidly made the jump towards true space-based reconnaissance platforms. The USA's first attempts at creating viable spy satellites centred around the CIA's Discoverer/Corona and the USAF's Samos programmes. Discoverer was essentially an Agena 'bus' modified to carry a camera and a film-ejection capsule which was to be snatched in midair over the Pacific by specially modified US aircraft. Discoverers 1 to 12 were all failures and it was only with Discoverer 13, launched on August 10, 1960, that the programme got into its stride. It continued until Discoverer 38 in 1962. The resolution obtainable with the Discoverer camera was about 12in. (305mm).

The USAF's Samos differed in using a direct transmission system for the return of the imagery to a ground station. The first successful Samos launch took place on January 31, 1961. In all, 30 Samos vehicles were launched, of which five failed. The imagery generated by the system is said to have been poor, with resolution varying between 20ft and 5ft (6m and 1.5m) during the course of the programme. Both Samos and Discoverer were superseded by a new generation of vehicles known by the generic term Key Hole, usually abreviated to KH. A total of 46 KH-5s were successfully placed in orbit.

Alongside the USAF-sponsored KH-5, the CIA developed the similar KH-6. The KH-6 camera system had a resolution of 12in. (305mm) and the exposed film

Above: This mid-air capsule recovery simulates the method used to recover film from the KH-9 satellite.
Below: The USA's Teal Ruby satellite tracks objects in low-earth orbit and transmits the data to AWACS aircraft.

was returned to earth in an ejection capsule. KH-6 was followed by the third generation area-surveillance KH-7 vehicle which was the first US reconnaissance satellite to be equipped with infra-red and multispectral sensors for imaging in poor light. Twenty-nine of these were launched from August 1966 onwards but it is believed

that the imagery they generated was not particularly good. KH-7 was matched by an equivalent similar-looking vehicle, the KH-8, which carried both a visible-light camera and an electro-optical suite similar to that used on the KH-7. A total of 52 such vehicles were launched between July 1966 and 1985.

KH-7 was followed by the fourth generation KH-9 area-surveillance vehicle which was also known as Big Bird. True to this appellation, the KH-9, at 50ft (15m) long, 10ft (3m) wide and 30,000lb (13,608kg) was the largest US reconnaissance satellite yet. At the heart of its capabilities was a 20-ft (6m) focal length Cassegrain telescope through which received energy was directed to a number of available sensors for recording on ejectable film. Alongside this suite, the vehicle was equipped with a twin-lens surveillance camera whose product was scanned for transmission to a ground station. The KH-9 also carried SIGINT equipment, was able to manoeuvre, and was also equipped to carry up to four small ferret vehicles for delivery into orbit.

The first KH-9 was blasted spaceward in June 1971, with the last being lost in a launch explosion on April 18, 1986. The KH-11 was an electro-optical system using Charged Couple Devices (CCDs) to capture radiated energy emissions across both the visible and non-visible parts of the spectrum. The use of CCDs made KH-11 the first US platform which could generate high-quality imagery for transmission in real time to a ground station. The first KH-11 was launched in 1976 and a fifth was orbited in August, 1985. However, on August 28,

Below: As reconnaissance satellites increase in number and usefulness, both the USA and the USSR have been developing anti-satellite (ASAT) missiles to deal with them. The US ASAT missiles are launched from USAF F-15s.

the sixth was lost in a launch accident. This, combined with the loss of the space shuttle *Challenger* on January 28, 1986, which put paid to the KH-12 shuttle-dependent successor to the KH-11, has left the USA with only one KH-11 on station. The KH-12, which has now been cancelled, was intended to solve the last remaining problem confronting US reconnaissance satellites – staying on station indefinitely. Although this would appear to have left the USA in a parlous position, the situation may not be as bad as it seems. If the Americans had believed that they were lacking one of the strongest cards in the arms control verification suite, then it is extremely unlikely that they would have signed the recent INF treaty. That there will be a successor to the KH-11 is not in doubt.

Soviet spy satellites

The USSR's reconnaissance satellite programme has followed generally similar lines, with improved vehicles succeeding one another. The first generation of such platforms began with the modified Vostok vehicle, Cosmos 4, which was launched on April 26, 1962. Starting with Cosmos 22, launched on November 16,

plagued by international terrorism, the sophistication of today's intelligence methods is a major force in the fight to defeat the men of violence. However, the intelligence and security organizations worldwide have a darker side. Perhaps more frightening for the ordinary citizen is their increasingly broad perception of who is an enemy of the state. Although it is true that the rise of terrorism has made more intrusive surveillance unavoidable, the question has to be asked, 'Where does it end?' With the technology available today, the individual citizen is totally at the mercy of the watchers. It is ingrained in such organizations to see treachery, threat and deceit everywhere, an outlook which, in the present state of the world, makes it virtually inevitable that today's democratic right of dissent will be perceived as tomorrow's threat to society. How we balance the need for surveillance against the rights of the individual has to be resolved now, if we are not to bring on ourselves the Orwellian nightmare in which 'Big Brother' really *is* watching.

Above: A Vostok rocket is prepared for launch at Baikonur, the Soviet space centre. The USSR's new SLW heavy-lift vehicle, will launch more powerful SIGINT satellites (left). Right: Winston Smith (played by John Hurt) watched by 'Big Brother' in the film version of *1984*. The intelligence-gatherers have helped to keep the peace – but their power may represent a threat to individual liberty.

1963, the second generation vehicles featured higher-resolution cameras and a longer mission duration (eight days instead of five). Cosmos 208 (March 21, 1968) marked the appearance of the third generation of Soviet reconnaissance satellites capable of carrying a piggy-back ferret into orbit. Cosmos 228 (June 21, 1968) saw such vehicles staying in orbit for up to 12 days, and Cosmos 251 saw the period extended to 14 days and offered manoeuvrability so that the onboard camera payload can be targeted with greater accuracy.

The fourth generation Cosmos 758 went into orbit on September 5, 1975; they are highly manoeuvrable and can carry six returnable film capsules for use in missions of up to a month's duration. An example of this is Cosmos 1504, which was launched on October 14, 1983, to observe the US invasion of Grenada.

Building trust between superpowers

Without the technology which has produced these space-based systems, the difficult job of establishing a basis of trust beween the superpowers would be that much harder and consequently the world would be that much nearer the nuclear abyss. Equally, in an age

Chapter 8

FORCES DIARY:
REVIEW OF THE YEAR

1988 was a watershed year for all those involved in deciding defensive and strategic policies, thanks to General Secretary Gorbachev's moves to revamp the USSR's defensive and foreign policy commitments. Of most importance was the INF Treaty: the Diary examines its implications for all in the West (and reports on disturbing evidence that the claimed reductions in nuclear weapons may not occur) and investigates why gaining a Treaty was so vital to the very future of the USSR. The USSR's new-look foreign policy, meanwhile, will affect many Third World nations – and may even indirectly bring about the end of apartheid in South Africa. These, and many other defence issues, both at home and abroad, are the subject of this year's Diary.

Factory workers march past a giant poster of Mikhail Gorbachev in Red Square, Moscow, during the 1988 May Day Peace Parade. Under previous Soviet leaders, the parade was used to display the USSR's military might.

Every statistic tells a story, and this year's Force's Diary examines a few in order to gauge what is happening not just in Britain and Europe as has been the case in previous Diaries, but also further afield, notably in the Soviet Union, the USA, the Gulf and some Central American and African countries – the trouble-spots of this larger political spectrum.

Just a few statistics offered by defence correspondents and other interested parties in the months of April and May, 1988, neatly indicate the staggering complexity of foreign defence issues today:

☢ In a new package of briefing documents entitled *Even Before the Bomb Drops*, offered at the Medical Campaign Against Nuclear Weapons Conference in Bath, Dr Robin Stott pointed out that, around the world, £2500 is now spent every second on nuclear weapons.

☭ In war-torn Afghanistan it is estimated that the USSR, who began a highly publicized withdrawal of 115,000 troops in 1988, have left some five million live mines behind as a memento of their stay. Sown at strategic points around the countryside, the mines will undoubtedly cause anxiety to those of the five million refugees (most of whom have been sheltering in Pakistan) who have been intrepid enough to return since the Russian soldiers moved out.

☠ Since the ill-starred Afghanistan war began more than eight years ago, 12,000 Russian soldiers are estimated to have been killed; some Afghanistan-watchers have even put the figure as high as 25,000. Double that amount of Mujahideen rebels may have fallen during the course of the war – although this can only be speculation, as not even the USSR is aware of the overall number of rebels, and so assessments of rebel casualties are even harder to establish with any accuracy.

☠ In Iraq, after a mere 34 hours of vicious fighting in the Faw peninsula, the Iraqis told visiting television and press crews that they reckoned to have killed as many as 30,000 Iranian Revolutionary Guards. Three days after the fighting, all the bodies had been bulldozed into the salt marshes, and only burnt-out tanks and vehicles remained as testimony to the terrible slaughter.

$ In Gulf waters, a further 12 US Navy ships were dispatched to reinforce the 7th Fleet; it was estimated that even before they arrived the escort operations were costing one million dollars (about £600,000) per day.

£ In Britain, the Executive Procurement branch of the Ministry of Defence (MOD) came under a continuing barrage of criticism from government and Parliament alike for managing to underspend by as much as £800 million of its 87/88 Financial Year budget, simply because it had marginally tightened its cost management and tendering policies. What had been happening before the tightening began?

Quoting statistics in this way can be guaranteed to raise hackles somewhere. Somebody, or, more likely, some committee, will argue with the interpretation put upon the statistics, and will produce different figures in support of their particular cause. Nevertheless, the list serves to illustrate not only the complexity of the defence issues of today, but also how quickly our world is now changing in both political and social terms. For the two months in question represented only a relatively insignificant period of time in an era which will doubtless be looked back upon with considerable interest in future years.

The broader picture

Last year, the media concentrated on the Intermediate Nuclear Forces (INF) Treaty, the Strategic Arms Reduction Treaty (START) talks, the US presidential elections, Afghanistan, the Gulf, the Israeli-Arab conflict and on modernization in NATO. Achieving a perspective is difficult when events are unfolding so rapidly but, overall, it appears that the majority of the small Second and Third World nations are having to jostle for position, vis à vis each other and the superpowers, spurred on by economic, racial and religious pressures. Meanwhile, the large continental powers – primarily Europe, Asia Minor, the USSR and the USA – are attempting to achieve peaceful solutions to their long-term quarrels.

For the superpowers, the stimulus to find new

Above: Soviet troops withdraw from Afghanistan. The war has been costly for all – some 12,000 Russian and as many as 25,000 rebel soldiers (inset) have been killed.
Below: Supporters in Honduras welcome Vice-President George Bush. US presidential elections always side-track American attention, and 1988's was no exception.

solutions is partly cultural. Generally, there is a desire for conciliation amongst people on both sides of the Iron Curtain; this is expressed in the increasing number of exchange visits, and in growing trade. There is also a growing cynicism about dogmatic ideologies, both Western and Eastern European. We have even witnessed television advertising in Moscow for the first time in the Soviet Union's history. However, the main reason behind the renewed search for solutions is practical: economic reform and growth are becoming the new priorities. The USSR is embarking on a process of radical domestic reform simply because she has no choice – a reason painfully clear to most members of the Communist Party as well as to the general public.

The Soviet Union is well behind in the economic and technological stakes, and spends 15 per cent of her Gross National Product (GNP) on defence, more than double that spent by the USA. To support this spending and maintain a powerful position in world affairs beyond the next decade will demand both consistent economic growth and a revaluation of expensive strategic commitments around the world. Soviet-backed regimes in Central and Latin America and in Central Africa have been happily milking the USSR for too long.

The USA, with its dominant role among the economies of all the major Western nations, was sidetracked last year by the run-up to the presidential elections. The elections always prove disruptive: the electoral machinery takes two years to crank into action, then it usually takes a further year for the new president to settle in to his position. The fall of the dollar, and the problems with the trade deficit, also shocked the world's stock markets, and caused the worst crash since the 1920s. In the background, Congress remained extremely concerned about the escalating costs and the technical difficulties of the SDI programme.

In too many small Third World countries, meanwhile, particularly in Central Africa and Central America, the power struggles and bloodshed continued, although they gained the attention of the Western press and media only intermittently.

Strengthening the WEU

In Europe, the main effect of the INF Treaty was to galvanize NATO and the Western European Union (WEU) into looking into ways of restructuring their conventional weaponry and nuclear defence systems. Both Spain and Portugal were invited to join the WEU, since the Spanish electorate, in particular, has given indications that it is not as firmly committed to maintaining a nuclear-free peninsula as it has been in the past. In the NATO spring-cleaning, a lot of the pet fears and hobby-horses were brought back to the surface. Denmark, for example, looked as if her position in NATO might be untenable, in view of the Danish people's hostility to British and US Navy vessels carrying nuclear weapons coming into her ports.

There were some improvements in the relationship between Turkey and Greece. The two nations have been uneasy allies under the NATO banner, and Greece was further angered by the prospect of Turkey becoming a member of the EEC. Economically, with the approach of the Single Market Act in 1992, all the European nations involved are preparing themselves to take advantage of the fantastic business opportunities it promises. Closer economic integration, of course, is likely to spur the EEC nations into considering further a pan-European defence alliance. It is noteworthy that Germany and France have already struck a mutual reinforcement and support agreement, and that France is particularly keen to develop the European defence pillar under the aegis of the WEU. Perhaps slightly to the concern of the USA, the revitalization and further strengthening of the WEU poses questions about the future of NATO itself. In last year's Force's Diary mention was made of US hostility towards any such European defensive alliance. Significant pressure is likely to be applied to NATO members in an attempt to get them to toe the Supreme Command line.

However, among all of this frenetic activity in the defence world the fluid state of East-West relations, due to the INF Treaty summit in Moscow between the superpowers, stands out as being of prime interest and a great deal of importance.

The INF summit

Shortly before the crucial summit talks between President Reagan and General Secretary Gorbachev were due to begin on May 29, 1988, the *Washington Post* published a tongue-in-cheek article outlining the astrological 'fitness' of each of the main contenders in the summit talks. To put this article in perspective, the USA has been swept by a revival of interest in astrology and, indeed, all things paranormal. Ronald Reagan himself, encouraged – we are told – by his wife Nancy, is alleged to have consulted the stars regularly since at least the early 1970s. Perhaps the White House gave the *Washington Post* its cue when it pointed out that Reagan, as an Aquarius, was 'in fat city' for the May summit talks in Moscow, and added: 'The zodiacal bottom line here is that Reagan's abilities to think and communicate (governed by Mercury) will rarely be stronger and his personal charisma should be at its peak. Whereas during the same interval, Mikhail Gorbachev, a Pisces, will be facing an astro-bummer of gruesome proportions.'

The stakes at play at the summit were high. The signing of the Treaty meant a phenomenal reduction of 50 per cent of strategic nuclear arsenals. Given the ratification, this means that in Europe alone some 464 of the USA's ground-launched cruise missiles are to be removed. And although there is a lot of groundwork still to be covered, the Moscow summit also involved discussions on strategic arms reduction (the START talks), which business was inevitably carried forward to the next summit. Some background to the political activity behind the scenes throws light on the importance of the Moscow summit held last May.

Before the summit even began, each side was jockeying for position in the propaganda war. Ever-conscious of the need to play to the Republican Party's right wing, Reagan, for example, attempted to shore up his conservative credentials by launching a sharp attack on the Soviet Union's global ambitions. These included plans 'to prop up their discredited, doomed puppet regime' in Afghanistan, despite the imminent withdrawal of troops. Reagan endeavoured to rouse US suspicions that the Soviet invasion in December 1979 was intended to furnish the USSR with air bases close to

Above: Reagan and Gorbachev in Moscow, May 1988.
Below: USAF aircrew at Greenham Common in June 1988, stand by a cruise missile deactivated under the INF Treaty.
Right: A South African boy with the flag of the right-wing AWB party. Soviet attempts to mediate in Angola could well be undermined by the stance of such extremist groups.

Iran, Pakistan and the strategic Straits of Hormuz: 'Have the Soviets really given up those ambitions?', he told a euphoric audience in Massachusetts. 'We don't know. We can't know – until the drama has fully played.'

However, so as not to jeopardize the results of the summit itself, the President tempered his nationalistic ardour by appealing to the US Senate not to disappoint him by rejecting the INF Treaty banning medium-range missiles in Europe and Asia. It was quite clear that at the end of his second term, and at the age of nearly 79, Reagan fully intended to bow out with dignity, with the Moscow summit representing a colourful and prominent feather in his political cap. He evidently has a great many supporters in the USA who think he is worthy of being awarded the Nobel Prize for Peace. This is ironic, given Reagan's warmongering reputation, especially at the outset of his presidential career, when he was known as 'Ronnie Raygun' by the press.

Gorbachev's new-look foreign policy

There are many people in the Soviet Union – and elsewhere – who believe that the Nobel Prize for Peace should be awarded not to President Reagan, but to General Secretary Gorbachev, who had a more difficult task at the time of the summit. Under the twin policies of *perestroika* and *glasnost*, Gorbachev has instigated a foreign policy revolution, of which the Afghanistan withdrawal was but one example. The USSR's domestic economic problems were – and still are – such that the Russians must concentrate on achieving domestic economic reform instead of on strategically outwitting the USA and her allies by funding friendly or potentially friendly nations. Cuba, Vietnam and Angola – to give but three examples – are estimated to be costing the Soviet Union as much as seven per cent of her GNP. In 1985 alone, the Soviets gave about £2500 million in support of Cuba.

In his new-look foreign policy, Gorbachev is intent on presenting an image to the West of the USSR as a peaceful, constructive power. The Soviet leader adroitly projected the withdrawal from Afghanistan as evidence of Soviet goodwill, and there are strong indications that this policy of 'goodwill' is being pursued on every front.

In Africa's war-weary state of Angola, meanwhile, the new Soviet approach has prompted hopes of a settlement. The forces of the South-West African People's Organization (SWAPO) and of Angola have been in conflict for years, and last year there were said to be as many as 40,000 Soviet-supported Cuban soldiers stationed in the country. A firm strategy of disengagement has yet to be seen in Angola, and because this part of the continent represents a relative-ly important strategic outpost for the USSR, it is unlikely that significant reductions in troop numbers will occur until some kind of dialogue can be established between the warring factions. But there is evidence that the Soviet Union may be prepared to apply enough

pressure to ensure that such a dialogue takes place. Indeed, the Soviet Union even approached her arch-enemy, South Africa, about holding tripartite discussions with Angola in an attempt to find a solution to the crisis there. This demonstrates just how eager the Soviets are to disengage from their expensive commitments around the world. In keeping with this policy of revaluating the amount of support given to friendly foreign nations, other countries in central Africa have been told to put their own houses in order, and not to look to the Soviet Union for assistance.

In Central and Latin America, the Soviet Union is also making friendly overtures to moderate states such as Mexico and Brazil, while attempting to cut back on financial support to the more volatile Central American countries. Gorbachev has even made a surprising offer to cease Soviet aid to the Sandinista government in Nicaragua, provided that the USA stops giving aid to the Contra rebels.

In Asia, the location of such traditional anti-Soviet countries as Malaysia, Indonesia and arch-capitalist Singapore, the Soviets are making significant attempts to create good relations. Vietnam, recently receiving a large amount of financial support each year from the USSR, has been told that there are limits to the amount of assistance available. In Cambodia (Kampuchea), the presence of Soviet-backed Vietnamese troops is causing the USSR particular embarrassment, and relations between Peking and Moscow have suffered because of it. If the Vietnamese were to withdraw their troops from Cambodia, a large obstacle to the achievement of a closer relationship between the USSR and China may be removed. Gorbachev is intent on pursuing a policy of détente with the Chinese, although most attempts have proved fruitless to date. Some observers believe that a summit between Gorbachev and Deng Xiaoping, leader of the People's Republic of China, may well happen before the end of 1989. China herself, of course, has severe problems, with very low morale in an ill-equipped, little-appreciated Army.

Mikhail Gorbachev is equally determined to gain a mediating position in any negotiations that take place to resolve the Israeli-Arab conflict. When Yassir Arafat, leader of the Palestine Liberation Organization (PLO), visited Moscow early in 1988, the old campaigner was told, in effect, that the PLO must eventually recognize the State of Israel, a move that runs deeply against the grain of PLO politics. The Soviet Union also appears to be moving cautiously in this direction. Notably, the Kremlin's backing of Syria – its traditional ally in this region – has been less visible for many months, and although Moscow's attempts to play the arbitrator between Iran and Iraq generally have borne little fruit, this too was a policy that further served to confirm their firm intention to play a peace-making role in the Middle East.

Improvements start at home

In the light of Gorbachev's recent activities, President Reagan's railings at the USSR's ambitions for global domination have a rather hollow ring. But such speechifying must be seen in its electoral and political context – as a demonstration of a continued commitment to a 'strong America'. Shortly after making the Massachusetts speech quoted above, President Reagan shocked his friends by referring to Gorbachev as the first Soviet leader to question the USSR's policy of aiming for global domination, and as the first since Lenin to have sound economic ideas.

Far left and left: The Contras in Nicaragua (far left) and the Vietnamese in Cambodia (left) have been backed by the US and USSR respectively – but both countries are now re-examining their costly commitments in the Third World. Above: To revitalize her stagnant economy, the USSR is encouraging foreign investment (for example, by Coca-Cola, above) and a limited amount of free enterprise (right).

In the USSR, the improvement of trade links with the West and attempts to stimulate growth within the Soviet Union's own economy are now the main priorities. The critical nature of these priorities cannot be overstated: they are essential if the USSR is to preserve its superpower position and not lose face in the event of its disentanglement from foreign military and political intervention. Gorbachev is desperately keen to present a new image of the USSR to the West; as he told British Foreign Secretary, Sir Geoffrey Howe, 'there are no bears left in Russia'. In line with this, Gorbachev's image has been carefully created. Soviet leaders have always previously appeared to be cold, distant figures, but Gorbachev presents himself as an affable, approachable family man.

Realists at the Kremlin are aware that it is highly important that Mikhail Gorbachev is effective at public relations. To pursue his policies he needs the support of the highly nationalistic Soviet press, of the old-style Politburo officials and of senior personnel in the Soviet armed forces. He also has to square his policy activities with other members of the Warsaw Pact and stimulate trade and general productivity at home without appearing to move overtly in a pro-Western direction. There has certainly been an explosion of interest in East-West joint ventures following moves by Eastern European countries to encourage Western investment. This involves products ranging from shoes to animated films and even the construction of a gambling casino.

The United Nations Economic Commission for Europe, in the first comprehensive study of East-West joint ventures published in April last year, says that by the end of 1987 there were 166 projects in operation or about to start, involving foreign investment of £1000 million. This trend looks likely to continue.

The USSR has suffered a grievous fall-back in real GNP growth for more than a decade. Gorbachev himself observed not long ago that were it not for revenues from oil and the sale of vodka, Soviet GNP would have stood still in the ten-year period preceding his accession to power in 1985. Recently, the crash in world oil prices caused the Soviet Union to suffer a fierce hard-currency squeeze. The 1988 collapse of the dollar – in which oil prices are reckoned – caused further problems, pushing up the price of importing vital goods, denominated in marks, yen and pounds. Compounding these domestic economic problems, the Soviet Union's earlier concentration on building up her nuclear arms to achieve parity with the USA, and the enormous enhancement of conventional arms and troops during the 70s and 80s, allowed great weaknesses to develop in the USSR's domestic technologies. These weaknesses can only be remedied with Western help. Some observers estimate that the Soviet Union is as much as ten years behind the major Western powers in technological terms.

Summit repercussions

In the light of this political background, the Moscow summit last May was undoubtedly the most important since the latest round of summitry began in 1985. To the Soviet Union, the INF Treaty was intended to indicate their good intentions to the world, hopefully signalling a period in which they could pursue the vital reforms necessary at home. The summit had certainly been friendly, but Gorbachev was quite critical afterwards of the slow and guarded approach of the Americans. Gorbachev wanted to move further, quicker. To the Americans, particularly to President Reagan, the summit talks represented the apogee of the policy of peace through strength. Reagan's part in the summit undoubtedly gave him a place in American presidential history, but observers may well feel that he was more concerned with his colours than with the highly complex technical and practical problems still needing resolution – principally verification procedures. To CND and other nuclear disarmament and freeze pressure-groups around the world, the INF Treaty ratification was perceived as a step in the right direction. Nevertheless, few of the groups have been prepared to claim that a great victory has been won – yet. In Britain, Prime Minister Margaret Thatcher appeared to be more concerned with augmenting and renewing NATO's nuclear 'umbrella' than with a treaty which, after all, still left the USSR with sufficient weaponry to destroy Britain several times over. Britain's independent strategic deterrent (in the form of the four new Trident submarines), is still on line. Added to this, Britain is to spend further colossal sums on the production of a new stand-off missile for the RAF.

Among the other commentators who are singularly dissatisfied with the prospect of reducing strategic missiles by 50 per cent is the author of a guide to nuclear weapons, Dr Paul Rogers from Bradford University. Dr Rogers has argued that such a reduction in the number of strategic missiles could paradoxically decrease rather than increase general stability if those that are left are to consist of 'counter-force' weapons. Because of their selective target-acquisition capabilities, he argues that there may be more temptation to use such weapons in a time of severe emergency. His preferred solution is to freeze the new deployment of strategic weapons and remove all the old systems.

Dr Rogers also points out that the number of medium-range missiles destined to disappear is comparatively small in relation to the total quantities. He concludes: 'The major conclusion of this documentation of nuclear arsenals is that their expansion and enhancement is continuing as if arms control negotiations do not exist.' Dr Roger's comments may not be unfounded, given the emphasis of the discussions of the Nuclear Planning Group (NPG) concerning the proposed structure of NATO's future nuclear armaments.

Modernization in NATO

Powerful conflicts were evident at the meeting of the NPG (Nuclear Planning Group) in Brussels. One side is determined to fight for a nuclear-free Europe; the other (represented mainly by the US and Britain), is pushing for the reinstatement of modernized nuclear weaponry at the centre of NATO's battlefield strategy. Mrs Thatcher in particular feared that Mikhail Gorbachev is plotting to promote the denuclearization of Western Europe, with the 'double zero' of the INF Treaty being followed by a Soviet-instigated 'triple zero' in which battlefield weapons would also be removed.

Such an option worried Prime Minister Thatcher, as

it would doubtless prove tempting to the Germans, in both the East and West, on whose soil a tactical battle would take place. Thatcher and the US defence administration are most concerned that a powerful NATO force, committed to the use of nuclear weapons, should be maintained. This point of view is based largely on the 'strong is secure' policy that has worked for more than three decades. It may also have something to do with the economic problems that would probably be caused by a severe cut-back in defence spending.

Faint-heartedness is definitely a factor in NATO's present make-up. The fact that last year's NPG meeting was held in Brussels rather than at Kolding in Denmark, was interesting in itself. The switch to Brussels was a last-minute decision, designed to avoid political embarrassment. For the question of whether or not the Danish would allow nuclear warships to visit Danish ports was tested in a snap general election in Denmark on May 10. The man who prompted the election, Social Democratic defence spokesman Mr Lasse Budtz, was the author of a controversial par-

Below: Margaret Thatcher and Mikhail Gorbachev meet briefly in London in 1988. The British Premier has always argued that the Soviets were only brought to the negotiating table by the strength of NATO's forces.

liamentary resolution that pointed to the unprecedented change of venue as evidence of what he claims is political interference by NATO and the USA.

Mr Budtz's resolution was intended to enforce a ban on all visits by nuclear-armed warships. It immediately drew severe criticism from the US and Britain, whose warships are the ones involved. Margaret Thatcher said that such a move would have grave implications for NATO, and warned that British ships would not be able to hold exercises to reinforce Denmark in a crisis. This warning was in fact motivated by a concern for British interests: if Denmark was to be occupied by Warsaw Pact forces in the event of war, they would have a formidable strategic advantage. By sea, Denmark is a gateway to the Baltic and Russian ports and by air the many airstrips in Denmark would give the Soviet and Warsaw Pact air forces a massive strategic superiority. Britain would be especially vulnerable. Current British plans call for a UK mobile force of 10,000 troops to reinforce Denmark in time of tension – a commitment costing about £275 million a year.

Fortunately, the eventual outcome of the Danish election allayed fears of an enforced ban for the time being. Nevertheless, an opinion poll demonstrated that the majority of Danes wanted guarantees that visiting

warships would not carry nuclear weapons – even if that policy weakened NATO. In addition, the question of protocol remains: should visiting vessels disclose to the Danes whether or not they are carrying nuclear weapons? Both the US and the British have so far followed a policy of refusing to confirm or deny the presence of nuclear arms on visiting vessels. The Royal Navy currently deploys a nuclear bomb, the WE-177, which can be dropped on sea, surface or land targets by Sea Harriers, or used as depth-charges by Sea King helicopters. In practice, these are only used on the three Invincible-class carriers and it seems likely that the British at least will be more readily able to disclose the nature of their arsenals on board.

The tension over the question of Danish anti-nuclear sentiment is an indication of more general concern about the restructuring and modernization of NATO's nuclear arsenal. This was the question tackled at the NPG's talks, headed by NATO's Secretary-General, Lord Carrington. It was agreed that a new stand-off air-launched cruise missile for NATO dual-capable aircraft is to be brought into commission in the 1990s.

Planning ahead

Regarding the updating of the Lance missile, US Defense Secretary, Mr Frank Carlucci, reckoned that Congress would approve funding for a successor, which would probably be based on the design principles of the US Army Tactical Missile System. A replacement is intended to be brought in by 1992. As Mr Carlucci commented: 'Dual-capable aircraft are being modernized. Nuclear artillery is being modernized. In terms of Lance, there has been a decision that there should be a follow-on. We haven't yet determined what the range should be, nor what the requirements are. But we are some time away from any deployment decision, so there is no need for the Alliance as such to make any decision right now.'

The 'Alliance as such' has been subjected to certain pressure from the USA – with the unstinting approval of Margaret Thatcher – to modernize and re-equip forces to a very significant extent. US defence experts were well-prepared for the meeting of the NPG, which they pre-empted by providing member defence ministers with a highly informative, classified briefing session. At the briefing session they demonstrated that US reconnaissance satellites had produced evidence that the Soviet Union is carrying out tests to shorten the range of some of their Intercontinental Ballistic Missiles (ICBMs) so that they can be retargeted on Europe.

George Younger, British Secretary of State for Defence, was singularly impressed by the briefing – and particularly by the knowledge, deriving from US sources, that while the West was uncertain about what steps to take to restructure their arsenal after the INF Treaty, the Soviet Union had made up its mind. The ministers learned that the USSR has tested a shortened version of the SS19 ICBM. This is codenamed 'Stiletto'

by NATO and, deployed in 1982, it carries six 550-kilotonne independently targeted warheads. During the tests the missile's normal range of 6250 miles (10,000km) had been reduced to between 1450 miles (2300km) and 1625 miles (2600km). At the meeting, the Americans disclosed that Stiletto itself is being updated by the new rail-mobile SS24 missiles and road-mobile SS25 missiles with a variable range. These, the Americans claimed, were targeted on Europe. However, another US Defense Department source commented that there was no proof that the shortened SS19 versions were to be targeted on Europe.

Pointing to other developments, the US intelligence officers at the briefing revealed that there were more short-range SS21 missiles replacing the Frog 7, and many more dual-capable strike aircraft, especially the Su24 Fencer. The latter is a supersonic swing-wing fighter with similarities to the USA's F-11 bomber.

Frank Carlucci did not hesitate to press home the warning that the post-INF deployment of more mobile missiles with a shorter range presented an 'increased threat to Europe' – a warning not dissimilar to the pronouncements of Bradford University's Dr Rogers.

A communiqué published after the meeting summarized the policy decisions taken, and it shows that there was a tighter accord after the US briefing. It read: 'We have confirmed that the forces remaining after the INF Treaty must be kept survivable, responsive and effective and structured in an adequate and balanced way. We also endorse our step-by-step approach towards the measures necessary to achieve our objectives and have provided further guidance on the way ahead.'

Below: US Defense Secretary, Frank Carlucci, and another official conduct a briefing session in May 1988. At a NATO NPG meeting, Carlucci warned that the Soviets were preparing to re-target some of their ICBMs on Europe.

Somewhere in Afghanistan

Even as these pronouncements were being made, Russian tanks rumbled towards the northern border of Afghanistan in mid-May as the first troops pulled out of the country after more than eight years of occupation, which had resulted in severe casualties among both Soviet and rebel troops.

In a situation that could be closely paralleled with the USA's ignominious withdrawal from Vietnam, Gorbachev had to justify the withdrawal to the Soviet public and to the army. Many of the new commanding officers of the Soviet army have won their service colours in Afghanistan, and have mixed feelings about the wisdom of the retreat. It was evident to all sides that the communist People's Democratic Party government in Kabul, propped up for ten years by the Soviet Union, was unlikely to survive for long. And the seven Mujahideen rebel groups – under the newly elected leader Mr Gulbuddin Hekmatyar – have confidently stated that President Najibullah's communist government could be wiped out with relative ease. A new all-Islamic state would then be installed.

The Mujahideen leaders were represented at the United Nations talks in Geneva at which the USSR's removal had been secured. Pakistan was also involved, and the US representatives made great play of their nation's involvement in the process. Gorbachev may have had his hand forced by the continual pressure from the UN and the West, but it is well known that he had wanted to get out of Afghanistan from the time of his accession to power in 1985. Until that time, and until late in 1987, the USSR's position was categorical: they would pull out of Afghanistan only if the USA and other Western nations stopped supplying arms to the rebels. Without these arms, particularly the Stinger and Blowpipe anti-aircraft weapons, which had been fed into

Above: The first Soviet troops leave Afghanistan across the 'Friendship Bridge' on the Afghan-Soviet border in May 1988. The disastrous Soviet experience in Afghanistan has been compared to that of the USA in Vietnam.

the country in large quantities (even last year), the rebels would doubtless have had little success against the powerful Soviet air force. Until 1984-85, the latter had been successfully, even cruelly, putting paid to rebel outposts throughout the country. Were the CIA-led arms supplies to have stopped, the many Russian lives lost in the débâcle would have been justified by the Communist Party leadership as sacrifices made in a successful defence of the USSR's allies. But, in the event, the Soviet Union's position changed enormously, and they decided to withdraw while rebel arms supplies were still being maintained.

This about-turn in policy made the Kremlin's justification for the war particularly difficult. It is one of the reasons why so many Afghanistan-watchers in the West were keen to suspect that the USSR would maintain a buffer zone of some sort on the northern boundary, and continue to support the fading communist government by other means. The Geneva agreement does not necessarily restrict the USSR from giving further military assistance to the government in Kabul. In the event, Soviet troops were withdrawn following an orchestrated farewell ceremony, staged for the media; the ceremony was heavily guarded against hostile rebel activity. After pulling out, the USSR still needs to save face, and considerable assistance will be given in the form of help with the maintenance of sophisticated weapons, the training of government troops and the delivery of military supplies. It is also highly important to the USSR to watch the common border with Afghanistan and to prevent the Mujahideen from trying to stir up Islamic sympathy in the south-Asian region of

the Soviet Union. It is a sad fact that the only feasible way in which Gorbachev (and his many supporters in the Kremlin) can demonstrate to senior army officers that he has not sold out in Afghanistan is by placing yet more Soviet troops in jeopardy.

By all accounts, irrespective of the withdrawal, the bloodbath will continue until the Kabul government is on its knees. At that stage the political battle will become a religious one.

Whether or not the people of Afghanistan want to be communist is one thing; whether they will want to be controlled by an Islamic theocracy is yet another. Whatever happens, observers may speculate about the use of more than 1000 Stinger missiles (possibly a lot more, since 600 Stingers were delivered in 1987 and the US has said that the full 1988 quota had already been delivered before the Soviet troops departed). A significant number of the more expensive Blowpipe anti-aircraft weapons were also sent to Afghanistan. A highly effective system (they are also used by British forces), Blowpipes are deadly, and in bringing down Soviet aircraft they have proved their capabilities time and time again. The Afghanistanis are also well versed in the use of Stingers, but it appears that many of the $50,000 missiles have failed to reach their intended destination; many have disappeared en route to the rebels, in Pakistan. Into whose hands have these missing Stingers fallen?

The repatriation of the five million refugees who have been sheltering in Pakistan, and of the further three million refugees displaced within Afghanistan itself, is another question causing concern to authorities in the

Below: An Afghan rebel with a Stinger missile. First supplied by the US in 1986, the missiles helped to tip the war in the rebels' favour, with as many as eight out of ten firings bringing down a Soviet aircraft.

area. Pakistan wishes to repatriate the large numbers of men, women and children in border refugee camps as soon as possible. However, the refugees themselves have so far shown some reluctance to return to devastated border areas which now offer little or no livelihood. It looks as if aid from the West will be taking on a new form – that of money and 'self-help' packages – for a long time to come.

International chemistry

NATO has estimated that the Soviet armed forces possess stockpiles of between 200,000 and 500,000 tons of gas-filled shells, bombs and rockets. The USA has about one tenth of that amount, mostly dating from before 1969 (1000 of these are said to be leaking, according to information supplied by Democratic Senator John Glenn to the Senate armed services strategic weapons sub-committee). Britain destroyed its own offensive stocks in the 1950s. Not surprisingly, Margaret Thatcher places chemical weapons particularly high on her multilateral disarmament shopping list. The British Government has been arguably the most forceful in calling for a solution. Unfortunately, the talks taking place at Geneva have been going on for ten years, with very little success. Indeed, there are particular problems when it comes to limiting chemical weapons, for domestic and agricultural chemicals are widely used and these can easily be reformed to make lethal gases and microbiological toxins.

Mr Graham Pearson, Director of the Chemical Defence Establishment at Porton Down has, for example, warned that the 40-nation conference in Geneva which has been attempting to gain a treaty for so long, had to cope with the shadowy zone between chemical and biological weapons. In particular, the poisonous botulinus toxin, which is 1000 times more toxic than nerve gas, was in the past produced biologically but can now be man-made as a chemical weapon. The USA was experimenting with the toxin in the 1960s, before it was banned as a biological weapon. Mr Pearson worried that the USSR may well know

Above: Soviet officials visit Britain's chemical warfare research establishment at Porton Down in May 1988. Britain destroyed its stocks in the 1950s, but the USSR holds between 200,000 and 500,000 tons of chemical weapons.

about the technology involved. He added that it was too easy to get round the prescription or ban of a particular chemical by slightly altering its formula.

Verification was another major problem, particularly with agents such as hydrogen cyanide, which has industrial uses. Ominously, at the same time as this warning was given, a row blew up in Ankara over the export of chemicals from Turkey to Iraq. It had long been suspected that chemical 'precursors' (components), carried into Iraq at the crossing-point at Habur, were used in the production of chemical weapons rather than for agricultural use, as the shippers alleged. The Turkish newspaper *Hurriyet* investigated the trade for six months before divulging that the quantities involved were far above what would be normal for agricultural purposes. Diplomats in Ankara recognized the chemicals, including chlorine, as being among those that the British Government is trying to have restricted. As one diplomat commented: 'They are all seemingly innocuous, but it is surprisingly simple to turn them into something lethal.'

The trial continues, as they say in the papers.

Diary – Events of 1988

Jan
11-16 Nordic observers invited to Soviet navy manoeuvres.
17-19 Soviet Foreign Minister Shevardnadze declares USSR ready to negotiate on conventional forces reductions in Europe.
22 Agreement to create Franco-German troop brigade signed.
28 Egyptian President Mubarak arrives in USA with 5-point plan for international conference on Middle East.
29 Thatcher and Mitterand agree to allow French nuclear subs to visit British ports.
30-31 Greece and Turkey agree to hold annual meetings on main areas of dispute in Aegean and Mediterranean seas.

Feb
8 Gorbachev announces phased withdrawal of Soviet troops from Afghanistan, beginning in May.
14-16 Anglo-Soviet talks on arms control and drugs trafficking. Agreement on drug trafficking signed on 15th.

18-25 Further Nicaragua/Contra talks in Guatemala City.
23 US Navy Secretary Webb resigns in protest at cuts.
25 USSR begins INF withdrawals from East Germany and Czechoslovakia.
27 Gulf War: missile attacks on Tehran and Baghdad continue throughout March.

Mar
2-3 NATO summit agreement to update nuclear weapons.
3 US House of Representatives approves $30 million (£18 million) aid to Contras.
7-31 Operation Fire Focus in Falklands tests rapid reinforcement capabilities.
16 In Beograd, Yugoslavia, Gorbachev proposes freezing naval forces in Mediterranean.

Apr
9 Gorbachev tells PLO leader Arafat in Moscow that recognition of Israel is essential to settlement of West Bank problem.
14 Election in Denmark over issue of visits by NATO ships carrying nuclear weapons.

Equipment and service highlights

The computer command project, which was supposed to provide the new British Type 23 frigates with the capability to meet sophisticated enemy threats, has been scrapped after several years and £30 million spent by the MOD on the project. A replacement system has been demanded as quickly as possible. The Assistant Under-Secretary in charge of Navy material at the MOD commented of the new system: 'It had jolly well better work.'

£400 million has been spent on the new Air-Launched Anti-Radar Missile (ALARM) for the RAF. Unfortunately, the RAF themselves say that they do not particularly want it.

Last year was a bad one for the MOD's Procurement Executive, whose defence equipment buying policies have been carefully scrutinized since the National Audit Department's highly critical report in 1987. Since the Nimrod fiasco, there has been the Type 23 computer cancellation, the Marconi fraud investigation, and the scandal over the tendering policies by means of which defence contractors achieve new orders. Under the directorship of Peter Levene, however, improvements have been made in purchasing and control methods.

After spending $12 billion (about £7000 million) on development of the Strategic Defense Initiative (SDI), an authoritative document from the Congressional Office of Technology Assessment has severely criticized the computer software involved in the highly sophisticated 'Star Wars' system. The software is the most complex ever written, and the COTA's fear is that it will never be able to meet the demands made of it. 'There may always be irresolvable questions about how dependable software would be', says the OTA report. Defense Secretary Frank Carlucci responded: 'It's like saying 10 years before we had helicopters that helicopters were doomed to failure.'

Scientists in California have developed a nuclear bomb that is capable of burrowing deep into the earth before delivering a blast ten times greater than that of a conventional nuclear device. The building and testing of a full-scale bomb, as yet, awaits US Government approval.

The first flight of the US's highly secretive Stealth bomber – the B-2 – took place last year, when the bomber flew to Edwards Air Force Base for extensive testing.

Jane's Military Communications claims that the Soviet Union is taking a lead in submarine communications. The USSR has developed the ability to communicate with submarines deep beneath the Polar ice cap. The USSR has been able to develop its Extremely Low Frequency (ELF) communications systems largely because it has many uninhabited tracts of land where experimentation can continue without disruptive protests by environmentalists.

Last year Britain sold nine warplanes to Botswana, which was seeking to strengthen its defences against South African cross-border raids aimed at African National Congress (ANC) troops on Botswanan territory. The planes, second-hand Strikemasters, are Botswana's first combat aircraft and first jets.

The much-loved English Electric Lightning was finally phased out in May 1988, after 30 years' service as a high-altitude RAF fighter and interceptor. A commemorative service was held at RAF Binbrook in Lincolnshire to mark the occasion. The Lightning is being replaced by the Tornado F3.

A new élite US helicopter squadron will be based at RAF Woodbridge in Suffolk as part of a new anti-terrorist crack force forming the 21st Special Operations Squadron. There will be 125 men in the Squadron.

18-19	Western European Union (WEU) half-yearly session in the Hague – ministers invite Spain and Portugal to join.
18-20	Gulf War – Iraqi offensive in south re-captures Faw peninsula; US attacks Iranian ships and oil platforms.
25	Britain announces willingness to co-operate with France, Italy and Germany on new fighter aircraft.
27-28	US-Canada talks – Reagan agrees not to obstruct British tender to supply nuclear subs to Canada.
30	US vows to protect neutral shipping in Gulf.

May

4	US/USSR monitoring of US conventional explosions/tests.
6	Frank Carlucci, US Defense Secretary, calls for more European defence spending.
13	Soviet troops begin withdrawal from Afghanistan.
16	George Younger, British Defence Minister, reveals that Britain is to replace free-fall nuclear weapons with air-launched stand-off bombs.
17	Details revealed of Stealth B1 bomber. 135 B1s on order.
24	Supreme Soviet ratifies INF treaty.
31	US Senate ratifies INF treaty.

Jun

1	Shultz-Shevardnadze agree on test and missile monitoring.
9	Soviets show MiG 29 at Farnborough.
11-13	Denmark announces decision to freeze defence spending.
23	Israeli security forces go on full alert to forestall trouble during a general strike and 'day of arson'.
25	NATO agrees to create a 5000-man multinational force, earmarked to reinforce northern Norway in times of crisis.
27	Iraqis drive Iran out of crucial oil regions.

Jul

3	Iranair Airbus flight 655 to Dubai shot down by USS *Vincennes*.
9	Britain signs £6 billion Saudi arms contract.
12	Nicaragua orders US ambassador and 7 diplomats out of country, accusing them of inciting revolt.
18	Iran agrees to UN resolution 598.
21	South Africa, Angola and Cuba announce agreement on principles to end Angolan war.
25	British Government announces that British Aerospace will receive no further funding for HOTOL project.
26	Iranian opponents of Khomeini's regime launch offensive.

INDEX

Picture Credits

F/cover	Aerospace Publishing
2/3	Soldier Magazine
4/5	COI
6/7	US Navy/MARS
10/11	US Navy/MARS
14	US Navy/MARS
16	US Navy/MARS
17	A. Workman/MARS
19	US Navy/MARS
20/21	US Navy/MARS
22/23	US Navy/MARS
24	US Navy/MARS
25	MARS
26/27	MARS
28	Martin Windrow
29	Kobal Collection/John Kobal
31	Martin Windrow: RT, ECPA: LT
32	Martin Windrow
33	Imperial War Museum
34	SIRPA/ECPA: LB, Salamander Books/MARS: RT
35	SIRPA/ECPA
36	SIRPA/ECPA
37	SIRPA/ECPA
38	SIRPA/ECPA: RB, Frank Spooner Pictures/Gamma, LT
39	SIRPA/ECPA
40	SIRPA/ECPA: LB, Frank Spooner Pictures/Gamma: RB
41	SIRPA/ECPA: LB, Frank Spooner Pictures/Gamma: LT
44	Frank Spooner Pictures/Gamma: LB, Topham Picture Library: RT
45	Frank Spooner Pictures/Gamma: RB
46	Associated Press: M, MARS: LT
46/47	Associated Press: B, MARS: T
47	MARS: RB, Associated Press: LB, M, LT, RT
49	Sipa Press
50	Frank Spooner Pictures/Gamma: LB, Sipa Press/Rex Features: B
51	Frank Spooner Pictures/Gamma: LB, RB
52	Frank Spooner Pictures/Gamma: RM, Topham Picture Library: RT
53	Sipa Press: T, Frank Spooner Pictures/Gamma: RM
55	Sipa Press: LB, LM
56/57	MARS
57	Vickers Shipbuilding Group Ltd/MARS
58/59	Fleet Photographic Unit/Crown
59	Department of Defense/MARS
60	MARS: LT, Associated Press Ltd: RT, Sipa Press Ltd/Rex Features: LM
61	Associated Press
62/63	Salamander Books
64	MARS
65	MARS
66	MARS
67	MARS
68	Bundesarchive, Koblenz/MARS: RB, MARS: LT
69	Imperial War Museum/MARS: RT, MARS: RM, Robert Hunt Library: RB
70	Central Press Photos: RT, US Navy/MARS: RB
71	Salamander Books: LT, Imperial War Museum/MARS: LB, MARS: RB
72	Department of Defense: T, The Press Association: RB
73	Salamander Books: LT, MARS: RT
74/75	Salamander Books
76	London Express News Service
77	MARS: LT, London Express News Service: LB, RM
78/79	John Bruce
80	Mark Dartford/MARS: R, Imperial War Museum: LB
81	Bundesarchive/MARS
82	Jill Wiley
83	Vickers Ltd/MARS: RM, MARS: LM
84	Imperial War Museum
85	British Aerospace/MARS: RT, RAF Museum/MARS: RB
86	Imperial War Museum/MARS
87	British Aerospace/MARS: RT, The British Aircraft Corporation: RM
88	Crown Copyright (MOD-RAF)/MARS: RM, RB British Aerospace/MARS: T
89	British Aerospace: LB, Crown Copyright (MOD-RAF)/MARS: RB
90	Duxford/MARS
91	Crown Copyright (MOD)/MARS: RT British Aerospace/MARS: RT
92	British Aerospace/MARS
94	Panavia/MARS
95	British Aerospace
96/97	GKN
98	Imperial War Museum
99	Imperial War Museum: LT, MARS: RT
100	MARS
102	Rheinstahl GmbH/MARS
105	MARS
110	Short Brothers Ltd/MARS: RT The Press Association/Colonel Dewar: LB
108	Colonel Dewar
109	GKN
111	MARS: LT, GKN: RB
112/113	MARS
114	Imperial War Museum/MARS
115	Robert Hunt Library: T MARS:B
116	Camera Press
117	Mark Dartford/MARS: T Camera Press Ltd: B
118	Martin Streetly
119	Crown Copyright (MOD-RAF)/MARS: B Crown Copyright (MOD):T
120	British Aerospace/MARS: T Camera Press: B
121	Martin Streetly
122	USAF/MARS
123	Crown Copyright (MOD-RN)/MARS: T Lockheed California/MARS: B
124	Department of Defense/MARS: T Associated Press: B
125	USAF/MARS: T MARS: B
126	Department of Defense/MARS: B MARS: T
127	TASS/MARS: T Kobal Collection: B
128/129	Ingrid Gavshon
130	MARS: M
130/131	Frank Spooner Pictures/Gamma
131	Department of Defense/MARS: M
132	Frank Spooner Pictures/Gamma: RT
132/133	Guardian
133	Ingrid Gavshon: LT
134	Frank Spooner Pictures/Gamma
135	Ingrid Gavshon: RB Coca-Cola Eastern Europe GmbH: TL
136/137	Camera Press/Bryn Colton
138	Department of Defense/MARS: LB
138/139	Camera Press (TASS)
139	Sipa Press/Rex Features: RB
140	Guardian
B/cover	Ingrid Gavshon

Artwork

12/13	John Hutchinson
15	John Hutchinson
18	Patrick Semple
28	John Hutchinson: RT, Daily Star: RB
29	Patrick Semple
30	Richard Scollins
34	Sandy Cameron
42/43	Daily Telegraph
48	Patrick Semple
77	Richard Scollins
80	John Hutchinson
81	W.R.R. Hardy
82/83	W.R.R. Hardy
90	W.R.R. Hardy
92	Barbara Leaning
95	John Hutchinson
101	Aerospace Publishing
103/104	Aerospace Publishing
106/107	Aerospace Publishing
108/109	Aerospace Publishing
118	Martin Streetly
121	Martin Streetly
130	John Hutchinson
141	John Hutchinson

The Contributors

MICHAEL DEWAR was born in 1941 and was educated at Worth and Downside Schools, the Royal Military Academy, Sandhurst, and Pembroke College, Oxford. He was commissioned into the Rifle Brigade in 1961, and has served with the British Army in many capacities all over the world. He is the author of five books and has written many articles in defence publications.

CHRISTOPHER DOBSON is a war correspondent and author, winner of the IPC Award of International Journalist of the Year in 1967 for his coverage of the Six-Day War in the Middle East and of the Tet offensive in Vietnam. He lectures at the Police Staff College, Bramshill, and has written a number of books on terrorism.

GILES EMERSON was educated at Oxford, and specializes in science and defence-related subjects on a full-time freelance basis; he also writes scripts for radio. He worked for several years with the Central Office of Information, producing publicity and recruitment material.

BILL GUNSTON was a pilot and flying instructor with the RAF. Since leaving the service, he has acted as an adviser to a number of aviation companies. He is an assistant compiler of *Jane's All the World's Aircraft*, and was formerly Technical Editor of *Flight International*.

HUGH LYON has had a lifelong interest in naval matters. After research into the British shipbuilding industry, he has written or co-authored 17 books on navies and warships in the past decade, including *The Encyclopedia of the World's Warships* and the warships section of *The U.S. War Machine*.

MARTIN STREETLY is an aviation and electronic warfare historian who has contributed widely to various military and aviation publications, including *Jane's Defence Weekly* and *Defence* magazine, both as writer and technical illustrator.

LT. COL. DAVID WRIGHT qualified in medicine from St. Thomas' Hospital, London, in 1970. He joined the Royal Scots Dragoon Guards as Regimental doctor in 1975. He commanded a field medical unit in Germany and has recently been Chief Instructor at the Royal Army Medical Corps Training Centre.